THE
CLASSICAL
TRADITION
IN
POETRY

GILBERT MURRAY

THE
CLASSICAL
TRADITION
IN
POETRY

THE CHARLES ELIOT NORTON LECTURES

VINTAGE BOOKS : NEW YORK

1957

PUBLISHED BY VINTAGE BOOKS, INC.

REPRINTED BY ARRANGEMENT WITH HARVARD UNIVERSITY PRESS

FIRST VINTAGE EDITION

PREFACE

___

WHEN I RECEIVED, IN 1925, AN INVITATION FROM HARVARD
University to give the first course of lectures for the
Charles Eliot Norton Chair of Poetry, just founded by
Mr. Chauncey Stillman, I accepted the honour with quite
peculiar pleasure. Apart from the personal enjoyment of
revisiting Harvard, I felt that, amid the whirl of new doc-
trines and old misunderstandings about art and poetry,
there was need for a restatement of the "classical" view,
and that a Chair bearing the name of Mr. Norton was an
ideal place from which to make it. What I mean by
"classical" will become clearer in the course of the book;
provisionally I mean the view of one whose training and
tastes lead him to regard literature as one, and the great
Greek and Roman writers as central forces in it.

Secondly, I welcomed the opportunity of expounding a
belief which I have long held about the overwhelming influence wielded over the art and thought of mankind by
unconscious imitation and tradition. This view is expressed
chiefly in chapters II, VII, and VIII.

It is a dangerous luxury for a scholar to venture out into
regions where he is an amateur, and of course that is all
I am in a large part of the field covered by this book. But
perhaps it would be a sad thing if literature were delivered
over entirely to the hands of the professional expert.

G. M.

PREFACE TO THE SECOND EDITION

PRACTICALLY NO CHANGES HAVE BEEN MADE IN THIS SECOND edition beyond the correction of a few errata. I have, however, added an analysis of the general argument of the book and would venture to ask any readers who feel a difficulty in my use of the term "classical" to look again at the explanation given on p. 6. There is, of course, a sense in which Pope and Racine are "classical" while Chaucer, Shelley and Ibsen are not: but that is not the sense in which I use the word. I did think of saying "The Greek Tradition," or "The Central Tradition"; but the first seemed unduly to omit the Roman and Hebrew influences and the second to be lacking in clearness. In emphasizing the immense antiquity of our poetical Tradition, and generally in championing the Tradition with its attitude of loving discipleship as against the Fashion, with its continual changes and self-assertions, I know I am stirring the ashes of many controversies; my main purpose, however, is not to confute my betters, but merely to expound a view which seems for temporary or superficial reasons to be in danger of being neglected.   G. M.

INTRODUCTORY

A SHADOW HAS BEEN CAST ON THE INAUGURATION OF THIS
Professorship by the sudden and untimely death of the
founder, before he could either explain to the first professor his conception of what a Chair of Poetry ought to be,
or see, with the normal mixture of sympathy and disappointment, this first imperfect realization of the adventurous idea which he had had so long at heart—the dream
that silently haunted him through a life apparently absorbed in the preoccupations of great business. I never met
Mr. Stillman. He actually came to Oxford, where I live, a
few weeks before his death; but by an unfortunate chance
I was then at Geneva, attending one of the committees
of the League of Nations; and by the time I returned, it
was too late.

I have to be guided chiefly by two things; by the word-
ing of the trust deed, which shows in every sentence careful consideration and understanding; and by my knowledge
of Charles Eliot Norton, in whose memory the chair is
founded and in whose teaching Mr. Stillman, I know,
found throughout his life a living inspiration.

I met Mr. Norton only a few times and that twenty
years ago; but I remember him vividly. Distinguished, critical, courteous and a little aloof, breathing an atmosphere
of serenity and depth of thought, he possessed to an exquisite degree the taste that is rightly called classic; that is,
his interest lay, not in the things that attract attention or
exercise charm at a particular place and moment, but in
those that outlive the changes of taste and fashion. His
eyes were set toward that beauty which is not of to-day or

vii

yesterday, which was before we were, and will be when we are gathered to our fathers.

It is a high responsibility to undertake to speak before this great University, of poetry in the sense in which it was understood by Charles Eliot Norton. It would be more so still if I attempted to give to the word poetry the full meaning which he gave it in his last lecture at Harvard, and which seems to be reflected in the language of the trust deed. He spoke of poetry as a spirit that exists not only in literature, but in art, in music, in human activity, and doubtless in the whole of life—something almost the same as beauty itself, that magical presence which a man from time to time feels surrounding him everywhere, not quite out of sight, not quite out of earshot, but for the most part unheard and unseen amid the roar of the world and the grinding of our own egotisms.

I shall not venture, except for a few pages in my last lecture, to treat of poetry in that wide sense; I shall speak only of poetry as a form of literature and shall concentrate on one particular question concerning it. We know that tastes in poetry change; they change in fact with exceptional violence and speed. Every generation, or at least the more excitable element in every generation, conscientiously stones the prophets of its fathers. I want to consider how far there is, underneath all these changes of fashion, a central and permanent tradition, from which every age and every individual may make particular and temporary divagations, but which remains somewhere at the heart of all styles so far as they are truly poetical. The research leads us to Greece, as research into art or literature usually does. And when we get to Greece, of course I feel more at home and less insecure in my judgements. But the subject of my book will not be Greek poetry but poetry itself, and poetry as it has manifested itself amid changing circumstances in the long line of tradition which begins with some nameless predecessor of Homer and Hesiod and reaches to the verses in to-day's newspaper.

ANALYTICAL TABLE OF CONTENTS

ix

Contents

X

Contents

CHAPTER V

Contents

CHAPTER VIII

CHAPTER IX

Contents

THE
CLASSICAL
TRADITION
IN
POETRY

I

WHAT IS MEANT BY TRADITION

SOME SEVENTY YEARS AGO, A TRAVELLER IN THE AUS-
tralian bush, riding up at nightfall to a solitary wooden
cabin in the district between the Murray and Murrumbidgee rivers, would have found the owner sitting alone
at a rough and frugal dinner, in complete evening dress.
He wore evening dress for the sake of its associations,
because he and his people had done so at home. It was
to him part of a tradition of thought and conduct and
social atmosphere which he valued and which he felt
himself to be in danger of losing. He wore it with
emphasis and deliberately, though it was, in his present circumstances, a habit both unusual and inconvenient.

For somewhat similar reasons he ordered regularly
from London a large chest of books, the recent books
that were there considered most interesting and important. He did this because at home his people had usually had the most interesting recent books, as they came
out. That also was part of the tradition, though, of
course, he also valued the books themselves.

These two observances of tradition, no doubt, excited
notice and comment from the man's neighbours. This
was because they stood out as unusual; they were not of
a piece with the ordinary texture of life in that neighbourhood. But the man was at the same time doing
innumerable other things for exactly the same reason,

3

except that he did them unconsciously and without effort; and all the people about him, without exception, were doing the same. He wore clothes, except for a few changes due to climate or circumstances, formed on the model of the clothes he had worn at home. He had his hair cut the same way; he used a sponge and a tooth-brush and a saucer bath, as a matter of course and without ever reflecting what extremely curious instruments they all were. He spoke English, and spoke it with an aristocratic and slightly Irish accent. He practised a religion which to many of his neighbours seemed highly erroneous; he had distinguished and somewhat ceremonious manners. And there were other practices beyond number which he followed not because he had thought them out or had found them specially convenient, but because they formed parts of his whole inherited tradition and no compelling reason had arisen for throwing them off. He was conscious of the tradition only when it conflicted with daily convenience or with the new customs among which he found himself. Otherwise the whole of his normal life was shaped and determined by the ways in which his family, neighbours, and ancestors had lived, long before, on the other side of the world.

Meanwhile his average neighbours in the bush probably thought of him as very "conservative" or dependent on convention, because of his English books and his evening dress, whereas in the countless ordinary actions of life they were fully as dependent on tradition as he. Indeed, they were more so; because, for one thing, he was a thoughtful man, a leader and a pioneer, who often consciously devised new methods to meet new conditions, and also because, in many of the cases where he followed tradition, he chose carefully the tradition that he wished to follow. The mass of them acted without any thought or selection at all, and followed the manners of speech and thought and behaviour which happened to be prevalent at that date between the

4

Murray and the Murrumbidgee. Tradition really held sway over all of them.

But there was a difference in the attitude of different people toward the tradition. All were bound by it. But to most men, at any rate to those of the lower type, it was an unconscious bondage. They spoke and ate and smoked and spat in the ways to which their fathers had been accustomed, because it had never occurred to them to do otherwise. They made and laughed at the same jokes, because it is notoriously difficult to make, or to see, new ones. They mostly resented innovations, at any rate when they involved effort. But they had no deep basis of conviction to prevent them from following the line of least resistance.

To the man in evening dress, on the other hand, the tradition represented an ideal. The tradition expected him to be an educated man and a gentleman, to keep his word, to control his desires and passions, and as part and parcel of the same attitude, to sit down as clean at his meals in the remote bush as he would in his father's house. And all kinds of small things which were associated with that ideal were dear to him for its sake, as a man may love some indifferent sound or smell because it is associated with his home or childhood. The tradition represented a memory which he loved and was proud of, and to which he intended to be true. No doubt he idealized it, and thought of it as something finer than in practice it had really been.

Of course there is always the possibility, or rather the certainty, in ordinary civilized life, that in some points the tradition may be, not too high, but too low for a man's critical conscience. He will then consciously rebel against it because he wants to raise the standard, and reform things. But, so far as I know, that question did not often occur in the society of which I am speaking. The question there was between trying and not trying to live up to a standard which was difficult to maintain, among people who had mostly lost or never possessed the sense of it. To a visitor from another planet or another civilization, the difference between my hero and his neighbours would have been very small. They were all living according to the habits and ways of thought which they had derived from their ancestors on the other side of the world. But the average feeling was: "One need not be so particular here as at home, thank goodness!" His feeling was: "I was once a better man than this, and living among better men. I must not fall below the old standard."

The parallel may help us to understand the effect of the classical tradition in English poetry. I mean particularly the Graeco-Roman element in that tradition; for in the full sense the classical tradition is the whole stream which comes down from the ancient civilizations and gives form and unity to our own; a stream which comes from Greece, through the Roman Empire, through Christianity, with affluents from the pre-Christian Hebrew and the barbaric North. The Hebrew tradition is in practice often more familiar, though inwardly less akin to us, than the Greek; the Northern stands beside the Greek in epic and heroic quality. But the Graeco-Roman element forms the main stream. It comes from great minds. It is a stream from which commonness has been strained away. It has formed the higher intelligence of Europe. At the same time it is ubiquitous and unescapable. Even the librettist of musical comedy, even the bombastic mob-orator, is under the spell of it, though he has assimilated only those parts of it which come easy to him and eluded all that he felt to be difficult or "above people's heads." The poets of the higher style—Milton, Pope, Shelley, Keats, Tennyson, Browning, Swinburne—accept the classical, and especially the Greek, tradition as an ideal which they love and to which, however they may adapt and develop it, they endeavour to be faithful. It will help us to understand what this tradition is, if we consider it first in an extreme and obvious form, and then, so to speak, in a disguised form, where it is overgrown and hidden by new matter. I will take it first in Milton, and then—more briefly—in Shakespeare.

Every reader can see that Milton—apart from his Hebrew elements, which I am not now considering—is steeped in Greek and Latin literature; he makes direct classical allusions, he uses peculiar Latin or Greek words and phrases; still more, he frames the syntax of his sentences on a model which is rather Latin than English, or at least which belongs by right to a highly inflected language, not to one whose inflections have mostly decayed; to a greater degree still he uses tropes and turns of speech which he could never have used unless he had learned them in Greek or Latin poetry; and even his treatment of metre is demonstrably influenced by classical rules and feelings. But we can go into the matter more closely than this. The whole form of his great poem, an "epic" divided into twelve "books," is directly taken from the form of Vergil, as Vergil took that from Homer; and we know that Milton doubted long whether to adopt this form or the still more marked and characteristic form of a Greek tragedy. Even his subject, which no doubt he thought to be Christian or Hebraic, consists of an old Greek subject, the *Titanomachia*, or Battle of the Gods and Titans, intertwined with, or followed by, the story of the Fall in Genesis. There was no genuine Hebrew legend about Satan: Milton's hero, though bearing the Hebrew name of Satan, is really Greek—part Typhon and part Prometheus. And it is perhaps noteworthy also how, on the whole, the later books of *Paradise Lost*, where the poet is following Christian and Hebrew originals, are inferior to the earlier books, in which he was more free to indulge his natural love for Greek memories. But let us look at some of these points in detail.

Of man's first disobedience, and the fruit
Of that forbidden tree, whose mortal tast

> Brought death into the world, and all our woe,
> With loss of Eden, till one greater Man
> Restore us, and regain the blissful seat,
> Sing, Heav'nly Muse.

This long period, with the verb at the end, is in the manner of the Latin epic: the subject of the poem is stated in the first words in an oblique case, with the verb of narrating left to follow when it will, just as it is in Vergil, Lucan, Statius, and others, who take it from the Iliad and Odyssey. The verb, when it comes, is a prayer addressed to a Graeco-Roman goddess, and takes the form of requesting her to "sing," though, of course, it is really the poet himself who is about to perform, and in the ordinary sense of the word there is no question of anybody singing. There is nothing wrong. In the old poetry which Milton loved, and in which his memory delighted, the Greek or Roman poet was accustomed to think of his poem as something "inspired," or "breathed into" him, by this goddess, and deliberately to describe it as a "song," though the word did not denote his own practice, but had come down to him from the practice of ages long before.

It is worth realizing that Milton was quite serious in his prayer to the Muse. He appeals to her in language taken partly from the ancient Stoics, partly from Theocritus (XXII, 116):

> Thou, O Spirit, who dost prefer
> Before all temples the upright heart and pure,
> Instruct me, for thou know'st,—

and one is not, or ought not to be, surprised to find that the prayer has passed imperceptibly from the throne of the Muse to that of the Holy Ghost.

He proceeds:

> Sing, Heavenly Muse, that on the secret top
> Of Oreb or of Sinai . . .

Why "secret"? Because of a tradition dating from the time when Hesiod's Muses walked Mount Helicon hidden from mortal eyes in deep mist (*Theogony*, 8).

But to continue:

> Or if Sion's hill
> Delight thee more, and Siloa's brook that flowed
> Fast by the oracle of God. . .

Why all these choices, these alternatives? Because the old Greek gods, since each of them was normally an amalgamation of beings worshipped in different tribes or cities, are regularly invoked in that way. You cannot be sure at which of his seats of worship your god will be, and you may be crying to an empty throne. So you call to him in every place. Dozens of instances will occur to the classical scholar: the Apollo who may be at the Spring of Castaly, in the forests of Lycia, or the isles of Delos or Patara; the Nymphs who failed to watch over Daphnis because they were away, perhaps in the mountain valleys of Tempe or perhaps of Pindus,[1]

> οὐ γὰρ δὴ ποταμοῖο μέγαν ρόον εἶχετ' Ἀνάπω,
> οὐδ' Αἴτνας σκοπιάν, οὐδ' Ἄκιδος ἱερὸν ὕδωρ.

But, to go back, what did the Muse do on Oreb or on Sinai?

> that on the secret top
> Of Oreb or of Sinai didst inspire
> That shepherd, who first taught the chosen seed
> In the beginning how the Heav'ns and Earth
> Rose out of Chaos:

"Inspire": purely classical. "That shepherd, who first taught the chosen seed": a trick of ancient style, bringing the action more vividly before our minds than would the simple name "Moses." And what did he teach them? A subject that recurs again and again in ancient poetry,

[1] Horace, *Odes*, III, 4, 64; Theocritus, I, 66.

9

in "Orpheus," in Hesiod, in Apollonius, in Vergil, of course in Lucretius, even in Aristophanes and Ovid [2]— the greatest and most mysterious of subjects to teach:

> In the beginning how the Heav'ns and Earth
> Rose out of Chaos.

So he invokes the Muse to give aid to his adventurous song "that with no middle flight" (an ancient poetical phrase) intends to "soar" (the consecrated ancient metaphor) "above the Aonian Mount" (that old Greek mountain where the Muses lived), while it pursues

> Things unattempted yet in prose or rhyme;

which it does because Horace similarly had uttered

> carmina non prius
> Audita Musarum sacerdos;   (*Odes,* III, 1)

because Lucretius had exclaimed,

> Avia Pieridum peragro loca, nullius ante
> Trita solo;   (I, 926, and IV, 1)

and their various models had said much the same before them.

In those first fifteen lines, there is not a phrase, there is hardly a word, which is not made deeper in meaning and richer in fragrance by the echoes it awakens of old memories, old dreams, old shapes of loveliness.

Presently (line 33) we find a question and answer:

> Who first seduc'd them to that foul revolt?
> Th' infernal Serpent; he it was, whose guile, etc.,

just because Homer at the beginning of the Iliad had similarly asked and answered:

[2] The *Orphica,* the *Theogony, De Rerum Natura;* also Aristophanes, *Birds,* 684 ff.; Vergil, *Georgics,* II, 475 ff.; *Aeneid,* I, 740 ff.; Ovid, *Metamorphoses,* I.

What God had cast those twain to clash in strife?
The son of Zeus and Leto.[3]

Later on, we find many speeches beginning in a very peculiar way, with a formal address followed by the word "for" or "since":

> Powers and Dominions, Deities of Heav'n,
> For, since no deep within her gulf can hold
> Immortal vigor, though opprest and fall'n,
> I give not Heav'n for lost. From this descent, etc.;
>
> (II, 11)

or

> Native of Heav'n, for other place
> None can than Heav'n such glorious shape contain.
>
> (V, 361)

Why does he write thus? Because this opening is a well-known mannerism of Homer, regularly noted by the scholiasts.[4]

Elsewhere, though this form is not observed, speeches generally begin with some similar classical turn, like the magnificent first words of Satan to Beelzebub:

> If thou beest he; But O how fall'n! how changed.

Turn from speeches to similes: there is a well-known peculiarity of Homeric similes, that when the poet says that A is like B, he proceeds to describe B in detail, adding points about it which have nothing to do with A. For example, Athena makes a light to blaze from Achilles' helmet:

> As from an island city, seen afar,
> The smoke goes up to heaven, when foes besiege,
> And all day long in grievous battle strive

---

[3] *Iliad*, I, 8:

Τίς τ' ἄρ σφωε θεῶν ἔριδι ξυνέηκε μάχεσθαι;
Λητοῦς καὶ Διὸς υἱός . . .

[4] A vocative followed by a γάρ clause. *Iliad*, I, 123, VII, 328, etc.; cf. *Ibid.*, I, 353, VI, 333, 382.

11

> The leaguered townsmen from their city wall:
> But soon at set of sun, blaze after blaze,
> Flame forth the beacon fires, and high the glare
> Leaps, that in other islands they that see
> Perchance may launch their ships and come to save.
> (*Iliad*, XVIII, 208)

Just so Milton, when comparing Satan stretched on the burning flood to Leviathan, goes on to describe how "the pilot of some small night-foundered skiff" is apt to mistake the sleeping Leviathan for an island and to cast anchor in the lee of him—all of which has nothing to do with Satan.[5]

Sometimes, further, one of these added details is made by Homer the starting-point of a new simile; for example:

> Out then they two *charged and fought* in front of the gates, *like wild boars on a mountain*, who abide the oncoming throng of men and hounds, and charging sidelong break the underwood about them, tearing it rootwise up, and through all else *comes the noise of gnashing tusks*, till some man strikes and slays them; so *came the noise of clashing bronze* about their bodies.　(*Iliad*, XII, 145 ff.)

This usage explains the double simile in Book I, 303. The legions of fiends lying on the burning flood are like the leaves in Vallombrosa,

or scatterd sedge

> Afloat, when with fierce winds Orion arm'd
> Hath vext the Red-Sea coast, whose waves orethrew
> Busiris and his Memphian chivalrie,
> While with perfidious hatred they pursu'd
> The sojourners of Goshen, who beheld
> From the safe shore their *floating carkases*
> *And broken chariot wheels*, so thick bestrown,
> Abject and lost lay these, covering the flood,
> Under amazement of their hideous change.

[5] Cf. the similes in *Paradise Lost*, I, 768, 781.

From Homer, too, comes the effective use of repetitions
(Book XI, 259 ff.; cf. 48, 97 f.) of phrases, or of particular lines like

> Thrones, Dominations, Princedoms, Vertues, Powers.
> (X, 460)

Even more marked are the un-English, but often beautiful, turns of syntax: like Adam's words,

> O *miserable of happie!* is this the end . . .
> *Accurst of blessed.*[6] (X, 720)

> Dust I am, and shall to dust returne;
> O welcom hour, *whenever!*[7] (X, 771)

> Yet one doubt
> Pursues me still, least *all* I cannot die.[8] (X, 782)

Sometimes these are heaped one upon another till the
sentence must be difficult to understand for those who
do not know Greek and Latin:

> Unwarie, and too desirous, as before,
> So now of what thou know'st not, who desir'st
> The punishment all on thyself; alas,
> Beare thine own first, ill able to sustaine
> His full wrauth whose thou feelst as yet lest part,
> And my displeasure bearst so ill. (X, 947)

After this, one scarcely notices the Greek idiom of

> Adam the goodliest man of men since born
> His sons, the fairest of her daughters Eve;[9]
> (IV, 323)

or Satan's words to Gabriel:

> Then, when I am thy captive, talk of chains;
> (IV, 970)

---

[6] Like τυφλὸς ἐκ δεδορκότος (Sophocles, Oedipus Tyrannus, 454).
[7] Cf. the use of utcunque, ubicunque, in Latin.
[8] From Horace's non omnis moriar.
[9] Like κάλλιστος τῶν ἄλλων, etc.

or

> Whom thus the Angelic Vertue answer'd milde;
>
> (V, 371)

or

> To whom the Virgin Majestie of Eve.[1]   (IX, 270)

These tropes and turns of syntax show more markedly Milton's intimate dependence on classical tradition than the many direct references to incidents in ancient poetry which are obvious throughout *Paradise Lost*, such as the famous lines about the infernal architect:

> Men called him Mulciber; and how he fell
> From Heav'n, they fabl'd, thrown by angry Jove
> Sheer o're the chrystal battlements: from morn
> To noon he fell, from noon to dewy eve,
> A summers day; and with the setting sun
> Dropt from the zenith like a falling star,
> On Lemnos th' Ægæan ile;   (I, 740)

or

> Enna, where Proserpin gathring flours
> Her self a fairer floure, by gloomie Dis
> Was gatherd;   (IV, 269)

or Satan sitting on the tree like a cormorant (IV, 196: cf. *Iliad*, VII, 60 *Odyssey*, V, 51); or the martial games of the Angels and Devils (II, 528, IV, 550: cf. *Aeneid*, VII, 162, *Iliad*, II, 774); or Eve, like Narcissus, looking at her reflection in the water (IV, 460); or the nine-days fall of the rebel host (VI, 872: cf. *Theogony*, 722 ff.); or the nectar that flows from an angelic wound, as ichor from the wound of Aphrodite (VI, 332: cf. *Iliad*, V, 340); or the myrrh and cassia and nard and balm which grow in the Garden, not because Milton had ever seen them growing on earth, but because they grew in ancient poetry; or the tremendous chariot-charge of the Messiah

---

[1] As one might say,

> Ἔπειθ' ἑλών με κόμπασον δεσμώματα,

or

> Εὔης δὲ παρθένωπον ἀνταυδᾷ σέβας.

14

in Book VI, when "O'er shields and helms and helmèd heads he rode," not because it was specially consonant with his Messianic character, but because Achilles in Book XX of the Iliad had made a chariot-charge just like that; or the sudden turn to the second person in a hymn to the Almighty,—"Thee, Father, first they sang" (III, 371),— because there is an exactly similar turn to the second person in a hymn to Hercules in the Aeneid.[2]

More really significant as signs of the deep saturation of Milton's mind with the tradition of ancient poetry are the passages where there is no concrete allusion to anything classical, but only a shade of thought or feeling, or even of rhythm, which comes to the classical scholar with the inward music of the old world:

> whereon Jacob saw
> Angels ascending and descending, bands
> Of guardians bright, when he from Esau fled
> To Padan-Aram in the field of Luz,
> Dreaming by night under the open skie,
> And waking cri'd, "This is the Gate of Heav'n."
>
> (III, 510)

There is the same vivid classical influence in lines like the Stoic *sententia*:

> To mee who with eternal famin pine,
> Alike is Hell or Paradise or Heaven;
>
> (X, 597)

or

> Millions of spiritual creatures walk the earth;[3]
>
> (IV, 677)

or

[2] VIII, 293:

> ut duros mille labores . . .
> Pertulerit: tu nubigenas, invicte, bimembres
> Hylaeumque Pholumque manu, tu Cresia mactas
> Prodigia.

[3] Cf. *Iliad*, XII, 326:

> κῆρες ἐφεστᾶσιν θανάτοιο μυρίαι.

15

> Unshak'n, unseduc'd, unterrifi'd;[4]   (V, 896)

or

> O Woods, O Fountains, Hillocks, Dales and Bowrs;[5]
> (X, 860)

or in the several descriptions of dawn and sunset, as much as there is in

> All is not lost; the unconquerable Will,
> And study of revenge, immortal hate,
> And courage never to submit or yield:
> And what is else not to be overcome.   (I, 107)

In the last line, no doubt, the average English reader is conscious of a shock to his expectations and will recognize something exotic; in the others he will notice nothing, the classical influence has sunk so deep, both into his consciousness and into the habits of English poetry.

Here, as in the rest of life, the unconscious and unnoticed influence of tradition is vastly more widespread than that which strikes the mind. Is there any possible way in which we can estimate that unconscious influence?

Perhaps a critic would usually think first of the judgements uttered about poetry in the *Poetics*, and would consider how far Milton was guided by them. Aristotle's first demand is for unity of action; an epic poem should have definite construction, so that the whole of it is about the same subject, like the Iliad or the Odyssey or a good Greek tragedy; it must not form a mere collection of amusing episodes, like the *Kalevala* or the *Decameron*,

---

[4] Cf. Sophocles, Antigone, 1071:

ἄμοιρον ἀκτέριστον ἀνόσιον νέκυν·

Euripides, Alcestis, 173:

ἄκλαυτος ἀστένακτος,

etc.

[5] Cf. Sophocles, Philoctetes, 936:

ὦ λιμένες, ὦ προβλῆτες, ὦ ξυνουσίαι
θηρῶν ὀρείων, ὦ καταρρῶγες πέτραι·

Theocritus, I, 115:

ὦ λύκοι, ὦ θῶες, ὦ ἀν' ὤρεα φωλάδες ἄρκτοι

etc.

or a modern revue. This is certainly a quality of *Paradise Lost*. One might also quote Aristotle for the approval of a special style of diction suitable for poetry, and differing both in vocabulary and in style from the ordinary language of conversation or of businesslike prose. Here, too, Milton is classical; as the late Sir Walter Raleigh has shown, he is the very originator of the current "poetic diction" of the ages that followed him. Again, Aristotle implies, though he never states it in so many words, a view of metre extremely different from that current in popular English or German poetry. He assumes, as a matter of course, that the rules of the metre in which he writes will be known and unerringly observed by the poet; he assumes also that the quantity of every syllable—long, short, or doubtful—will be definitely known, and that, whatever variety of metrical effect the poet may produce or aim at, it must always be a variety inside the rules of the art. Here, also, Milton, among English writers of blank verse, is conspicuously exact and wonderful in his varied music. There is perhaps one more "classical" quality which we can definitely derive from Aristotle: that is, the quality of being "heroic," or dealing with characters and actions and experiences which are, as he puts it, "greater than ourselves." The kind of poetry to which Aristotle gives the name of tragic—for he includes the Iliad under that head—deals habitually with kings, and gods, and "heroes," which is only the early Greek name for the mighty dead. And should anyone object that a king may not be a hero, or indeed any "greater" in character than a bootblack, Aristotle's answer would be merely that, of course, that sort of king is not a fit subject for heroic poetry.

After that, if we try to observe further the sort of characteristics that belong to Milton and also belong markedly to the Greek tradition in poetry, we shall have to leave Aristotle and notice some of the qualities which he did not consider worth mentioning, he took them so completely for granted. One is a vivid consciousness of values, of what is good or bad, high or low, right or wrong; a complete absence of the cynical or merely realistic spirit, which either does not feel disgust when its heroes or heroines act disgustingly, or is actually amused and pleased at making them do so. One whole tragedy of Sophocles hinges on the problem whether a young man will, or will not, tell a bad lie because he is ordered to do so; and quite a number of tragedies are concerned with the problem of Orestes' duty toward his father and mother. This attitude is, as it were, stiffened and exaggerated in the Puritan poet, with his overwhelming sense of the importance of acting rightly or wrongly, and his conviction that Sin is the mother of Death.

Two other characteristics of Greek poetry are less conspicuous in Milton, but, if one looks, are to be found in him. Lafcadio Hearn observes that one of the difficulties which the Japanese feel in appreciating English poetry is the immense—and to their minds unpleasant—importance which our poets attach to love between man and woman. Indians are said to feel the same difficulty. Our preoccupation with the subject may well be criticized; it is certainly often extravagant and morbid. But there can be no doubt that it belongs to the Greek tradition. Greek myth is full of love-stories where love is not a trivial but a tragic thing; where disappointed lovers die, or persistent lovers go through long ordeals; where maidens kill themselves to preserve their virginity, or because they have lost it; and where the observance of some rule of chastity leads to bliss, or its breach to disaster. This motive was, for various reasons, so immensely developed and exaggerated in the Middle Ages and in the Romantic Movement, that nineteenth-century writers fell into the habit of regarding romantic love as a modern invention with which the ancients did not sympathize; but such a view will not bear a moment's reflection. It cannot be maintained that the ancient poets and artists abstained from the romantic idealization of woman—Homer and the vase-paintings and the concepts of such goddesses as

Athena and Artemis disprove such a view. It cannot be maintained that women did not express their feelings: Sappho shows that they did. The truth probably is that something which in a large sense may be called the Romantic Movement began in Greece, but, partly because it was only beginning and partly because of the restraint and truthfulness that was natural to Greek art, it was free from those intensities and extravagances of sensibility which it developed, for example, in the *Vita Nuova* of Dante, or the novels of George Sand. It arose, also, in protest against that extremely unromantic and matter-of-fact view of woman which was probably normal in the stage of civilization out of which the Hellenic movement rose, and which still remains usual outside the narrow limits of the cultured Western or Hellenic tradition. And, lastly, we must always remember that, in the ancient world, when emotion rose above a certain degree of intensity, it regularly expressed itself, not as literature, but as religion. Why invent stories or compose rhapsodies about inspired and angelic young women, when it was so much easier to sing hymns to the Muse or the nymph Egeria, to Artemis or Pallas Athena?

The same thought throws light on another subject where modern criticism has notoriously gone astray. The Greeks are said not to have possessed our sensitive appreciation of the beauties of nature. The truth seems to be that our sensitiveness to nature is simply the old ecstasy of nature-worship sublimated and devitalized. Wordsworth wished, in his rapture, that he could catch sight of Proteus rising from the sea,

Or hear old Triton blow his wreathèd horn.

But the old Greeks, in their rapture, simply did so. Where we write long descriptions of the beauty of some mountain scene, they trudged to the mountain-top at dawn and gave sacrifice. Only gradually, as the cruder nature-worship died away, did the poets begin to describe natural beauty with much detail: there are flashes in Sophocles and

Euripides, exquisite pictures later in Theocritus, and eventually, toward the fall of Greek literature, elaborate descriptions in the novelists, Heliodorus and Longus. I speak with insufficient knowledge, but it seems to me that the long descriptions of nature in such mediaeval romances as *Aucassin and Nicolette* or even the *Romaunt of the Rose* are modelled, at one or two removes, on these late Greek novelists. At any rate, the thrill of nature, like the thrill of romantic love, is an essential element in the Greek tradition.

In Milton, then, it almost seems as if the occasional marked "classicisms," using that word to denote the striking and unusual imitations of Latin or Greek usage, were so conspicuous as really to divert a reader's attention from the main stream of classical tradition flowing through him. And it is the main stream that matters. Let us take the great antithesis to Milton in this matter, who is supposed to represent the English tradition at its freest, most removed from the learned or Graeco-Roman influence— Shakespeare. It will not be fair to take his poems: they are as deeply dyed in classical sources as Milton. The verse is strict; the diction poetic; the allusions, to an almost tiresome degree, mythological. We must take his plays, where the style, evidently of set purpose, is much looser and nearer to spoken language. And among the plays it would not be fair to take the definitely classical plays, like *Julius Caesar*, nor yet, on the other hand, the more trivial or fanciful comedies. The classical tradition shows best in the greatest works; let us take the opening scene of *Hamlet*.

First, there is the form of the composition. It is a "tragedy," a form invented by the Greeks; and written in five acts because in Shakespeare's time Greek tragedies were commonly believed to be so divided. And, like Greek tragedy, though it represents conversation, it is written in regular verse, and that verse iambic in character. The subject of a Greek tragedy is, without exception, taken from history, and almost always from remote and legendary history, away from the tyranny of exact information. It is never invented by the poet. It is practically always about kings, queens, and princes. *Hamlet* follows all these rules. We may also notice that Greek tragedy was never bound by narrow patriotic interests; the Athenian poet chose his subject indifferently in Argos, or Thebes, or wherever he might find it. So Shakespeare, though he also wrote a series of English historical plays, in his greatest works is as free as the Greeks. Here he chooses a royal family in the legendary history of Denmark.

The subject itself is a strange one: the old Hamlet having been murdered by a younger kinsman, his wife seduced, and his crown taken, his son is urged by supernatural warnings to avenge his father and eventually does so; but, overpowered by the horror of the situation, and especially by his feeling toward his mother, he becomes deranged in mind on the way. This is not only the regular tragic sequence of Old King, Young King, or Enemy, and Third King, or Deliverer: it is exactly the story of Orestes, the most typical hero of Greek tragedy. The father of Orestes also was murdered by a younger kinsman, his wife seduced, and his crown taken; Orestes is urged by supernatural warnings to avenge his father; he also eventually does so; but, overpowered by the horror of the situation, he also becomes deranged in mind on the way. The differences and similarities in detail are very striking, but these I propose to discuss more fully in a later chapter. Let us now take the actual opening of *Hamlet*—a very beautiful and famous scene.

A platform before a Castle at Elsinore; a sentry watching in the night. Just so the *Oresteia* of Aeschylus opens on a platform before—or above—the Castle of the Atreidae at Argos, where a sentry is watching in the night. Aeschylus then proceeds to explain the situation in a soliloquy of the Watchman; Shakespeare, following the practice of the later Greek tragedians, has, instead of the soliloquy, a dialogue between soldiers. The dialogue between two servants or retainers as a method of exposition seems to have been started in the *Medea* of Euripides, and has remained a favourite device ever since.

Shakespeare can use three speakers instead of two; and his verse is composed on a looser model than that of Aeschylus, Sophocles, or Euripides, unless indeed we consider the unfinished *Iphigenia in Aulis* of the last-named. That play initiated a movement toward freer and more colloquial dialogue, a movement developed afterwards with wonderful grace and daring by Menander, and copied much more loosely and heavily by Plautus. One might say that Shakespeare was just continuing the Menandrian tradition, and carrying it a step or two further.

At line 41, while it is still night, "*Enter the Ghost.*" A large number of our extant Greek tragedies begin with some supernatural being, a god or a ghost, in the darkness before dawn; after this being's departure there are usually some lines calling attention to the break of day:

> But look, the morn in russet mantle clad
> Walks o'er the dew of yon high eastern hill;

or

> Hark, the sun's first ray
> Awakens the clear song of morning birds,
> And the dark revel of the stars is still.

Shakespeare says one, Sophocles[6] the other; and, as it happens, it is the modern poet, not the ancient, who personifies and gives human form to the goddess of dawn.

Shakespeare's Ghost first enters after forty-one lines; most Greek ghosts or gods like to be there at the beginning, though the Ghost of Clytemnestra in the *Oresteia* enters at line 94 and departs at 139. Still, Shakespeare's Ghost, with its two entries and exits, moves a good deal more freely than the fifth-century ghosts, and more like those of the New Comedy.

The language of this scene is, of course, free from the elaborate classicisms which add dignity to the verse of

---

[6] *Electra*, l. 17.

Milton; for this is the language of a play, and a play, as Aristotle observes, must keep close to real life. It is meant to be spoken and to be rapidly understood. Some few phrases remind one of a Greek or Latin source—the dating of an incident, not by clocks or hours, but by the stars:

> When yon same star that's westward from the pole;

a deliberately Greek periphrasis for "the late King":

> That fair and warlike form
> Wherein the majesty of buried Denmark
> Did sometime march;

references to "the Fates" and "an omen": to

> the moist star
> Upon whose influence Neptune's empire stands;

and to the various signs and portents which boded the death of Julius Caesar, when

> the sheeted dead
> Did squeak and gibber in the Roman streets

—which they did, doubtless, because of those ghosts who "squeaked in thin voices like bats" in the Odyssey.[7] But I keep further details for a later chapter.

Of course there is no suggestion here of denying or minimizing the great differences of style and treatment which separate Shakespeare from his antique predecessors: the greater length of the play, the variety of incidents, the number of characters, the free admission of irrelevant matter, the lavish use of ornament and quip and quibble, the great flexibility with which the Elizabethan moves in and out of the tragic legendary world to visit the common world of to-day. Still less, I trust, will anyone imagine that this insistence on the element of tradition in Shakespeare, and still more in Milton, affects in the smallest degree the greatness of either poet's genius. It is one of

[7] Odyssey, XXIV, 6.

the very feeblest of critical errors to suppose that there is a thing called "originality," which consists in having no models. I have merely tried to show, first, that in an author of markedly classical leanings, like Milton, there is, besides the obvious classicisms, a great mass of classical influence—that is, extremely ancient traditional influence —which passes unnoticed; and next, that the same is true of a very different author, such as Shakespeare, who is commonly supposed to represent the opposite tendency. But we remain confronted by the difficulty that, when we try to reckon up the amount of unnoticeable and perhaps unconscious classical influence that exists in these authors, we have no proper instrument for detecting it. We do not really know what we are looking for. We can see the classicism that stands out as alien against the ordinary style of English poetry; but how are we to recognize the elements in that ordinary style which are the direct though unconscious fruit of ancient influence and have been in poetry from the beginning?

To answer this question, it may be helpful to begin at the other end, and try to discover what the origin of poetry, as known to the European or Mediterranean world, really was, and what elements seem to have been essential to it. If that can be made out, we shall gain some conception of the sort of subject, language, style, method, and spirit that originally made poetry, and that constitute its classical or permanent tradition; we may also observe the sort of variation from norm which has, at different times, for one reason or another, been tried and found unsatisfactory, or at least impermanent.

24

II

THE MOLPÊ

THE OLD HISTORIES OF GREEK LITERATURE USED TO BEGIN
with Epic Poetry, and proceed in order to Lyric and Dramatic. A romantic poet could even write: *Le monde naît,
Homère chante*; as if highly elaborate constructions like
the Iliad and the Odyssey, with a vast development of
both history and technique behind them, had been the
first utterance of an almost primitive society. That con-
fusing conception has passed away, and dark as the pre-
Homeric stage of poetry is, we can to some extent
penetrate into it.

The direct evidence is, of course, both scanty and
unreliable. Few scholars put much trust in the lists of
supposed poets who were earlier than Homer. But there
is a form of indirect evidence which, as far as it goes,
can be trusted. It is the evidence of religion. Anthro-
pologists have long established the principle expressed
roughly in the epigram that man makes his gods in his
own image; or, more exactly, that the instruments, gar-
ments, and characteristics attributed traditionally to a
god are generally a safe guide to those of the tribe which
worshipped or invented him. If Hephaistos, the divine
smith, has a hammer and an anvil, we may be sure that
a hammer and an anvil were used by human smiths among
his worshippers. If Apollo uses a bow and arrows, so must
his worshippers have used them; and if his caused disease

and pestilence, it is probable that theirs were poisoned. If Poseidon, the sea-god and fisher-god, carries a trident, we may conclude that it was usual among his first worshippers to spear fish with a three-pronged fork. By these instances we learn something of the habits of primitive Greek smiths, warriors, and fishermen. What can we learn about poets?

Most professions have created for themselves a divine ancestor. Smiths are children of Hephaistos; soldiers are children of Ares; heralds, of Hermes; doctors, of course, are sons of Asclepius, while kings are descended from Zeus. But what of poets? Poets are not the children of any one god or goddess:

> ἐκ γὰρ Μουσάων καὶ ἐκηβόλου Ἀπόλλωνος
> ἄνδρες ἀοιδοὶ ἔασιν ἐπὶ χθονὶ καὶ κιθαρισταί.

So says our very earliest witness, Hesiod (*Theogony*, 94): "From the Muses and far-shooting Apollo come bards upon the earth and harp-players." Apollo and the Muses together made the poetry of heaven: the bard and a chorus must have made that of earth. The poet—or at least the bard, for we may draw a distinction between them later —does not stand alone. He is the leader or director of a chorus, whose movements and emotions are attuned to his. Nor yet does his poetry stand alone; its words are caught up in music, and its rhythm deepened by the swaying of the dance; though, of course, both "dance" and "music" bore a different meaning in those days. Neither had been so specialized and developed. Both were far frailer and gentler things, and they also went always together. The Greek word Molpê means "dance-and-song."

We have many descriptions of the doings of these early bards. On the shield of Heracles, among the emblazonry, "there was a Dance of the immortals, and in the midst the Child of Zeus and Leto harped with a golden lyre so as to wake longing; and the divine Muses of Olympus started the song, like women lifting up sweet voices." (*Aspis*, 201.)

26

The word ἐξάρχειν, to "start" the song, is generally used
of the bard himself, especially of Apollo. But not always.
At the feast in Menelaus' house a bard was in the midst
of the chorus, harping; and there two special tumblers
"started" the dance, for the others to join in later. (*Odyssey*, IV, 17 ff.) On the shield of Achilles there was a
"labyrinth-dance"; there a bard "started" the dance with
his harping, and the professional tumblers merely added
to the entertainment. (*Iliad*, XVIII, 603 ff.) At the feast
at the castle of Alcinous the bard Demodocus was invited to sing a lay (or narrative poem), and he duly sang
one; but the procedure seems rather surprising. "So spake
Alcinous; and a herald went to fetch the bard's harp from
the King's house. And there rose up the chosen public
umpires, nine in all, and they made smooth the dancing
ground (χορός) and wide the meeting place (ἀγών). And
the herald brought the harp to Demodocus and he went
into the middle; and on either side of him rose youths
in their prime, skilled in dancing, and they beat the divine floor with their feet. Then he touched his harp and
began sweetly to sing." It is all intelligible enough, except perhaps why the floor should be called "divine."
Probably it was "divine" in the sense of "inspired" or
"inspiring"; because, when you came on to that floor,
after the nine public umpires had done their best to it,
you felt that you were bound to dance. There was magic
in it, or, as the Greeks said, some divine power. For the
rest, it is all intelligible, but it certainly is surprising.
When we ask a modern poet to recite his works to us,
we do not expect nine policemen to clear the ground.
It is the more curious, in that Demodocus did not sing
a lyric or a mere song; he sang a regular lay or narrative
poem.

It is probably from this sort of lay that the epic eventually arose. It came when the adventurers in the Sea Migrations wanted poetry, but had left their "dancing floors"
and bands of maidens or the like far behind at home.
Like Achilles in Iliad IX, they had only themselves and

27

their ship and their story; and the story grew, taking the place of the dance and song.

Usually in this early poetry we seem to find a choral song, and a choral dance or procession. For example, in the Hymn to Apollo we hear how that prototype of all poets conducted his business: "He goes forth harping on his way toward rocky Pytho, his raiment is fragrant and immortal, and his harp beneath the golden striker makes a sound that awakes longing; then up, swift as a thought, he springs to Olympus, to the Hall of Zeus. And straightway all the hearts of the immortals are full of harping and song. And the Muses in divisions answering one another sing with sweet voices. . . . And Apollo in the midst of them strikes his lyre, stepping fair and high."

What the Muses sang about we shall consider later on; but the method of their singing and dancing is already clear in outline. We can see the bard, in the midst, with his lyre or harp, "starting" or "conducting" the Molpê, and the choir around him performing it. Here it is Apollo and the Muses; at Delos, as Professor J. A. K. Thomson has shown in his fascinating study of this subject,[1] it seems to have been Homer and the Delian Maidens; in a Bacchic dance it is the God, or his human representative, and the Maenads: in each case a "conductor," with a chorus, generally female. It is interesting that Hesiod, who is inspired by the Muses of Helicon without the intervention of Apollo, is himself chosen by them as their leader and presented with a staff or sceptre of growing laurel. Hesiod, like Homer, is an inspired exarchon. (*Theogony*, 22 ff.)

We can make out something about the movements and the place of these dances. The harvest dances naturally took place on a threshing-floor. It was charged with the magic of fruitfulness; it was large and round and level, and there was normally one in every village. Indeed, the words ἅλως (threshing-floor) and χορός (chorus or dancing place) are sometimes used interchangeably. Then

[1] *Studies in the Odyssey*, chap. 10.

28

there were springs and altars: the Muses in Hesiod danced round the mountain spring of Helicon and the altar of Zeus. (*Theogony*, 1–5.) The chorus in tragedy danced round an altar; and one may presume that the Delian Maidens of the Hymn to Apollo did so, though it is not definitely so stated. And in very early times, before the days of temples, a spring was generally a sacred object and formed a natural centre for a dance. On vase-paintings the dance is often round an altar. But we hear a good deal also of a Molpê that is more like a march or procession, not merely a dance round some centre in a sacred place. Hesiod's Muses, for example, when they have bathed their soft bodies in the aforesaid holy spring, set up their dances on the highest top of Helicon, and then comes the best of it: they set off, through the night, unseen, only the lovely voices sounding through the mist, to visit all their haunts in the mountains.[2] We are not told their final destination; but when Apollo leads them in the Hymn (182 ff.), the dance moves from the altar of Delos in the sea to that of Pytho among the hills; then up, up, to the highest and most untrodden heights of Mount Olympus, and from there away to Heaven and the House of Zeus. It is the human "Mountain Walk," or *Oreibasia*, transferred to the gods.

The dancing was as integral a part of the bard's duty as his singing or his invention. That explains the punishment of Thamyris the Thracian, who boasted with his newfangled sort of poetry to surpass the Muses: "And they in wrath made him a maimed man, and took away from him his heavenly Song and made him forget his harping."[3] Scholars have taken the word πηρόν, maimed or lame, to mean something different, because to later ages lameness was no great disqualification to a poet. They thought Thamyris must have been struck blind

---

[2] Theogony, 8. Cf. the Song of Callicles in *Empedocles on Etna.*
[3] Iliad, II, 595 ff.:

> αἱ δὲ χολωσάμεναι πηρὸν θέσαν, αὐτὰρ ἀοιδὴν
> θεσπεσίην ἀφέλοντο καὶ ἐκλέλαθον κιθαριστύν.

or dumb. But a passage in Aratus' poem about the stars really settles the matter. He describes there a constellation called Ἐν γόνασιν, the Man on his Knees, and explains how this man trails wearily on one knee because he is lame; and the scholiast explains that the man is Thamyris. (Aratus, *Phaenomena*, 63 ff., and *Scholia*.) The curse of the Muses was terribly complete. Thamyris used to sing, to harp, and to dance; and they disabled him from all three. He developed, one may suppose, a really vicious style, and every talent he had was poisoned by it.

There is a word which occurs in two forms, οἶμος and οἴμη, derived from a root meaning "to go": it is a verbal noun and must mean "a going." In practice the masculine form generally, but not always, means a journey, or a wandering; the feminine means simply a song or lay. The two went always together: when you sang, you went. Just so in English the verbal noun from the root "dig" has two forms, "dyke" and "ditch," which are now divided in meaning, though they began by denoting the same concrete object, the dug ground. The reason is that, whenever you found a "ditch" dug, you found a "dyke" thrown up beside it. So with οἴμη and οἶμος. Demodocus, we may remember, sang, or at least recited, to the harp, his narrative poem; he can hardly have danced it. But the dancers were at their work before he began, and as soon as he finished two very special dancers took the floor. That is perhaps why the early poems that we call the "Homeric Hymns" were in Greek called προοίμια—"preludes," or things that come before the οἴμη, or, indifferently, before the οἶμος. The dance, of course, was not like our dancing. At times it may have been something with fixed steps and movements; at times we know that it was mimetic, trying magically to bring about some effect which it imitated. But in its essence it is only the yearning of the whole dumb body to express that emotion—the Greeks' would say that "longing" (ἵμερος)—for which words and harp and singing are not enough. The word constantly applied to all good singing or harping is ἱμερόεις, not merely "beautiful," but possessing that sort of beauty which makes the heart yearn. Ἵμερος and ῥυθμός, longing and rhythm, are the two special elements which the voice finds strengthened in the movements of the body.

It is difficult at this distance of time to estimate the relative importance in this early Molpê of the bard and the chorus respectively. In development, one would conjecture, the group came first and the individual after; and in later literature one certainly seems to find the individual gradually emancipating himself. We hear of competitions between separate choruses; also between bards who lead and conduct their respective choruses; while the special chorus of the Delian Maidens seems to have been at the disposal of all the various competing poets, and could sing in all the different dialects that were required. Fifth-century poets like Pindar and Bacchylides express themselves entirely through a chorus which they "teach"; so do the great tragedians, though in both cases the poet on particular occasions might conduct or lead the dancing himself. But at the same time, or earlier, the Lesbian poets and poetesses were singing or speaking their lyrics alone, and together with the cessation of the chorus the element of dancing seems to have disappeared or diminished. We hear also of the chorus being divided into "semi-choruses" or other groups, as in drama, for the purpose of a continuous performance, or perhaps of an epic lay. One half could rest while the other danced and sang; or at times, perhaps, the singers could rest while others danced. It is curious, and perhaps significant, that this "amoebaean" form of recital, in which one semichorus or group answered another, is the form that seems specially to be called ὁμηρεία or ὁμήρευσις—"Homer-ing." The Muses in Hesiod tell their story ἀμειβόμεναι ὀπὶ καλῇ | φωνῇ ὁμηρεῦσαι.[4]

What subjects were treated in this Molpê? The evidence is not very clear, because no doubt certain sub-

[4] *Theogony*, 38; cf. *Iliad*, I, 604, *Odyssey*, XXIV, 60.

31

jects were assumed to be obvious and natural. Hesiod and Homer do not define the subjects, but speak generally of them. The Muses of Hesiod, as they dance invisibly through the night, "sing of aegis-bearing Zeus and queenly Hera, and Athena, and Phoebus Apollo, and Artemis, and Poseidon, and Themis," and others, and, indeed, of "all the race of the Blessed who live for ever." [5] The Gods seem to form a great part of their song. But also they help the bard to sing "tales of men and women aforetime"; [6] they sing of the things "that are and that shall be and that were long ago"; they even sing of the "laws and good customs of the immortals." [7] But the great message which they gave to Hesiod in his vision consisted of a confession and a promise: "We know how to utter many false things that look like real; but we also know, when we choose, how to speak truth." [8] In the Hymn to Apollo, again, they sing "the immortal gifts of the Gods and the endurances of men—θεῶν δῶρ' ἄμβροτα, ἠδ' ἀνθρώπων τλημοσύνας." [9] Life consists, it would seem, of a long grey struggle to keep alive, and not to lose heart; but across the grey there flash on occasion such things as love and delight and victory and surprising deliverances— the "immortal gifts" of the Gods.

There is nothing very explicit in this. We know, of course, that there were Molpai for sowing and harvest; Molpai for rain or for sun; for fertility in man, beast, and fruit; for the averting of pestilence, and for most of the other things that people pray for. We hear of choric songs for marriage and death and victory and the like. But there is one choric celebration which was peculiarly old and has proved peculiarly long-lived, as well as extraordinarily important in literature, and which may perhaps fairly be taken as the most central and typical of its class.

We all know, since the work of Sir James Frazer, how

[5] *Theogony*, 11–21. [6] *Hymn to Apollo*, 160. [7] *Theogony*, 38, 66.
[8] *Ibid.*, 27, 28. [9] *Hymn to Apollo*, 190.

the whole religion of the Mediterranean world centred
on what we call agriculture: the ancients regarded it as
the action of divine powers blessing or cursing man
through his land and flocks. In particular, we find, almost
wherever we have any information, the worship of a being
who somehow typifies the vegetation or life of the year;
modern mythologists can call him a Year-Daemon or
Vegetation Spirit, or some other generic name; but to
the ancient villager he was, of course, a definite person,
often with a definite history. He was Attis, Adonis, Osiris,
Hippolytus, or one among many other heroes or fragments
of heroes—for, of course, these creations of the human
mind were as ready as clouds are to lose their fixed outlines and blend one with another, or disperse. But in the
Attic celebrations which ultimately led to tragedy and
comedy the divine being was Dionysus; and his *sacer
ludus*, or "holy playing," is said by Herodotus, who had
seen both, to be in almost every detail like that of Osiris.[1]
This *sacer ludus*, it is now generally agreed, was essentially
identical in subject with the "Mummers' Play" which still
lingers on, in a broken and degenerate form, among the
peasantry of northern Europe. The Mummers' Play shows
the birth of the Year-Child, his marvellous growth and
beauty, his successful combat and his marriage; then comes
a further battle with some dark enemy, discomfiture and
defeat and death, followed in most forms of the play by
at least some hint of resurrection. For, of course, the
year that dies in winter will rise again in the ensuing
spring. It has been, to my judgement, convincingly argued
by Mr. F. M. Cornford [2] that both comedy and tragedy
are derived from this Year-Play: comedy culminates in
the hero's *Comos* or Marriage-Revel, and tragedy in his
death and lamentation. Yet, though Greek tragedy does
not fear the "unhappy ending," none the less it is haunted

---

[1] Herodotus, II, 48; cf. 42, 144.
[2] *Origin of Attic Comedy* (Arnold, 1914); also my *Excursus on the
Forms of Greek Tragedy in Themis*, by J. E. Harrison (2d ed., 1927).

by the thought of some life after death, and the nearer it keeps to its proper Dionysiac form, the stronger is the note of rebirth.

Tragedies end in death. Comedies end in marriage. The rough rule is true of almost all Greek tragedies, and, if we understand rightly the word "marriage," of practically all Greek comedies. "Marriage" in English is a word of legal and ceremonial connotations; the marriage *Comos* of Greek poetry has little to do with legal forms. It is a union of lovers accompanied by an outburst of joy. Is it not at first sight amazing, and on further reflection profoundly instructive, to recognize that the same rule has remained generally true of all tragedies and comedies since? The poets and dramatists have not deliberately wished to end upon the note of rejoicing for love or of weeping for death. Thousands of them have tried hard to escape from so hackneyed an ending, and to prove themselves "original." But the tradition is too strong for them. There is one general joy greater than other joys, one universal fear darker than other fears; and the poet who throws himself on the stream of his song is borne almost inevitably toward the one or the other. Aristotle speaks of the Homeric epos as the fountainhead of tragedy; Longinus distinguishes the Odyssey from the Iliad as a "comedy of character." [3] Both judgements are easily explicable. The last line of the Iliad tells us: "So wrought they the burial of Hector tamer of horses." And the last line of the Odyssey, according to Aristarchus,— though in our present version there are many lines after it,—runs: "So came those two to the rite of the ancient Marriage-Bed." (*Odyssey*, XXIII, 296.)

Love and Death: those are the two chief subjects of this primitive Molpê. Next there is Strife, whether for defeat or victory. The Iliad and Odyssey are full of it; no ancient comedy is without it, and, properly understood,

---

[3] Κωμῳδία τις ἠθολογουμένη. De Sublimitate, IX, 15. Cf. Aristotle, Poetics, 1449a.

no ancient tragedy. Indeed, it is largely strife which gives to love or death its value. The world is not greatly interested in a marriage which has involved no difficulty and no opposition, nor even in a natural and expected death. It is Love won in spite of obstacles and enemies; it is Death in the midst of strife and glory, especially Death averted or conquered, that move us most.

Death can be conquered by heroism, by some quality of character or some expression of beauty so dazzling that death seems a small thing in comparison; but the easiest way—in fiction—to rob Death of his sting and the grave of its victory is, of course, through the revelation of some life beyond death, and the contemplation of the Immortals who are "deathless and ageless for all days." When Dionysus, who was torn in pieces and scattered in dead fragments over the earth, rises again in the spring with a new and glorified body, that is the full and complete conquest of Death—the only complete conquest. With Dionysus, being a god, the new life is of course a certainty; and no doubt the same "immortal gift" has come to the very great heroes; the gods would naturally see to it, and our fathers have told us that they did so. For us common men the case is different; but still, one may hope. One may at least think and wonder about it. And early Greek poetry thinks about it a great deal. There are visions of the world of the dead in both Iliad and Odyssey; there is the regular resurrection in glory of the Year-Daemon in the legends of his cult, and the remains of it are visible in many tragedies. In most of them there is at the end either a character made immortal, or one rescued from the grave, or at least some worship established which implies a continuance of life.[4]

Love, Strife, Death, and that which is beyond Death. Those are, it would seem, definitely the four themes about which our earliest bards sang, and, when singing was not

---

[4] E.g., in Euripides: someone made immortal at the end of *Andromache, Helena, Orestes, Bacchae*; back from the grave, *Alcestis*; worship established, *Medea, Heracleidae, Hippolytus*, etc.

enough to express all their stress of emotion, yearned and reached out their arms amid the dancers. But apart from these actual themes, there was an atmosphere in the early Molpê which was markedly characteristic and which has haunted nearly all poetry since. The whole Molpê was inspired by the worship of nature. The feast was a feast for sowing or reaping, for planting or harvesting; it was a magic rite to make sure that the dead Dionysus would rise again. Only a few years ago Mr. J. C. Lawson found in Greece during Holy Week an old woman on the verge of tears: "Of course I am anxious; for if Christ does not rise to-morrow we shall have no corn this year." [5] She was feeling what her ancestors had felt three thousand years before, the adoration of that mystery which makes the Life of the World.

People will say: "It was not the beauty of Nature that moved these primitive worshippers. It was simply the desire for food." But I think such a criticism is sophistical. The coming of spring is beautiful and thrilling to anyone; to one whose life or death depends upon it it certainly cannot be less thrilling, and I doubt if in any but a highly abstract sense it is less beautiful. The delight felt by the primitive Greek in the loveliness of the young vegetation which meant to him the reborn Dionysus was no doubt not a purely aesthetic delight; he did not isolate the impression of beauty and think about it. But the joy in beauty was surely present—it was not merely swamped and forgotten—in the flood of gratitude and gladness which he felt at being relieved of the dread of famine. We need not argue about the precise aesthetic quality of his emotion. He danced and sang both for joy in the spring and in order to make the spring richer and stronger. He knew the spring to be really a new-born God; and he danced to worship the God, and to express delight in him, and also to make him grow great and conquer his enemies. And surely it is a lineal

---

[5] *Modern Greek Folklore and Ancient Greek Religion,* p. 573 (Cambridge, 1910).

descendant of that feeling—a joy in beauty which is filled with mystery and worship and even magic—that has been characteristic of nature-poetry ever since; and not by any means a purely aesthetic appreciation of beautiful objects. When Wordsworth's heart filled with pleasure and went dancing with the daffodils, his emotion was not purely aesthetic: he was probably closer than he suspected to those far-off and much-envied spiritual ancestors of his who had in their time communed with spirits of the forest or heard the horn of a sea-god echoing amid the murmur of the waves.

The sense of Nature is there from the beginning; and I think we ought to notice one other element, not perhaps consciously present but haunting and transforming the atmosphere. As the dancers felt that the Dionysus for whose death they wept would after all return again, so they knew in their hearts that the new-born stranger over whom they rejoiced was really the same whom they had welcomed and wept over before. The Old King, long since cast out, humiliated, defeated, was now returning to his own. All that they were doing became like a dream: they had done this before, every cry, every movement, every throb of the heart. The magic of Memory was at work, Memory, ἱμερόεσσα, "waker of longing," the enchantress who turns the common to the heavenly and fills men's eyes with tears because the things that are now past were so beautiful. That is why they liked to dance in the place where they danced last year, and where others had danced before them; why they liked to cling to the old words that had always been used in these songs instead of the clearer and commoner modern words, and liked them perhaps all the better when people were not quite sure of their exact meaning but only felt the atmosphere and the fragrance, and of course the actual magic, that clung about them. There were words and phrases, full of music, which, as soon as they were uttered, brought back the feeling of the dance, the moon and stars and the dawn, and the wind tossing in the dancers' hair; surely

37

such words were better worth using than those which were used every day and carried no virtue. But of course one would use them only at the place and hour where they belonged.

Painters have delighted in efforts to depict this ancient Molpê, yet it is only with difficulty that we can imagine what it was like. We know something, but not much, of the tunes. We can conjecture from the metres and the vase-paintings something, but not much, about the steps. But it is worth while, for the help of our own imaginations, to realize how the bards themselves felt about it and what they felt themselves to resemble as they worshipped. They felt that they were like birds on the wing.

The Muses, Hesiod tells us (*Theogony*, 61), had carefree hearts. They could also free others from care. For when they have taught a bard, and he sings of the gods and the heroes of old, then even a man in fresh grief forgets his sorrow and remembers not his cares any more (*Ibid.*, 102). That explains, if it needs explanation, the cry of the bard Alkman, when his limbs fail him in the long nocturnal dance: "Would, would that I were the ceryl-bird, who over the flower of the wave floats among the halcyons, with never a care in his heart, the sea-blue bird of the spring." The ceryl-bird conducts a Molpê too, like the poet, except that the bird never wearies. The word Molpê itself is used of the halcyon in a similar prayer of another poet:

> Bird of the sea rocks, of the bursting spray,
>   O halcyon bird,
> That wheelest crying, crying, on thy way:
>   Who knoweth pain can read the tale of thee:
> One love long lost, one song for ever heard,
>   And wings that sweep the sea.

It is the singing and the dance together that make the likeness, and so turn the bird into an *Aoidos*. It is the same with the "minstrel swan," not ours but the Medi-

terranean swan, which utters a deep, bell-like note as it
flies; it is like the bard, or rather, it is what the bard
wishes to be like. (*Iphigenia in Tauris*, 1089, 1103.) The
same with the cranes in the *Helena* (1484), flying in
clamour high among the clouds: "O winged ones long-
throated," the poet calls, "I would I could join your
dance." Even the nightingale, which seems to us to do
very little in the way of dancing, having specialized entirely in song, seemed to the ancients to have a "dance"
of her own, a dance of hiding or flying, fugitive either
from some hungry hawk or from her own persecuting
memories. These song-birds[6] are all *Aoidoi*, making magical Molpai with their voices and their wings alike. They
show the poet what he should strive to be.

For it seems as if there were still one element which
we had forgotten, and one which the ancients counted
among the most important of all, the element of Mimesis, or imitation. In most of the dances, if not all, the
dancer ceased to be himself. He "imitated," or person-
ated, the god or hero of whom he sang, or it might be
the centaurs or satyrs or the wild beasts of the mountain. There was something outside himself which he
longed and strove to be, or at least to be like. In moments of ecstasy he actually felt that he had become it.
He forgot himself. He partook of the divine or magic life
which he celebrated, so that the hierophant in the mysteries regularly became identified with the god, the leader
of the Bacchic dance became Bacchos.

The word "imitation" is too unpretending to suit our
modern style. Our critics pour contempt upon it, and
speak of "creation" or "self-expression," or the like. But
the Greeks knew what they meant. *Mimesis* was the
striving to be like something which you longed to be:
an attempt, as Shelley, with his usual acuteness of divina-
tion, puts it, to be one with "that ideal perfection and
energy which everyone feels to be the internal type of

---

[6] *E.g.*, *Iliad*, III, ad init.; Sophocles, *Electra*, 146; Euripides,
Rhesus, 546, *Helena*, 1107; Aeschylus, *Supplices*, 63.

all that he loves, admires, and would become." Perhaps we can understand the word better when we notice that it is treated as practically equivalent to *Methexis* (Μέθεξις), which means participation or communion, and is especially used of those who, through inspiration or possession or sacramental communion, partake of the being of their God. "The Pythagoreans say that existing things exist by imitation of Number; Plato says, by participation in Number." So Aristotle tells us.[7] The exact meaning of the two words these philosophers have left undefined. But clearly both imply some transcending of the bounds of self, some "ecstasy" or "standing outside" of the prison of the bard's ordinary identity and experience.

Yet surely, a critic may say, there is a contradiction, or at least a paradox, in the whole of this argument. We think of a classical style as emphatically a correct and chastened style. The ancient writers are always recommending the *limae labor*. Horace exhorts the poet to keep his poem in his desk till the ninth year, to make sure that he has made it as good as possible. We hear of the infinite labour bestowed by Vergil on the Aeneid, and how at his death he ordered the manuscript to be burnt because it was so miserably imperfect. Even in prose we hear of Plato's leaving seven different versions of the first sentence of the Republic before he hit upon the present remarkable order. It is only an exaggeration of the same spirit when we hear of the fifty-six different versions of the opening of *Orlando Furioso*. Yet, if poetry is the inspired outpouring of a bard leading his dancers in ecstasy on the threshing-floor or the mountain-top, what has it to do with all this studious and painful elaboration?

To an early Greek the question would probably have seemed a simple one. An *Aoidos*, or bard, sings amid the dancers; and no doubt some specially gifted and experienced Aoidoi can start off on the pure excitement of the

[7] *Metaphysics*, I, 6; Cornford, *From Religion to Philosophy*, p. 254.

moment, with no previous preparation. But normally you need a *Poietes*, or maker, as well as a singer. The one constructs the Molpê, taking as long as he likes; the other performs it; though of course one person can, and to a certain degree must, fill both offices.

That is, I think, the orthodox classical tradition; and whosoever would be saved should, in some form or other, act upon it. Poetry needs ecstasy or inspiration; true, but the inspiration will not merely be imperfect, it will simply not come, except to a mind that has by some long process of thinking and feeling been prepared for it. The preparation need not be conscious or specialized. When Paul had his vision on the road to Damascus, or Augustine heard the words, "Tolle, lege," or Plotinus and St. Francis were uplifted into their special ecstasies, they had not, of course, been practising or rehearsing those ecstasies, but they had long been living the kind of life and concentrating upon the kind of thought or effort to which that inspired hour was a natural crown. A poet who tosses off some exquisite lyric, apparently on the spur of the moment, has almost certainly been so living as, first, to be exquisitely prepared for that particular mood or emotion, and, secondly, to have developed the technical skill which enables him to write what he wants to write. It is, if one thinks of it soberly, absurd to suppose that inspiration falls like the rain equally on him who lives among poetical thoughts and him who thinks only of his digestion and his bank balance.

Many believers in the "inspiration theory" of poetry would admit thus much. But they still rebel against the idea of the poet sitting at his desk and laboriously correcting and improving and rewriting. A poem, they protest, ought first to represent a "real emotion," and secondly it should be an inspiration, the flash of an intense moment. As to the first point, it is the old realist fallacy raising its head once more. It implies that poetry proceeds from direct experience, whereas really it proceeds from imagination. Direct experience, as a matter of fact, does not produce poetry: poetry is produced by remembered experience or imagined experience. But the demand for inspiration is a little more plausible, or the fallacy of it harder to make clear.

How can a poem which has the true quality of ecstasy be produced by laborious rewriting? Of course, it cannot be produced by labour alone; there must be the ecstasy or inspiration, at any rate, the flash of intense emotion, as well. But is there any difficulty in understanding that a man who feels some emotion intensely and delightfully should love to dwell in it, as a lover, for instance, spends a large part of his time consciously, and far more subconsciously, thinking about the beloved? Why should people imagine that an emotion which is felt vehemently for a moment and then thrown away is somehow superior, or more sincere, compared with an emotion which colours all a man's life for long periods? Vergil worked over and over the Aeneid because he loved doing so. What exactly it was that he loved would be, certainly for us and probably even for him, impossible to say: partly the whole atmosphere of the poem, partly the interest of particular stories or thoughts, chiefly—one would imagine—the mere artist's delight in his craft, in making the texture of his weaving more gorgeous or the fretting of his marble more exquisite.

The mistake comes, I think, from people's regarding "labour" or "study" as a disagreeable thing, associated with the idea of an imposed task. And no doubt among the innumerable ways of going wrong which lie open to every artist there is the possibility of trying to cover by labour, or still more by cleverness, a deficiency of inspiration. A man may often go wrong by laziness or carelessness: millions do so. He may go wrong by snatching too eagerly at the fun or the fame of having his book published before it is properly finished. He may go wrong by working long and hard with his mind set on the wrong object: for instance, on his desire to be a poet, or to dazzle his fiancée, or to outdo a rival, or to get good

reviews, or to be clever, or to shock the bourgeois, or
perhaps to do something that no other person, or at
least no other sensible person, has ever done, instead of
simply thinking about the work he is doing. There are
so many ways of failure that sensitive and impatient critics
are inclined to say that it is no good taking trouble. The
poem will be either good or bad, inspired or not inspired,
and there an end.

There is, no doubt, a difficulty in understanding the
exact psychological process by which a poet goes on, day
in and day out, working quietly and often happily at a
poem full, let us say, of tragic emotion and excitement.
I believe that a subconscious or repressed stream of excitement is present most of the time; that is what makes
imaginative composition so exhausting. In fact, one may
suspect that the poet is really in a state of what is loosely
called "double consciousness," such as is usual in actors
on the stage. I remember a company that was playing
Othello in a theatre which had last been used for panto-
mime and had a trapdoor on the stage, which was supposed to be not perfectly safe. In the height of a passionate scene, which both were feeling deeply, Othello
whispered to Desdemona: "Mind that beastly trap"; and
Desdemona answered: "I know. Can you move a step
up?" There the artists were mainly concerned with the
play, but kept a part of their minds on the trap. In
prolonged composition the poet is perhaps mostly concerned with mending or smoothing traps, but the thrill
of the poem is always present at the back of his mind.
And I think there can be no doubt, first, that the maddening exhaustion which results when the work goes badly
is in part due to the strain of emotion caused by poetical
imagination itself. It is quite different from the prosaic
worry caused by ill success with a cross-word puzzle. On
the other hand, I suspect that, when the work goes reason-
ably well, the labour itself helps to give peaceful release
to the emotion, while the beautiful words and rhythms
which are constantly in the worker's mind soothe him with

what Wordsworth calls "the co-presence of something regular."

At any rate, it seems clearly a misunderstanding to think of Vergil or Milton, or one of the later poets in the Homeric tradition, as working away at his desk in a perfectly cool state of mind, as if he were correcting his pupils' exercises. And it seems also that, for once, Shelley goes astray in his account of the matter. He suggests that the "toil and delay recommended by critics mean no more than a careful observation of the inspired moments and an artificial connexion of the spaces between their suggestions by the intertexture of conventional expressions." This sentence certainly gives a rather imperfect account of the facts; but if one remembers the condition of psychology in Shelley's day, not merely before William James, but before Bentham and James Mill, one may surmise that he meant by it something much nearer the truth than he succeeds in saying.

The classical tradition is practically consistent in demanding both ecstasy and labour, both the *Aoidos* and the *Poietes*, the singer and the maker. And one must not forget that, though in an abstract way the two can be divided, in truth every maker must be in his heart a singer, and every singer inevitably a maker, just as the dramatist must have the spirit of the actor in him; while the actor, by his interpretation, inevitably in part makes his own play. Neither can do his work without study, neither without inspiration.

Love, Strife, Death, and that which is beyond Death; an atmosphere formed by the worship of Nature and the enchantment of Memory; a combination of dance and song like the sweep of a great singing bird; all working toward an ecstasy, or a transcending of personality, a "standing outside" of the prison of the material present, to be merged in some life that is the object of adoration or desire: these seem to be the subjects, and this the spirit and setting, of that primitive Molpê which is the fountainhead of ancient classical poetry. The tradition, if there is a tradition, rises there. It can be traced in later Greek literature, and through Greek into Latin, and on into the higher style of verse in mediaeval and modern Europe, a thing permanent amid changes innumerable, creating still, as it created many thousand years ago, the indefinable result that we call poetry. And I would suggest that the difference between that modern poetry which we feel to be in the main stream of great art and that which, however attractive or startling, seems to be pursuing a byway or a backwater, may lie in the following or the forsaking of the paths shown by this age-old and almost eternal Molpê.

III

DRAMA

DRAMA WAS HELD BY ARISTOTLE TO SPRING SPONTANE-
ously from the needs of human nature, which loves imi-
tating and loves rhythm and therefore is pretty sure to
indulge in rhythmic imitations. And it seems to be
found, in one form or another, among most peoples in
the world who are not debarred from it by some religious
scruple. Yet it is well to remember that all the things
that we habitually do seem to us to spring from human
nature, while a great many of them in reality owe their
present form to a quite complicated and fortuitous historical process. The drama that we know in Europe is
historically derived from Greek sources; and the same
may perhaps be true of Indian and Chinese drama as
well. The dates at any rate permit of it.

Now the peculiar characteristic of classical Greek drama
is the sharp and untransgressed division between tragedy
and comedy. The two styles are separate and never combined. No classical author is known to have written in
both. At the end of a rather voluminous literature which
has appeared recently about the origin of the Greek
drama, I think we may accept the general conclusions
reached in the preceding chapter: that both forms of
drama have their origin in ritual; that the ritual was
connected with the cult of what is sometimes called a
Year-Daemon, or a Vegetation God, or a Life Spirit,

46

which everywhere forms the heart of Mediterranean religion; and, lastly, that we can find a sort of degraded survival of the original form of drama in the Mummers' Play, which still survives among the peasantry of Europe. In that play there are two main elements. The hero, like the typical Year-Daemon, appears as a child who grows tall and strong with surpassing swiftness and is married amid a revel or *Comos* of rejoicing. Secondly, he fights various enemies and eventually meets some dark antagonist, by whom he is killed, though he shows a tendency to come to life afterwards. We know from Herodotus that tragedy represented the sufferings of Dionysus, and that these were, except for certain details, identical with those of Osiris. And Osiris, we know, was slain by his enemy, the burning Set; torn in pieces as a corn-sheaf is torn and scattered over the fields; bewailed and sought for in vain during many months, and rediscovered in fresh life when the new corn began to shoot in spring. Tragedy is the enactment of the death of the Year-Spirit; and comedy is the enactment of his marriage, or rather of the *Comos* which accompanies his marriage. The centre of tragedy is a death; the centre of comedy is a union of lovers.

Thus Greek drama starts, not as a mere picture of ordinary life, or even of ordinary adventure, but as a re-creation, or *mimesis*, of the two most intense experiences that life affords; a re-creation of life at its highest power. The purpose of the drama was—it is generally agreed—originally magical. The marriage *Comos* was intended actually to produce fertility; the death-celebration was the expulsion of evil from the community, the casting-out of the Old Year with its burden of decay, of the polluted, the Scapegoat, the Sin-Bearer. It is well to remember that dramatic performances were introduced into Rome *inter alia caelestis irae placamina* in order to cure a pestilence.[1] This occurred actually during the lifetime of Aristotle. But Aristotle himself has forgotten

[1] Livy, VII, 2.

as completely as we have that tragedy was ever a magical rite: he treats it simply as an artistic performance, and judges it, not for any concrete effect it may have on the public health, but simply on aesthetic grounds. And this shows us that, for whatever reason it was created, drama persisted and increased because it answered to some constant need in human nature.

It was a *mimesis*,—what we call an "imitation,"—and the word always disappoints us. We feel that art must be more than mere imitation, and modern critics tend to deny that it contains any element of imitation at all. I think myself that Aristotle is right. Art is a *mimesis*; and we quarrel with the statement only because we do not see the exact meaning of the term. If you fought with a wolf yesterday, you go over the fight in your mind. You re-create the fight; but it is not the same fight: it is an imitation fight, a fight in your imagination. If you are to fight the beast to-morrow, you go over the coming fight beforehand, and very likely feel it intensely. But this also is not the real fight: it is an imagined or an imitated fight. And Aristotle tells us expressly that the characteristic of poetry and drama is that it imitates, not the particular thing that is or was, but the sort of thing that might,[2] or would under certain conditions, be.

In the particular case we are considering, drama takes the two most intense experiences, for good or evil, that normal life affords; it goes over in imagination the great obvious joy, the great obvious terror. It intensifies experience. And also, by emphasizing one part of the thing experienced and ignoring or belittling another, it transfigures experience. It selects its facts and details. It practises that art so much praised by ancient orators, of making things small or great at will. It provides the blessed, the indispensable, element of illusion. In the *Comos* it provides not merely the suggestion that love will endure: that may quite possibly be true; but the more thrilling illusion that the intense joy of the mo-

[2] *Poetics*, 1451b. See note on p. 117.

ment when love is won will continue as a permanent element in life. It is like the illusion which a study of the various apocalyptic writings has revealed in their descriptions of Heaven. The heavenly life, as described in most of them, is conceived on the model of the crowning moment of the Mysteries, the topmost hallelujah of inspiration, prolonged through all eternity.

Tragedy in the same way, facing a still more pressing need, hides or adorns the "coming bulk of death," magnifies the glory of courage, the power of endurance, the splendour of self-sacrifice and self-forgetfulness, so as to make us feel, at least for the fleeting moment, that nothing is here for tears, and that death is conquered.

Thus drama does not merely select the most intense experiences of life; in those experiences it intensifies the elements that it desires to have increased and belittles or ignores those that it does not want. It exercises the ordinary selective power of art. And this explains one of the most striking judgements of Aristotle. To him the fundamental difference between tragedy and comedy is not that between tears and laughter; it is that between high and low. Tragedy, he says, deals with those better than ourselves, people whom we must needs look up to; comedy, with those lower, whom we can patronize and laugh at. Now why should people at a funeral be nobler in nature than people at a wedding-breakfast? Only because, if tragedy is to get the full artistic value and beauty out of death, the death must be met and faced and somehow or other, amid all its terrors, conquered on its own ground; if comedy is to get full value out of its revel, it must be a revel enjoyed to the full and not spoilt by any tiresome temperance or prudential considerations of the morrow. Death, to yield its full value in art, demands heroism. A frolic, to yield its full value, demands a complete surrender to frolic.

A complete surrender. A scholar who never writes without deepening his reader's understanding, Mr. Cornford of Trinity College, Cambridge, has pointed out the close

49

similarity of doctrine here between the old classical critics and the new psychologists, between Aristotle and Freud. Aristotle finds in tragedy, in comedy, in certain kinds of music and other forms of art, what he calls a *katharsis*— a cleansing or riddance or purgation. Your nature is choked up with various tendencies, or "affections" ($\pi\acute{a}\theta\eta$), which must, for the soul's health, be given vent and allowed to discharge themselves harmlessly. In boys, for instance, various pugnacious and bloodthirsty instincts, which would cause trouble if exercised in real life, are satisfied by playing Red Indians and revelling in stories about spies and pirates. This is exactly the Freudian theory of repressions and release. Many things in the history of comedy are explained by it. Comedy originated, so the archaeologists tell us, in a sort of May-Day festival intended to increase the fertility of earth and flocks and man. It involved not only an imaginative release, but a real and practical indulgence, of physical desires and passions which had to be restrained for the rest of the year, but on this festival were in place and fulfilling their cosmic purpose. And one can see traces of this origin clinging about comedy, not only in Aristophanes and Menander, but in Terence, Shakespeare, Molière, Congreve, Labiche, and every transient musical comedy which is from time to time approved in London by a censorship which has condemned Tolstoy and Sophocles.

When I first visited America, foreigners had to sign a paper answering the questions: "Are you an anarchist? Are you a polygamist?" And we all, so far as I have heard, indignantly repudiated both insinuations. Yet we all know that, if the same question were put by the Recording Angel who observes men's hearts and not their actions, the answer would be very different. At the best it would be: "Of course, at heart, I am both, as a being of your vast and unique experience must well understand; but I mostly try not to behave as such." The anarchist and the polygamist, close-prisoned and chained in ordinary life, enjoy their release in comedy.

The anarchist laughs to see the Clown burning the Policeman with the hot poker, or the cinema hero knocking people into tubs of whitewash, just as in ancient Athens he joined in flinging mockery at magistrates and generals and divine beings; as in the Middle Ages he used to dance in the Feast of Fools and mock at bishops and nuns and the holy chalice itself. He identifies himself with the rascalities of some Xanthias or Sosias or Scapin, and the irresponsible mystifications of Figaro and Don Cézar de Bazan. He sides shamelessly with the young lovers who deceive and rob sundry meritorious persons, such as guardians and creditors, and in general all the elderly and orderly.

As for the polygamist, if he retains some shreds of decorum, he merely goes to the theatre with the intention, or at least the hope, of falling imaginatively in love for an hour or two with the heroine, whoever she may be; but in general he goes much further. Comedy provides him with an atmosphere in which young lovers, like himself as he appears to himself, have everything their own way, and husbands are recognized as ridiculous and wives as a nuisance; where Captain Macheath and Don Juan and *Célimar le bien-aimé* find a world that exactly suits them. I think it is worth noticing here how great a difference is made in comedy by the actual quality of the language. So long as the language is clean and refined, the licentiousness of comedy may remain a thing remote and unreal, projected on to a further plane, and existing only in the imagination. One can enjoy a play of Labiche in which two perfectly grotesque lovers write messages to each other in white chalk on the back of an unsuspecting husband, or where another husband is drenched in scent so that his proximity can always be detected, even when he is hidden and silent in a cupboard; one can enjoy such a play as a matter of pure fantasy to which serious judgements do not apply. But if once the language becomes gross, as in the English Restoration comedy,—Aristophanes is different,—the licentiousness

51

has passed out of the realm of fantasy into that of fact: and in the realm of fact it is disgusting. The crimes and escapades of the characters, however unedifying, are only make-believe; but the words of the characters are really spoken, and there is no getting over it.[3]

The truth is that the inward anarchist and polygamist, who are let out of prison for a treat on the Comic Festival, are really on ticket of leave and under supervision all the time. Even in the most ancient times the license in fact was a strictly limited license. And by now, if ever they allow themselves to act as if the license given them were more than imaginative, the inward censor, if not the external policeman, is down on them at once. The release is only a release of imagination.

Thus comedy seems fairly intelligible, regarded as affording a *katharsis*, or release. It gives an imaginative release or satisfaction to various instincts of primitive man which are starved by the humdrum rigour of civilized city life, and which are, on the whole, not hard to identify. But tragedy is much more difficult. Why is it that people should find not merely enjoyment, but a very high kind of enjoyment, in scenes of death and anguish, the disappointment of human hopes, the terrific punishment of slight errors, and generally the overthrow of the great? Aristotle, in his abrupt style, like the style of a telegram, speaks of "pity and terror," and then says that tragedy affords a purgation of "affections of that sort." [4] Perhaps, if we possessed his explanation of what he meant by "affections of that sort," we should understand this better. In default of that, let us try to conjecture what elements of primitive instinct, ordinarily repressed by our sense of duty and the needs of social intercourse, can possibly find release, or *katharsis*, in the spectacle of *Oedipus* or *Macbeth* or *Hamlet* or *Athalie*.

[3] R. L. Stevenson makes somewhere the interesting remark that his pirates in *Treasure Island* never actually use a bad word, yet they make the requisite blood-curdling impression. That is Art.
[4] *Poetics*, 1449b.

First, let us remember how Greek tragedy dwells on the danger of greatness and the envy of the gods. Sometimes the poets are at pains to explain that it is not greatness in itself that brings on disaster, but only the pride or cruelty that is often associated with greatness. But in the main popular conception there is no such subtlety: life is seen in the tragic pattern. As the Sun every year and every morning begins weak and lovely, then grows strong and fierce, then excessive and intolerable, and then, by reason of that excess, is doomed to die, so runs the story with trees, beasts, and men, with kings and heroes and cities. Herodotus sees the history of the Persian War in the same tragic pattern: Xerxes, tall, strong, beautiful, lord of a vast empire, became proud and desired too much, was led into Atê and stricken down. Thucydides sees the history of Athens in the same pattern: incredible achievements, beauty, splendour; then pride, battle, determination to win at all costs; crime, brutality, dishonour, and defeat after all. That is the essential tragic idea, however we translate it into modern language, climax followed by decline, or pride by judgement. Why do we enjoy it?

It may perhaps be suggested that the envy in question is perfectly real, only it is the envy of our own hearts and not of the gods. It is a pleasure, everyone knows it, to hear anecdotes telling how proud people were "scored off," or made to look small. There was a great Spanish nobleman in *Candide*, whose mien—as Voltaire puts it—was so distinguished, whose bearing so magnificent, whose blood so blue, that no ordinary man could be ushered into his presence without immediately conceiving a desire to kick him. There is a pleasure in hearing of the defeat of the great Spanish armies by the Dutch, or the great Burgundian armies by the Swiss, and, generally, in the downfall of the proud. At every fight the sympathy of the onlookers tends to back the little 'un. We identify ourselves with the under dog, just as we always think of ourselves as more oppressed than oppressing. Such little

53

injuries as we may have done to other people are really so pardonable and easily forgotten and even, if looked at in the right spirit, humorous; but the wrongs done by others to us are different and do demand some imaginative satisfaction. It is worth while remembering that it is to sects and nations that have suffered persecution that we are indebted for almost all our information about Hell. It is thus quite conceivable that there is in the mass of mankind a subconscious sense of unredressed injury. Still, I doubt if such a feeling goes far in accounting for tragedy. As a rule, such a sentiment is more comic than tragic; it is amused by small mishaps to the unduly dignified, but it is no longer amused if the mishaps become painful.

However, if we have faced that unamiable element in our instinctive subterranean nature, let us also face something worse: man, differing herein from most other carnivores, takes pleasure in torture and cruelty. Savages torture their prisoners; children in most countries torture animals. The Roman games, the sports of the Middle Ages and even of the eighteenth century, the records of the burning of martyrs and of public executions, not to speak of certain elements in the late war and the succeeding revolutions, are more than sufficient to show that there is in man an element which lusts for the infliction and the sight of pain. It enables us to understand many extant forms of sport, and I think also part of the fascination of certain scenes in such plays as Flecker's *Hassan*, Sardou's *Théodora*, and the stamping on Gloucester's eyeballs in *King Lear*.

We must allow, then, for the instinctive cruelty of man; we must allow for vindictiveness or *Schadenfreude*. We must allow for the mere excitement of looking on at a game where the stakes are high. But I do not think that, between them, they amount to much. Doubtless the just vengeance of the gods is an imaginative projection of our own desire for such justice; but the supposed tragic φθόνος, or envy, of the gods is not, I think, a projection of our own envy, but of something quite different. The envy of the gods is a projection in personal anthropomorphic form of the dead pitiless and overpowering forces of the vast alien world in which man finds himself so isolated, and his well-being so precarious. It is really not envy, but indifference, the indifference of dead material things; but it seems to our imagination like personal malignity. It seems as if some personal law or will created this tragic pattern, which ordains that all life shall fail and die. I think we shall agree that the emotion with which we regard the fate of Oedipus or Macbeth or Othello consists genuinely of "pity and fear," and not in the least of *Schadenfreude*. Pity for the great man overcast; fear, because we partially identify him with ourselves and realize through his fate the precariousness of our own. We feel, as we look on the overthrow of the tragic hero, that man himself has here no abiding city.

I would suggest that there is perhaps one further element in the tragic emotion besides this pity and fear. There is a curious suspicion that the brutal and meaningless disasters inflicted by Fortune are, in some mystical way, not quite unjust. We are almost like dogs who feel that they must have been naughty if they are accidentally trodden upon.

Aristotle makes an acute remark on this subject. He points out that, while tragedy demands the fall of the great, the hero must not be absolutely wicked, nor yet utterly innocent. If he is merely wicked—like an Elizabethan villain—the theme loses grandeur as well as interest and reality. If he is entirely innocent, the story becomes what Aristotle calls μιαρόν, or "revolting." He must commit some offence, he must show some flaw—not enough, by human standards, to justify his punishment, but enough to let us feel that Nature or Fortune or the gods are, after all, according to their own inhuman rules, playing the game. Such a conception makes these powers less blind and dead, but all the more terrible.

We see the hero doing exactly the things calculated to get him into trouble, and feel that he can hardly complain of the consequences. We all know how Fortune is apt to behave; and the hero who boasts, or shows pride, or forgets proper precautions, with that knowledge in front of him, is like a man who carelessly drinks the water in his bedroom in a town where there is known to be typhoid. He is not exactly a wicked man, but really he almost deserves what he gets.

But let us look further, and we may find an explanation of these curiously divergent impressions.

Two recent writers—Dr. Janet Spens in 1916 and Mr. Cornford in 1922[5]—have independently brought out a most significant fact about ancient tragedy toward which I also was groping. It is that the tragic hero (embodying as he does the good Vegetation Spirit torn and scattered, and at the same time the evil Old Year cast out) presents a curious combination of contradictory qualities. It is quite in accord with the strange but well-known confusion which exists in the Bacchic ritual and the sacramental feast. Is it the god himself who is torn and devoured, or is it the god's enemy? To avoid the horror of murdering your god, you can say that the figure you tear is the enemy Pentheus and not the god Dionysus; but you know in your heart that it is only the life of Dionysus himself that will have any true magical effect, and you show your knowledge of this by arranging that the image which you call Pentheus shall be shaped and dressed in every detail so as to be like Dionysus. In later ages we have distinguished the hero and the villain, but there are no villains in Greek tragedy and the villain's fate is normally suffered by the hero.

Put briefly, it seems that historically the tragic hero is derived both from the Life Spirit—call him Dionysus or what you will—who comes to save the community

---

[5] *Shakespeare and Tradition*, by Janet Spens, 1916; Lecture on *The Origin of the Drama*, by F. M. Cornford, Conference on New Ideals in Education, Stratford, 1922.

with the fruits of the New Year, and from the polluted Old Year, the *Pharmakos* or Scapegoat, who is cast out to die or to wander in the wilderness, bearing with him the sins of the community. Every Year-Spirit is first new and then old, first pure and then polluted; and both phases tend to be combined in the tragic hero. Oedipus is the saviour of Thebes, the being whose advent delivered Thebes from death; Oedipus is also the abomination, the polluter of Thebes, the thing which must be cast out, if Thebes is to live and be clean. Orestes is the saviour who comes to redeem the House of Atreus from the rule of murderers; Orestes is also the murderer, the matricide, whose polluting presence must be removed from all human society. Pentheus, the stricken blasphemer, is, as we have seen, identical with Dionysus, the sacrificed god. The conflict between two rights or two commands of conscience, which is said by Hegel to be the essence of tragedy, is already present in the tragic hero himself.

The emotion which the striving and the death of such a hero rouses in the normal man must be far from simple. We feel love for him because he is a saviour and a champion, a brave man fighting and suffering to redeem those who without him would be lost; we feel horror toward him because of his sins and pollutions, and their awful expiation. And both feelings must have been intensified in ancient tragedy by the subconscious memory that the sins he expiates are really ours. The Greek hero, when he suffers, almost always suffers in order to save others.[6] And the artist knows how to make us feel that such suffering is a better thing than success.

It is only through sacrifice and suffering that courage and greatness of soul can be made visible, and the drama-

[6] This point has not been sufficiently realized. Thus Oedipus suffers for Thebes, Orestes for his father, Alcestis for her husband, Prometheus for mankind, Eteocles for Thebes, Menoikeus for Thebes, Antigone for her brother, Iphigenia in Aulis for Hellas, Macaria for her brethren, etc. Some suffer for the Gods or for duty, but nearly all suffer for somebody or something. The tragic hero is thus affiliated to the Suffering God and the Babylonian "Faithful Son." Cf. Langdon, *Tammuz and Ishtar.*

tist who knows his business knows how to make the beauty of such sacrifice resplendent while hiding away the ugliness of the mere pain and humiliation. He shows the beauty of human character fighting against fate and circumstance; he conceals the heavy toll of defeats and weaknesses and infidelities which fate and circumstance generally levy on the way.

If this analysis is historically correct, and I believe it is, it goes far toward answering our whole problem about "the pleasure of tragedy." First, no doubt, tragedy implies the contemplation, not of mere suffering and disaster, but of the triumph of the human soul over suffering and disaster. So much seems certain, but it is not very characteristic. That pleasure one might receive from any exciting drama or story of adventure in which the bad people seem to hold all the cards but the good people eventually win. What is really characteristic is that, from the very beginning, the tragic conflict has in it an element of mystery derived ultimately from the ancient religious conceptions of *katharsis* and atonement. The contest takes place on a deeper level of reality. It is not to be estimated in terms of ordinary success or failure, ordinary justice and injustice, but in those of some profounder scheme of values in which suffering is not the worst of things nor happiness the best. A tragedy is true to type when one can sincerely say at the end of it, "Nothing is here for tears," as one does at the end of *Samson Agonistes* or *Othello* or *Lear* or *Oedipus* or *Antigone* or *The Trojan Women*. Only one can never say such words except under the inspiration of some more or less mystical faith or some high artistic illusion.

And here we have the explanation of another characteristic of the tragic art. As tragedy, if it is to be bearable, needs fineness of character in the sufferers, so it needs beauty of form in the execution. Greek tragedy more than any other insists on an extreme severity of form, and I think it is true to say that severity of form implies and corresponds with purity of experience. The test is that it must not be interrupted. A great tragic effect is spoilt by any irruption of incongruous words or incidents or snatches of prose amid the poetry. Comedy does not mind such things; in some ways they make a funny situation funnier. I think the reason is that tragedy is based on an illusion which is always precarious. It must show beauty outshining horror, it must show human character somehow triumphing over death; and it can create and maintain that illusion only by high and continuous and severe beauty of form.

It is interesting to notice the history of this classical insistence on purity of form. The Gothic tradition rose and clashed with it; and I suppose on the whole the Nordic races, so far as there are such things, like their art rather Gothic and consequently rather loose and diversified. But not always in the same way. In *Faust* there is a hodge-podge of different subjects and tones, but the form in any given scene is strict. In Shakespeare there are many different degrees of form, ranging from an intense and almost lyric severity in the most tragic or poetic passages to a loose and somewhat verbose style in the dignified but less interesting scenes, and to mere prose in those that are comic or unimportant. This is very different from French tragedy, in which the tradition of severity lives on. Racine is not merely as severe as any Greek, he is as rigid in his rules as Ovid or Horace. Every line scans and rhymes and has its caesura in the same place. There is never a syllable *extra metrum*, never a word that is outside the poetic convention. Such severity goes far beyond Goethe's *Iphigenie* or Shelley's *Prometheus* or *Hellas*, or, so far as I can speak with knowledge, any modern Italian drama. One can scarcely find a parallel to it except in such purely lyrical tragedies as Swinburne's *Locrine* or Metastasio's *Morte d'Abel.*

In comedy it is much harder to preserve a severe form. Comedy always tends to imitate actual conversation. Yet it is interesting to see what an immense additional charm severe form adds even to comedy. In Aristophanes the exquisite writing is fully half the fun. In Menander, though the form is much more colloquial and there are no lyrics, the style remains exquisite. The few comedies in older English literature outside Shakespeare that really live are those of Sheridan and Goldsmith—every line of them polished and exact. Molière's prose has something of the same polish. And at the present day it would hardly be a paradox to say that, while the man in the street ridicules the very idea of a comedy in verse, the most successful and vital comedies current are perhaps those of Rostand in France and W. S. Gilbert in England —verse to the *n*th degree, a verse that revels in its own art.

In another respect also the Greek tradition insisted on a severity of form from which the modern world has largely fallen away. It insisted, as will be explained more fully later on, on architecture, on unity. It produced plays like the *Medea* or the *Oedipus*, in which there is not a single scene which is not active in building up the main story of the play, not a single passage of mere eloquence or mere theatrical effect, which does not at the same time serve a further purpose. Here again the French tradition has been nearer to the Greek. The French dramatists, from the seventeenth century onwards, did set themselves to write "well-made plays"—*des pièces bien faites*. They may be mechanical, they may be narrow in interest and poverty-stricken in psychology; but the play knows where it is going, and the whole forms a unity. It is really astonishing to read several of the rather soulless and unintelligent plays of Scribe, and find how interesting they are made by the mere fact that they tell one definite story without interruptions or irrelevancies. English writers, on the other hand, seem to find it peculiarly difficult to manage their construction or architecture. The twenty-five volumes of Mrs. Inchbald's *British Theatre* will bear this out for the seventeenth and eighteenth centuries: and most contemporary plays, admirable in detail and stagecraft as they often are, have weak last acts.

Similarly, in the novel, which always takes greater liberties than the drama proper, you find a number of writers who can give exquisite studies of character, delicious conversations and individual scenes, but very few who can construct a story with a definite unity of effect and a proper climax or, to use the Greek term, "catastrophe." One might almost say that they leave that high quality to the writers of detective stories.

Why has this severity of form so strangely broken down in modern times? In part, no doubt, because the great modern Babel of literature, made up from many tongues and climates and centuries, has less clarity of taste than ancient Athens. But also, perhaps, for a more legitimate reason. We said above that severity of form goes with purity of experience, or definiteness of artistic conception. The fifth-century Greeks kept the severe form because they wrote either tragedy or comedy and not a mixture. They set before themselves as an ideal the intensest expression of the tragic or the comic emotion. Only to a slight extent did they amuse themselves by copying closely actual details of real life. Theirs was in the main a *mimesis* of imagination, not a *mimesis* of observation.

But the *mimesis* of observation followed quickly. In the third century B.C. pure tragedy and comedy had almost ceased to exist, supplanted by what was called the "New Comedy" of Menander and Philemon. This was comedy in the modern sense, not the ancient. No doubt some trace of the original feast or revel remained,[7] but in the main the New Comedy developed a general *mimesis*, neither tragic nor comic, of ordinary human life, in so far as it happened to present an interesting material. An ancient epigram addresses Menander: "O Menander and life, which of you has imitated the other?" Menander

[7] In Menander the Chorus takes the form of a band of revelers outside the action of the play; in the Middle Comedy there are frequent descriptions of feasting. Cf. the essay on Menander in *New Chapters in Greek Literature*, Second Series, Clarendon Press, 1927.

61

is a delightful writer, refined and witty and at the same time touching; the style of play which he introduced was more pliable, varied, easy to read and to follow, more amusing to the average lazy man, than ancient tragedy; it paid only the penalty of not rising to anything like the same heights of intensity or of beauty. And we, as we naturally would, have followed Menander.

It is a mistake, of course, though a mistake frequently made, to imagine that an artist can take life at random and let it tell its own story. I doubt if even the most mechanical photograph can do that. The artist is there to select and interpret, to emphasize, and distort, and when necessary to falsify—without being discovered. And the realistic artist, if he is a good artist, just as much as any other. It is a question, as Sophocles long ago pointed out, of presenting things, not as they are, but in the right way.[8]

Not as they are, but in the right way: the Greek artists certainly realized this principle. The columns of their temples, we all know, produce the illusion of slender straightness, while in fact they are curved so as to swell in the middle according to some highly subtle rules. Their bas-reliefs sometimes produce an effect of absolute naturalness, combined with a grace which is somehow not often met with in real life. In reality, the sculptor has again and again sacrificed the true human proportion to certain rules of symmetry and rhythm. A distinguished modern sculptor recently explained to me that he altered the real planes and contours of the head in order to produce this or that effect of colour and even of life. A head exactly equal in its measurements to the real head would be lifeless.

The realistic artist needs this lore, if he is to be a good artist. Next, I am inclined to think that what matters most to a writer of the realistic type is to have a sound general judgement of moral values. A writer of lyrics or intense tragedy can be eccentric or half mad

[8] Ar. *Poetics*, 1460b 34.

without much loss: one may think of Dostoievsky, or, some people would say, of Blake. But a realistic artist ought to be sensible if he can possibly manage it—and so few of them do! As an artist he is always selecting and emphasizing, and as a realist he is always showing what he thinks important and true. Consequently he reveals all his follies and weaknesses and obsessions.

Menander, the creator of the lifelike play, lived, I think, up to this maxim. His judgements of life—I mean the judgements implied in his selection of incident and his treatment of plot—are sane and kindly and fair. I am always reminded of him when I think of Diderot's famous treatise on the *genre sérieux*, where he pleads for a form of play which shall not set out to be either funny or sad, but just to illustrate truly and interestingly the serious facts of life. This common sense and this kindly sympathy are qualities much despised by the more high-brow artists and critics; but the ordinary reader values them, and I venture to think that they are qualities which not only appeal widely to the ordinary public of the day, but also tend to secure immortality. They are qualities which you find in Menander, in Plutarch, Chaucer, George Eliot, Dickens, Trollope, and among contemporaries, in Arnold Bennett; they are conspicuously wanting in Congreve and Wycherley, in Maupassant and Strindberg. At any given epoch there is a fashion for some particular forms of foolishness or one-sidedness; but they become extremely tiresome after a generation or so, whereas the normal and sensible does not lose much of its charm as it grows old. Of course, a brilliantly exciting or original view of the world, if genuinely held, is nearly as good as a sensible one. I would not say a word against the *Weltanschauung* of Shaw or Ibsen. But neither is exactly a realist.

I think one might say that modern drama has branched out in two opposite directions from its classical origins. Ancient tragedy and comedy tried to re-create the highest or intensest moments of experience: that has developed or decayed into Romanticism. The New Comedy, the *genre sérieux*, tried to represent external life with the utmost illusion of naturalness, so that, if nothing was ecstatically sublime, everything was convincing. That has developed, or—again, let me admit the possibility—decayed, into Realism.

Both extremes are rather easier to follow than the true classical mean, in which you have to be both reasonable and intense. A flat realism is easy, because it needs no strong effort of imagination or construction. It is easy also to invent the preposterous romantic feats of cinema heroes, because you are not chained by the needs of probability or consistency. In general, I think, there has been in our own times an increasing looseness of form parallel with a decline in intensity of imagination. This is, roughly, what we call Realism. It is no good being unsympathetic toward this tendency. Most cultivated people, when they are feeling vigorous in mind, infinitely prefer the *Agamemnon* and *Paradise Lost* to *An Old Wives' Tale* or *Love and Mr. Lewisham*. But one's mind is not always vigorous, and realism of the right sort has a very strong case to make for itself, so long as it does not imagine that it is real realism. It is all right so long as it is consciously dishonest.

The main reason for Realism is to produce illusion, and particularly to keep up the illusion when it is in danger of breaking down. If you wish us to weep with your heroine, do not overstate your case: do not make her more beautiful or more good than seems probable. Do not make your villain impossibly wicked, as the Elizabethans did. Even the tactful introduction of a suitcase or a cold in the head, or a purse containing seventy-five cents and a trolley-ticket, has often saved an exciting situation which would otherwise have been incredible. And, of course, extraordinary value can be obtained by the use of extremely simple or even commonplace language in tragic scenes. The spectator is apt to have in the back of his mind a feeling that poets lie, and the conventional language and manner of poetry is associated in his mind with falseness: a sudden break-away from the poetic convention often produces an air of sincerity, by which the cunning artist can make doubly sure of his victim.

One motive which leads to realism or romanticism, as the case may be, is, as I have suggested, lack of energy. It is difficult to make both a consistent and credible story and also a series of moving incidents or extraordinary characters. Therefore it is easier to do one and let the other drop. Another, and more vicious, motive is ennui. Ennui is the enemy of all good art, as of good thinking or good living. You are sick of the existing good plays, or poems, or pictures; so you try something bad for a change. It is only by accident that this at the present day produces excessive realism. At other periods it has led, just as easily, to the sensational and fantastic. Its true object is to get away from that of which one has had too much. And so it breaks the convention. This is well enough if carried out with extreme skill; but it is a dangerous doctrine. It is this that makes the unwary artist, in his eager desire to be in the mode, write deliberately ugly verses, or use by preference words that most poets have considered obviously unsuitable; or make his heroine really plain and morally repulsive, or his story really boring or nasty—or somehow unlike the successful stories, heroes, and heroines of whom he has seen too much. Thus the young and innocent realist ruins himself and his work, while the crafty old traditional artist knows how to produce the illusion of all these things without paying the price. He obtains all the verisimilitude and solidity of plain heroines and boring lives while privily contriving that the reader or spectator shall be both fascinated and thrilled. It is all a question of fixing your convention and then, at chosen moments, slightly transgressing it.

What then is the real difference between the art that we call in the true sense realistic—I leave on one side the art that is ugly or unclean, and is called realistic by euphemism—and that which may be called romantic or ideal? It is, I believe, a difference of psychological motive. Romantic art is a reversion to classical tragedy and comedy with the checks and controls removed—especially the control of the intellect. Romantic or ideal art in its extreme form offers a release to our uncensored dreams; it enables us to identify ourselves with heroes infinitely strong and brave and beautiful, who are also great artists and poets, as well as exquisite swordsmen, and makers of incomparable repartees, and who deservedly win the love of heroines worthy of their steel. Or, it may be, with Napoleonic tyrants, dark-browed and irresistible, if our weakness happens to be megalomania; or with injured and misunderstood persons of heroic saintliness, if we are more attracted by the ecstasies of self-pity. And, of course, beside our dream selves—ourselves as we ought to be if we had our deserts—there is apt to be placed our dream enemy, the villain. Our hate, envy, resentment, fear, or whatever it may be, is free to depict him in his ideal blackness. Romance gives an illusion of fulfilment to our day-dreams.

Realistic art, on the other hand, depends on the interest of observation, and rejects the luxury of dreaming. It is also less concerned with self, and the projection of the artist's own feelings into his characters. It generally observes and depicts the outside world and other people. It may seem hard or cold, but all good observation implies understanding and sympathy. Even satire, if it is good satire, and not a mere outpouring of ill-will, implies an effort to understand. All good parodies try to catch the secret of the beauty of the original. And apart from satire, almost the whole effort of this type of art is an effort to understand others, and not merely to observe them from the outside, but to realize them by entering into their feelings. It is by no means inconsistent with this remark that when, in a modern novel or play, the author depicts himself, or some parts of himself, the picture is nearly always satirical: it gives you Sir Willoughby Patterne, or Tommy in *Tommy and Grizel*, or possibly—so people say—Peer Gynt or the Master-Builder. That is the usual result of observing dispassionately the one person about whom you possess intimate and almost unlimited information and from whom, no doubt, you are always apt to expect too much.

Thus, in the main, realistic drama is based on the interest of observing and understanding other people, as they are; and of course they cannot be understood without sympathy and imagination. In the main, romantic or ideal drama is based on the imaginative enjoyment of the highest moments and most thrilling possibilities of life; and these cannot be fully enjoyed—they will only be grossly caricatured—without some real observation and understanding. Consequently neither style can entirely neglect the other. The greatest achievements of ideal tragedy and comedy are, I think, reached when the scene that is so terribly moving or so irresistibly absurd also impresses the spectator as exactly true to life; while it is almost obvious that the greatest triumphs of realism are those in which the common stuff of human life, such as we live or observe day by day, is revealed as possessing the same spiritual value as the doings of great heroes, and perhaps at the same time the ridiculousness of puppets. Here we are in the true classical tradition. Bernard Shaw makes on the drama a high demand—not always satisfied, as he would be the first to admit, in his own works—that it should treat no character as a mere outcast or enemy, but every one as at least potentially a "temple of the Holy Ghost." It seems to me that Greek tragedy, on the whole, with rare exceptions, lives up to this lofty rule. It presents us with no villains, no monsters—no one who has not some real point of view for us to understand or, at least, some plausible case for us to consider. That is the explanation of those long scenes of argument which superficial critics have attributed to the Athenian taste for litigation.

The Classical Tradition in Poetry

William Archer, whose profound knowledge of the drama and whose clear and unvacillating judgement made him rank in his lifetime, and will, I think, establish him hereafter, as a classic among critics, once said to me that he thought one of the greatest changes taking place in human society, at any rate among the more advanced nations, was the spread of psychological sympathy through the reading of novels and plays. The average novel readers of to-day have the material for understanding people different from themselves which a century ago lay only in the power of individuals of special imaginative sympathy. Even the most popular newspapers occasionally have articles or short stories of which the point is to explain and make sympathetic the behaviour of someone who seems at first sight remote or absurd or definitely repulsive. The effect is superficial, of course. It is swept away in a moment by any real personal feeling. But it does familiarize the great public with the notion, normally strange to them, that they ought to try to understand people different from themselves. And it is an added advantage that the understanding is achieved not by analysis and reason but by the force of sympathetic emotion. There is an element of that ecstasy, or rising beyond oneself, which has been from the earliest origins the special characteristic of *mimesis*.

Ecstasy—ἔκστασις, the power of standing outside ourselves, or outside this immediate material present which is our prison—ecstasy is the essential quality of drama, and the great element of value which it, in especial, contributes to our spiritual and social life. In pure tragedy or pure comedy, of the classical Greek type, we rise outside the material commonplace present to relive, or to live beforehand, the great moments which life at its highest intensity has to offer, the moments of Strife, Love, Death, or the things beyond Death; in the mixed form to which we are accustomed at the present day, and which we can associate with the name of Menander or of Diderot, we get outside that bundle of desires and

68

beliefs which we call our own mind and are able to enter into the minds of other people. To understand and live the great moments of life, which come, after all, only to those who are capable of them; to understand and live the lives of those people, different from ourselves, who fill the world and on whom we are so strangely dependent—those are the two kindred and contrasted adventures on which drama, or, at least, such drama as is descended from Athens, seems to me to be leading the human race.

IV

METRE

IF WE SEEK IN IMAGINATION TO RECONSTRUCT THIS AN-
cient Molpê, what instruments do we possess? The dance
has vanished. At best we have on vases a few pictures
of various dances as they appeared at particular moments. The music is utterly gone. Even the few fragments of musical scores that have survived—a Delphic
Paean, a few lines of a lyric in the *Orestes,* and the like
—seem to me to be barely intelligible in the absence of
the musical instruments to which they refer. The one
element that remains to guide us is the metre.

Metron means "measure" or "measurement"; and the
things measured are the "feet" or "steps" on which the
words of the song moved. For the words themselves were
supposed to dance: if they did not dance, how could they
join in the general rhythm of the dancers? The words
took long and short steps in some regular recurrence or
pattern, just as the dancers made long or short movements. Here we strike on one of the fundamental principles of classical poetry, and one which is constantly
overlooked or misunderstood. The total rhythmical effect
of any dance or song or poem is based on a harmony
between different movements, and every harmony implies
a contest or clash overcome. Even in the simplest "dance,"
such as a march, though it may seem that there is only

one absolutely simple rhythm given by the sergeant's command, "left-right-left-right," there are really two: there is the sergeant's "left-right" and there is the actual placing of each foot on a rough road, with occasional stones or puddles to step round. And consequently there is harmony or conflict between the two. Similarly, in the songs that go with reaping, washing, milking, and the like, there is a definite attempt to make the rhythm of the action coincide with the rhythm of the song; an attempt and therefore sometimes a failure, a harmony and therefore a conflict. And further, in the song itself, the natural pronunciation of the words can never be exactly the same in rhythm as the pronunciation required for the rhythm of the song. The tune, so to speak, is free and imposes its law; the words are material objects and therefore more or less recalcitrant. They seek to obey the law, but having an independent life of their own, they obey it always with a difference. They achieve a harmony which is also a clash.

This explains the relation of the words of any poem to the metre. The metre is an ideal pattern which is, as a rule, uniform throughout the whole poem, though no single verse or stanza, as spoken, is exactly identical in rhythm with any other. In every verse the words conform to the metre with more or less variation. This variation is not a regrettable "license." It is from the outset an essential element in the total rhythmical effect, and if it were not there, much or all of the beauty of rhythm would be lost. Thus, there is no doubt that Milton conceived the verse of *Paradise Lost* to be a line of five iambics, with certain permissible variations; and if we take the first three lines of *Paradise Lost*, we find that they all conform to that general type, though not one of them could be exactly so scanned.

Of man's first disobedience, and the fruit
Of that forbidden tree, whose mortal tast
Brought Death into the world and all our woe:

71

Each line conforms generally to the pattern

$$\smallsmile - \smallsmile - \smallsmile - \smallsmile - \smallsmile -$$

and can be felt and understood by means of that pattern. Whereas if, instead of seeing the metre as a constant pattern to which the verses resistingly conform, you attempt to make it an exact description of the measurement of each verse taken severally and pronounced as in ordinary speech, the result is chaos. The first verse becomes something like

$$\smallsmile - - \smallsmile\smallsmile - \smallsmile\smallsmile - \smallsmile\smallsmile -$$

(iambic, dactyl, dactyl, anapaest)

a verse unintelligible in itself, and bearing no intelligible relation to those that follow.

Similarly, it has been observed that in English blank verse one at least of the stresses is apt to be very faint, so that most verses in Shakespeare have only four strong stresses, and many only three. This is an interesting observation. But to erect it into a metrical rule only darkens counsel. It is one of the natural and legitimate varieties which come under the rule. I may be wrong, but in my judgement many modern writers on metre have gone wildly astray through mere misunderstanding of the meaning of the classical terms as the poets in the classical tradition have accepted them.

The above applies to ancient and modern verse alike. But there is otherwise a great general difference between the Greek and Latin practice and that of any modern language known to me, and I propose in the present chapter to discuss that difference. Greek and Latin poets had perfectly fixed rules, with fixed "licenses" or variations. These rules were, by respectable poets, never broken; or if they were, it was simply a mistake and had to be corrected, like a mistake in addition or a false note in music. Similarly, the quantity or length of every syllable was known; one long was reckoned equal to two short, and the permitted varieties in pronunciation were notably few. A modern poet, however bad his verse or his ear, can seldom be convicted of a "mistake"; he can always say that he knows what he is doing, and that by doing it he is producing some peculiarly rare and exquisite irregularity of rhythm, or, at the worst, expressing his own personality—a confession which no doubt is true. Similarly, the quantity, or length, of syllables—at any rate in English—is not fixed; and normally the "length," or stress-value, of any syllable in a verse depends not on itself alone, but on its relation to the syllables before or after it. (Thus we say "The climber turns | to thé | ascent," contrasted with "Forward, forward | tó the | mountain," and the like.) But of this more later.

A highly inflected language must have each syllable clearly spoken, because every syllable up to the last may seriously alter the meaning. This is perhaps the reason why, in Latin and Greek pronunciations, quantity was the chief variable; while modern uninflected languages have fallen back more and more on the easy careless method of stress. In English, it is often considered enough to pronounce clearly only the accented syllable of a long word, and there is a marked tendency in the colloquial language to reduce all words to monosyllables. A very strong stress generally devastates the values of all unstressed syllables in its immediate neighbourhood, and reduces their vowels to the indeterminate "ə," as usually heard in the last syllable of *painter*, or *table*, in the first and last of *amusement*. (For example, it would be impossible for even such simple words as "regīnă" or φιλάνθρωπος to live in modern English; we should say "rəgīnə," and either "fíllənthrópəs" or "filánthrəpəs.")

The pronunciation of classical Latin is fairly well ascertained, and can be reproduced. That of classical Greek is still obscure. The main facts are that in classical times the one element in speech that was sufficiently noticeable to determine the rules of verse was "quantity," which meant, apparently, the difference in duration between different syllables. One cannot of course be sure that when they spoke of "duration" the Greeks meant nothing but duration, and paid no regard, for instance, to volume of sound. The fact that the difference between "long" vowels and "short" vowels was originally a difference between "open" and "close" sounds seems to suggest that there was something in it besides mere duration. That is, ω represented the sound in *aught* or *hot*, ο that in *boat* or *but*; η the sound in *bête*, or the first sound in *air*, ε that in *bait*. And many small phenomena in verse would seem to suggest the presence of a slight stress-accent more or less like that which is traditional in Latin, Italian, English, German, and most Indo-European languages: that is, a tendency to stress the penultimate when it is long, otherwise the antepenultimate: to say "regína," but "impossíbilis." For instance, such a word as πατέρα, the accusative of πατήρ, occurs most usually in verse in such a position that the stress naturally falls on the first syllable. (Normally, χαίρεις ὁρῶν φῶς, πατέρα δ᾽ οὐ χαίρειν δοκεῖς; rarely, τί γὰρ κακῶν ἄπεστι; τὸν | πατέρα | πατήρ.[1])

---

[1] The chief argument for this view is the treatment of tribrach words like πατέρα, ἔλιπε, φόνιος, κτλ. These, according to the normal Indo-European manner, would be pronounced with a slight stress on the first syllable; and in verse, if they had two of the short syllables treated as equivalent to one long, would take the place of a trochee, not of an iambus; that is, they would be pronounced roughly like πάτρα, ἔλ᾽πε, φόνγος. If, on the other hand, they were pronounced with no stress at all, one would expect them to be treated indifferently as equivalent to either an iambus or a trochee. Now the fact is that they are regularly treated as trochees, only exceptionally as iambi. We commonly find lines like

ὅτ᾽ ἔδραμε ῥόθια πεδία βαρβάρῳ πλάτᾳ,
ὅτ᾽ ἔμολεν ἔμολε μέλεα Πριαμίδαις ἄγων (Helena, 1117),

or

λάβῃ σε, θάνατος ξένιά σοι γενήσεται (Ibid., 480),

but never one like

πεδίον ἔμολεν ἄβατον ὄν, ὡς ἄφοβος ἄγαν.

In the first scene of the *Prometheus* the only tribrach words are ἄβατον (ἄβροτον), Θεμίδος, ψάλια. All are stressed metrically on the first syllable. In the *Bacchae*—to take a play most markedly contrasted

The matter is complicated by the existence in Greek of a variation of musical tone in the pronunciation of ordinary words, comparable more or less to the several "tones" in Chinese and to certain musical phenomena in, for instance, Swedish and Norwegian. One syllable in any long word was apt to be spoken on a note higher than the rest; our authorities say that in extreme cases it could be higher by a whole fifth.[2] This peculiarity had apparently no effect on metre in classical times and was not marked in any way in the script. But during the Hellenistic period, when the civilization and language of Greece were spreading rapidly over all the Mediterranean world, foreigners found this "tone" difficult to reproduce. Hence the marks of acute, grave, and circumflex "accents," or "tones," were introduced into Greek writing in order to help the barbarians to speak correctly; and, as one might have expected, the barbarians first carefully learned their accents and then pronounced them all wrong. Instead of speaking the "tone" syllable on a higher musical note they merely spoke it with a violent stress. And this stress-accent, apparently unknown to classical Greece, gradually prevailed in most parts of the Mediterranean world, and had completely driven out quantity

---

with the *Prometheus*—the tribrachs in the first scene are: ἄβατον, θυγατρὸς, ἐλάταις, θυγατρὸς, θέμενος, ἔρυμα, παρέδρους, stressed on the first syllable as in Latin or English (= trochee), and μιγάσιν, θίασος, the other way. One may also notice the quadrisyllables τυφόμενα, ἀθάνατον, ἀναφέρειν, μετέβαλον, ἐκόμισα, scanned $\cup - \underline{\cup}$, although it is easier to find a place in the verse for such quadrisyllables in the form $- \cup -$. Facts of this sort, which are very common, seem to show that, in doubtful cases, the poets prefer to let the metrical stress fall on a syllable which in most European languages would, as a matter of fact, have the regular oral stress. It has been suggested that, since tribrach words are often proparoxytone, the Greek tonic accent may be concerned in this metrical stress. But the evidence is weak, and the complete disregard of the tonic accent is one of the most obvious characteristics of ancient Greek verse. The trochaic position is about twice as common as the iambic. See *Classical Review*, XLIII, 5 and XLIV, i (Nov. 1929, Feb. 1930).

[2] Dionysius of Halicarnassus, *De Compositione*, XI: διαλέκτου μὲν οὖν μέλος ἐνὶ μετρεῖται διαστήματι τῷ λεγομένῳ Διαπέντε, ὡς ἔγγιστα. καὶ οὔτε ἐπιτείνεται πέρα τῶν τριῶν τόνων καὶ ἡμιτονίου ἐπὶ τὸ ὀξύ, οὔτε ἀνίεται τοῦ χωρίου τούτου πλεῖον ἐπὶ τὸ βαρύ.

from the spoken language by about the fourth century A.D. It is extremely strong in modern Greek.

Metrical verse has, of course, a growth and a history; and its development in European poetry can perhaps be best appreciated if we begin by a word or two on non-European systems, for instance, those of the Hebrews or the Chinese.

A great deal has been written of late years about Hebrew metre, and it may be that some discovery will be made which will completely change our conception of it. But, on the existing evidence, it seems that the verse of the ancient Hebrews cannot be called metrical. It had not really analyzed words into syllables. Following ancient Babylonian models, it was content with the rhythm produced by parallel clauses, generally in sets of two; true, these clauses are expected to be approximately equal in length, but it is equally important for them to be cognate in meaning and parallel in grammatical structure. Thus it is not the metre that makes the verse: it is a general parallelism, in which a rough similarity of length is one factor. For example, Job, XXII, 9:

> Thou hast sent widows away empty,
>> And the arms of the fatherless have been broken.
> Therefore snares are round about thee
>> And sudden fear troubleth thee.
> Or darkness that thou canst not see
>> And abundance of waters cover thee.

In Hebrew it is probable, although not traditionally assured, that each line has three strong stresses, and therefore each couplet equals 3 + 3. This rule is said to hold throughout the book of Job, whereas in Lamentations and elsewhere a long line is followed by a shorter one, probably three stresses by two; as in Amos, V, 2:

> She is fallen to rise no more:
> The virgin of Israel.
> She is forsaken upon her land:
> None to raise her.

It is worth remarking that Josephus, who had the Greek conception of metre and was anxious to argue that his own nation was quite equal to the Greeks, describes the 3 + 3 form of Hebrew poetry as a hexameter. It would be at any rate an extremely rude one. It is curious to see how Hebrew poetry was held back in its development by this initial lack of artistic analysis: it never analyzed words into syllables. It produced all sorts of other devices: metaphors and traditional phrases; acrostics and anagrams (Psalm 119, and others; Lamentations, I–IV); alliteration, and an extremely elaborate system of semi-musical accentuation; but with all its richness and variety of sound, as well as its passion and elevation of feeling, it never produced what we should call metre in the full sense of the word.[3]

The Chinese system, again, presents an even stronger contrast to the classical. The Chinese poetry undoubtedly attains great beauty and delicacy of expression. One can see that from Mr. Waley's translations. But its methods are curiously different from those of our own models.

Homer and Vergil operate with a highly constructed syntax, a rich and exact system of inflexions, words of widely varying length divided into short and long syllables, and a variety of metres in which each syllable has its value in the pattern, and the lines vary greatly in individual rhythm while remaining within the rules, and can run to sixteen and seventeen syllables without need-

---

[3] A very similar parallelism is found in Greek, in the highly antithetical rhetoric of Gorgias, but it counts there as prose.

> What was lacking in them
> That men ought to have?
> Or what present in them
> That men ought to lack?
> Would I could speak what I desire,
> Would I could desire what I ought,
> Rousing not the nemesis of the Gods
> And escaping the jealousy of men!

Cf. Wilamowitz, *Griechische Verskunst*, p. 23.

Metre in the strict sense is said to occur in the Jewish poetry of the Middle Ages, introduced doubtless from the Arabic.

ing the assistance of rhyme to make them intelligible to the ear. Chinese poetry—so far as one entirely ignorant of the language can understand what scholars say of it—has no syntax, no inflections, no words longer than monosyllables, and no metre beyond a plain counting of words —or of syllables, since there is no distinction between the two. No lines are longer than seven syllables, while five-syllable lines are the commonest, and four-syllable lines are recognized as classic. The seven-syllable and five-syllable lines are divided by a regular caesura. So far it would seem as if Chinese poetry was deficient in almost all the elements that to us make rhythm or music in verse. On the other hand, it insists on rhyme, presumably because it has so little metrical structure that even a poem of four-syllable lines cannot maintain itself to the ear without rhyme. And it also insists on a quality which has no equivalent at all in our verse: every syllable has to have its musical "tone," and the sequence of tones has to follow definite rules.[4] This sequence and alternation of tones must, one would imagine, be the main difficulty in composing Chinese verse, and must make the most essential and obvious difference between verse and prose. Yet it is a property which our European poetry does not possess at all.

The earliest form of Indo-European verse known to us is to be found in certain poems of the *Avesta*. In these the word is already analyzed into syllables, and the syllable used as a unit of measurement. The verse which is regarded by many scholars as the most ancient consists of sixteen syllables with a pause in the middle, or two sets

[4] E. g., a five-word stanza may run, marking the caesura as o, and reading downwards,

sharp	flat	flat	sharp
sharp	flat	flat	sharp
flat	sharp	flat	sharp
o	o	o	o
flat	sharp	sharp	flat
sharp	flat	sharp	flat

of eight. Professor Sonnenschein[5] quotes a translation by Professor Charlton M. Lewis as illustrating this verse-form:

> Who was the first of all mortals
> To honour thee on earth, Hôma?
> Vivaswan was the first mortal
> To do me honour upon earth.

This gives far greater exactitude, and far greater promise of future advance, than the Hebrew. But although the Zend language is said to have possessed at this time distinctions both of accent and of quantity, the *Avesta* poets have not yet made use of the distinctions.

In the earliest Greek verse the unit is no longer merely the syllable, but the "short syllable," and on this precision of phonetic analysis the whole development of European metre is based. Syllables were divided into two classes, short and long, and the long was conventionally accepted as equal to two short, while an elided syllable was not counted at all. The ancient metricians knew that this rule was merely conventional; Dionysius of Halicarnassus (*De Compositione*, XV) discusses the obvious inequality in length of the first syllables of ὁδός, Ρόδος, τρόπος, στρόφος, though all count equally as "short," the length of the initial consonant sounds being conventionally disregarded. It is not the case that all long syllables are equal: σπλὴν in Greek must be longer than ἤ, *sons* in Latin than *os*; nor yet are all short syllables equal: ὁ is shorter than ὅς, and *id* than *quid*. Nor yet is a long syllable, apart from some exceptional coincidence, exactly equal to two short; sometimes a long was treated by the Greeks themselves, in lyrics, as equal to three or four units; and modern measurements by a kymograph, recording actual English speech and measured in hundredths of a second, show very great variations in the length of

---

[5] *Rhythm*, p. 42.

syllables.[6] That is to say, the rule that one long equals two shorts is not like a law of science, which attempts exactly to state the truth; it is like the rule of a game, a convention according to which the game is to be played. Such a rule, if it is to work well, must, on the one hand, allow reasonable variety in the play, and on the other hand, be near enough to the truth to avoid shocking the player's sense of what is fitting. The rule that — equals ‿ ‿ was greatly modified in practice by the admission of "doubtful" or indifferent syllables in certain parts of the line. In those places, so far as the rule went, one syllable was as good as another.

Verses are made of words. And we have seen that words in Greek and Latin had much firmer and sharper outlines than modern English words. In the first place, the termination was important: ἄνθρωπος, ἄνθρωπον, ἀνθρώπου, ἀνθρώπῳ, would all mean different things; so the last syllable must be clearly spoken by one who wished to be understood. English people are always apt to slur the last syllable of such a word and to talk of "Hellǝny" for "Helenê" or "Pǝseidǝn" for Poseidōn, just as they say Jezzǝbǝl for Jezebel and Sattǝdy for Saturday. In the second place, every syllable had its definite length; a long syllable did not become short whenever it met another long, so as to make the pronunciation easier, as in English; a short did not behave as if it were long just because it had another short on each side of it. The edges of words were more clear-cut, and the value of each syllable more definite, than with us. Consequently, many metrical effects are possible and even easy in Greek which are practically impossible in English—not because our ears cannot catch them or our lips pronounce them, but because, with our habits of pronunciation, nine readers out

[6] Cf. Sonnenschein (*Rhythm*, p. 32), who quotes a kymographic record taken by himself of Tennyson's line:

The	long	light	shakes	across	the	lakes.
12	31	27	45	7 34	9	55

of ten will turn them into something easier and commoner.

A fairly common Greek metre is the dochmiac; in its most regular form ⏑ — — ⏑ — (ἁμαρτημάτων, in hāc māchinā). This is almost impossible in English because it brings two long (or stressed) syllables together. Boys are taught for illustration a supposed English dochmiac:

> The wīse kāngaroōs despīse leāther shoēs.

But you soon find the less careful ones saying

> The wīse kāngarŏōs despīse leāthĕr shoēs

like

> Alās for the deēd, alās for the dāy.

Again, a common Greek device in lyrics is to leave out a short syllable where one is expected between two longs; and so to produce a strain or tension on the syllable before (syncopated iambic):

> Ἰδαῖά τ' Ἰ—δαία κισσοφόρα νάπη.
> ἐπάθομεν, ὤ, τὰ κύνατ' ἄλ—γη κακῶν.[7]

If one tries to represent the metrical effect of the first of these lines by

> And Īda, dārk Īda, where the wīld īvy grōws:

where "wild" and "dark" are each equal to two syllables (— ⏑), there will be a tendency to turn it into

> And Īda, dărk Īda, where wīld ĭvy grows.

One can make sure of the metrical effect only by bringing in the help of tune, by making song help speech; for example:

> Grāsshopper sīttin' on de sweē' p'tāter vīne.

[7] Euripides, Troades, 1066, Supplices, 807.

81

That is, in English the words themselves have not a sufficiently definite metrical form to make the rhythm clear or to overcome the general unconscious expectation that two strong syllables do not come together.

Similarly, in a generally trochaic rhythm (for example, that of *Hiawatha*) Greek gets very beautiful effects by the use of what are technically called ionics *a minore* with anaclasis: the commonest form is the Anacreontic:

> πολιοὶ μὲν ἡμὶν ἤδη
> κρόταφοι, κάρη δέ λευκόν.

The charm of this metre depends on keeping the first syllable short; but an English reader, expecting as a matter of course an alternation of long and short syllables, will often make it long, like four trochees. If a verse is written in ionics, like

> For his kíngdom, it is thére,
> In the dáncing and the práyer,
> In the músic and the láughter
> And the vánishing of cáre,
> And of áll befóre and áfter,

there will be a strong tendency in English to stress the first syllable in every verse, and thus ruin the rhythm, merely because (1) that gives a commoner metre, and (2) the initial syllables, though certainly short, are not —and in English cannot be—definitely and unmistakably short.

Again, there is a very charming and lightly tripping metre in Aristophanes in which the place of _ ◡ _ ◡ is taken by _ ◡ ◡ ◡ . This gives three short syllables together. The verse is like an ordinary long trochaic—

Dreary gleams about the moorland flying over
Locksley Hall

with a short syllable in place of a long in the second, fourth, and sixth beats:

πῖνε κατάκεισο λαβὲ τήνδε φιλοτησίαν.
(*Acharnians*, 985.)

Or, in English:

Rōamĭng ăs ă | rōvĕr ŭpŏn | īnfĭnĭtĕ ĭm|mēnsĭtĭĕs.

Effects of this delicate sort are extremely difficult to produce in English, except in comic verse, where an exaggerated emphasis is permissible.[8] However well they may be built, the tendency of the ordinary English reader will be to destroy them. Our words pour out in a semi-liquid stream, melting into one another like wax; the speakers of a highly inflected language, like Greek or Latin, built their speech of clearly shaped marble blocks.

One interesting result of this difference is the prevalence of rhyme in modern languages. Greek and Latin could do without rhyme because they had such clear metres. Rhyme is needed to mark clearly the end of the line and to provide the ear with fixed resting-places. Without such divisions the metrical form would become dull and obscure. The hearer would not be sure where one line ended and the other began; he might not even be sure whether he was listening to verse or prose. Indeed, in some of the more loosely written scenes in Shakespeare the editors differ on both these points; they divide the lines differently, and some print the scene as prose and some as verse. It is worth noticing that Latin took to rhyme when it had begun to lose the sense of quantity; a mediaeval monk who could not catch the rhythm of Vergil could at least distinguish a verse in

Hac sunt in fossa Bedae venerabilis ossa.

---

[8] Cf. the Dragoons' Song in Gilbert and Sullivan, *Patience*, which is written in feet of the form —∪∪∪ | —∪∪∪ or ∪∪∪ | ∪∪∪

"They're | pósitively | snéering at us, | fléering at us, | jéering at us!
Prétty sort of | tréatment for a | mílitary | mán!"

Chinese insists on rhyme because it has no metre. The prevalence of rhyme in English country songs and ballads seems to have made admissible a certain laxity in their metre. On the other hand, the renewed popularity of rhyme in the time of Dryden followed upon an ever-increasing looseness in the treatment of blank verse by the later Jacobean dramatists, and was part of a general reaction toward severity of form.

In Greek verse, then, the definiteness of the metrical values of words made the outlines of each verse much clearer. But besides that, though the Greeks did not use rhyme and appear not to have been sensitive to it,[9] they did take special pains to mark off the beginnings and ends of verses. The question chiefly arises in the two main continuous metres, dactylic hexameters and iambic trimeters. In hexameters the final dactyl-spondee or dactyl-trochee is sufficiently marked; also there are some subtle rules, Wernicke's law and the rest, which seem intended to prevent the ear mistaking a spondee in the fourth foot or the second for the final spondee. A verse never has dactyl-trochee with a pause after it in the fourth foot, nor yet dactyl-spondee if the last vowel in the spondee is short; it never has $- \cup \cup - \asymp$ with a pause after it in the second. That characteristic is definitely kept for the end of the line. Similarly in the iambic, the metre of the last two feet is kept particularly exact, while that of the first foot is particularly free. Very rarely indeed, and never without deliberate intention, is the verse so written as to obscure the end of the lines.[1] I will not dwell on the methods used; but one may compare the use in English blank verse of a trochee instead of an iambus in the first foot as a means of marking sharply the end of the verse before:

[9] If they had been, the orators, who are so careful about euphony in other matters, would not have admitted the somewhat ugly rhymes and half-rhymes which sometimes occur in their artistic prose.

[1] Sophocles sometimes has elision at the end of a line—τί ταῦτ'| ἄλλως ἐλέγχεις; the other tragedians, never. The same freedom occurs in the fragments of Achaeus of Eretria.

> The calf in Oreb: and the rebel kīng
> Doublĕd that sin in Bethel and īn Dān,
> Līk'nĭng his Maker to the grazéd ox.[2]

In French, where metre has gone back to mere syllable-counting, and the syllables are sometimes long musical diphthongs and sometimes so short as to be really mute, metrical rhythm has practically disappeared. The consequence is, first, that rhyme has become an absolute necessity, and next, that the verse has to be cut up into small, regularly recurrent lengths in order to remain intelligible. The Alexandrine, for instance, has both to rhyme and to be divided in half; and the two halves again tend to be halved. This divides each Alexandrine into four bars of three syllables each, and some modern French metricians maintain that the actual rhythm of the Alexandrine is normally four anapaests. This seems an exaggeration. No couplet of Racine sounds much like *Young Lochinvar*:

> For she looked | down to blush, | and she looked up
>   to sigh,
> With a smile | on her lips | and a tear | in her eye,

though one is not so far away from it in

> Je deviens | parricide, || assassin, | sacrilège.

Sometimes, however, the original iambic rhythm positively asserts itself, as in the first verse of

> Je meurs; j'ai fait couler || dans mes brulantes veines
> Un poison | que Médée || apporta | dans Athènes,

and the last of

> Abolir | tes honneurs, || profaner | ton autel,
> Et venger Athalie, || Achab et Jézabel.[3]

---

[2] *Paradise Lost*, I, 482.
[3] The passages are from *Andromaque*, *Phèdre*, and *Athalie*.

It is interesting to observe that an English ear generally finds the verse of Racine monotonous because of its metrical rigidity, and somewhat unmusical because of its lack of uniform rhythm, while a French ear finds English verse monotonous because of its clear rhythm, and untidy because of its comparative lack of rules.

In English the condition for doing without rhyme is that the metre must be uniform and clear; the term "blank verse" with us generally is taken to mean the Miltonic five-iambic line, because that is the one form in which rhymeless verse is really successful. The largest license that is common in English blank verse is the hypermetric syllable at the end:

> I know that virtue to be in you, Brutus,
> As well as I do know your outward favour, etc.,

and even this irregularity serves the purpose of making the end more unmistakable. It prevents the ear from running on from one line to the next. Irregular verse without rhyme, like *Queen Mab* and some of Southey's and Matthew Arnold's poems, has, in spite of Milton's wonderful attempts in *Samson*, not commended itself to imitation. It is too obscure to the ear, except possibly where, on the model of the Greek, it is written in strophe and antistrophe, or in stanzas of uniform metre. The exact repetition of a rhythm enables the ear to catch it, and subsequently to expect it. It seems to be almost a necessity in good verse that the ear should subconsciously expect a certain pattern, and have its hopes alternately, or varyingly, suspended and fulfilled. And the more clear this ideal subconscious pattern is, the more variety, as a rule, can be enjoyed within its limits. Take some of the most irregular lines in Milton. A five-iambic verse like

> Why are you vexed, | Lady? | Why do you frown? [4]

or

[4] *Comus*, 666.

86

Light from above, from the | fountain | of light;

or

> Eternal wrath
> Burnt after them to the | bottom|less pit;[5]

or

Yet fell: | remember and | fear to transgress,[6]

would be metrically unintelligible if they stood alone.
Coming in the midst of crowds of other lines, all con-
forming, with variations, to the uniform five-iambic pattern, they are naturally read in accordance with that
pattern. Perhaps the most remarkable case in English
literature where a chance set of words, of quite peculiar
rhythm, is taken by a poet, and the rhythm of those
words repeated until it becomes accepted as a perfect
and satisfying pattern, is Swinburne's poem,

> By the waters of Babylon we sate down and wept,
> > Remembering thee,
> That for ages of agony hast lain down and slept,
> > And wouldst not see.

It is a marvel of metrical skill to produce this effect in
English; in Greek the verses would be difficult to write,
but once written they would be unmistakeable.

The truth is that, putting aside the iambic trimeter,
which is said to "imitate conversation," ancient metres
are much nearer to the dance than ours are, and consequently not only more exact, but far richer and more
sonorous. If one asks why Dryden's translation of Vergil is so utterly unsatisfying, it is partly, no doubt, because Dryden is apt to miss or coarsen the delicate poetry
of his original, but even more it is that he substitutes
for a deep and sonorous music a sort of thin impetuous
rattle of sound. The same is true of all translations of

---

[5] In a Greek text critics would restore the metre by a transposi-
tion: "to the pit bottomless."

[6] *Paradise Regained*, IV, 289; *Paradise Lost*, VI, 866, 911.

Homer, particularly, perhaps, of Pope's. It is curious that Wordsworth speaks of Pope "charming England with his melody." There is reason to think that recitation was more careful and varied in the eighteenth century than it has become since. But even so, how very little of what we should call melody Pope's form of verse admits! Take a moving passage in the *Letter of Heloïse to Abelard*:

> Unequal task! A passion to resign
> For hearts so touched, so pierced, so lost, as mine.
> Ere such a soul regains its peaceful state
> How often must it love, how often hate!
> How often hope, despair, resent, regret,
> Conceal, disdain—do all things but forget!

Brilliant and moving poetry, by all means, and Pope's rhythm at its best. But for music or sonority put this so-called "classical" style of English verse beside a "Romantic" passage:

> O Love, my Love, if I no more should see
> Thyself, nor on the earth the shadow of thee,
>   Nor image of thine eyes in any spring,
> How then should sound along life's darkening slope
> The ground-whirl of the perished leaves of hope,
>   The wind of Death's imperishable wing!

In mere variety and richness of sound this is much nearer to the classical models, though I think one must never expect from the English language a sonority like that of Greek and Latin. The words "love" and "death" may have as much magic beauty as "mortem" and "amorem," but they have not the same volume of sound, and a word like "imperishable" or "inevitable," with its tripping run of short syllables, cuts a poor figure beside "inēvītābilis."

Turn to a simple Vergilian line like

Infandum, regina, jubes renovare dolorem; [7]

or, to take a passage similar in subject to those we have quoted above:

Ipse cava solans aegrum testudine amorem
Te, dulcis coniunx, te solo in litore secum,
Te veniente die, te decedente canebat; [8]

or take

Νηλεές, οὐκ ἄρα σοί γε πατὴρ ἦν ἱππότα Πηλεύς,
οὐδὲ Θέτις μήτηρ· γλαυκὴ δέ σε τίκτε θάλασσα
πέτραι τ' ἠλίβατοι, ὅτι τοι νόος ἐστὶν ἀπηνής. [9]

We notice two differences. First, the vowel sounds in English are not so full, long, and sonorous as in the Latin or the Greek. This might be different in other European languages. "La Belle au Bois Dormant" has far more richness and beauty of sound than "The Sleeping Beauty"; German has wonderful long vowels. Italian also is certainly no less sonorous, if more languid, than Latin.

But, secondly, the metre itself counts for more in the Greek and the Latin than in English, and unless my ear fails me, immeasurably more than in other European languages. It is perhaps difficult to make this clear to those who do not know or feel the rhythms of Vergil and Homer. But one may notice, first, that in English a given verse might often be mistaken for prose: "How often must it love, how often hate" might conceivably occur in a prose sentence, and many lines, even very fine lines, of Wordsworth or of Shakespeare much more easily, because their metre is less emphatic and regular.[1]

---

[7] Aeneid, II, 3.   [8] Georgics, IV, 464.   [9] Iliad, XVI, 33.
[1] Again, one may often find in a passage of English prose not merely an occasional blank-verse line—that could be paralleled in Greek—but several continuous lines of blank verse. For example, in Bleak House, vol. iii, chap. 5:

No waking creature save himself appears,

It would be inconceivable that any of the above lines
from Homer, and almost inconceivable that any of those
from Vergil, could pass as prose. They would stand out
from ordinary prose as a burst of song would stand out
from ordinary conversation.

Again, if one rewrote Pope's words in a different order:
"It would be an unequal task, for a heart so touched,
so pierced, so lost as mine, to resign a passion," the loss
would not be overwhelming. The rhythm would have
gone, but the information, so to speak, would remain,
and be moderately interesting. But rewrite the Vergil,

Ipse, amorem aegrum testudine cava solans,

and it is absolute destruction. So much beauty has de-
parted that one cannot go on.

A third test, though not a certain one, is the effect
produced on the ear of a hearer who does not know the
meaning of the words. Accidents and idiosyncrasies may
upset the test, but on the whole such a hearer will generally recognize a fuller and more varied music in the
Greek or the Latin when compared with the thin liveliness
of the English.

I would not be misunderstood. What is called "music"
or beauty of rhythm in poetry is an extremely subtle
thing. The late Frederic Myers even suggested that what
we call "music" in language is not a matter of sounds
heard but of sounds articulated. The pleasure is a pleasure
in the movements of the vocal chords. Certainly it may

Except in one direction, where he sees
The solitary figure of a woman,
Sitting on a door-step. He walks that way.
Approaching, he observes that she has journeyed
A long distance, and is footsore and travel-stained.
She sits on the doorstep in the manner of one
Who is waiting, with her elbow on her knee,
And her bag upon her hand. Beside her is
A canvas bag or bundle she has carried.
She is dozing probably, for she gives no heed.

The sixth line is perhaps a little "licentious," but the rest would pass
muster. No Greek or Latin passage of anything like this length could
pass as verse.

be feared that every poet enjoys speaking verse far more than most people enjoy hearing it. However that may be, a form of verse which is comparatively thin and prose-like may often achieve a beauty of rhythm more magical, and thus possibly more intense, than that of a form which is more sonorous. I have heard good critics say that the most musical verse in English poetry is

After life's fitful fever he sleeps well.

Evidently they are counting as elements in the music not merely the sounds but the associations of the various words, and probably also the contrast of rhythm between this line and the other blank verse lines round about it. In that sense one may value the music of Shakespeare's line more highly than that of

Μή μοι γᾶν Πέλοπος, μή μοι χρυσεὶα τάλαντα,[2]

or

Altitonans Volturnus et Auster fulmine pollens.[3]

I only suggest that the classical verses are, first, more sonorous, and, secondly, far nearer to dancing and music and more remote from the rhythm of common speech. The test case, perhaps, is that of the Greek Anthology, in which there are many poems, particularly among those of Meleager and Paul the Silentiary, which attain an indescribable and as it were diaphanous beauty by almost nothing but their rhythm, the sweet insistent beat of the elegiacs and the long melody-saturated words. The sonnets of Petrarch have words equally sonorous, but nothing like the same beauty of metre.

The above remarks apply chiefly to the metres which are used continuously in long poems: blank verse, heroic couplets, the four-iambic or eight-syllable line of *Marmion*, and so on. Exceptions would have to be made for the Spenserian stanza, the stanza of *Don Juan*, and the like, in which the metre certainly forces itself on a

[2] Theocritus, VIII, 53.   [3] Lucretius, V, 745.

reader's attention. But of course there have been attempts in English to find a continuous narrative metre which should have a swing and sonority comparable to that of the ancient hexameter. First, there are accentual hexameters or elegiacs—I leave aside the attempts at quantitative verse, for the present. There are Longfellow's *Evangeline*, Kingsley's *Andromeda*, Clough's *Bothie of Tuober na Vuolich*, and the very interesting elegiacs in Clough's *Amours de Voyage*. And one might for most purposes add Goethe's *Hermann und Dorothea*.[4]

These, it is fairly obvious, have to struggle with several difficulties, of which I will mention three. First, the hexameter starts of necessity on a strong syllable; English verse finds it very difficult to start continuously on a strong or accented syllable, at any rate in trisyllabic verse. It either needs what is technically called an anacrusis, that is, one or two unimportant syllables before you get to the first strong one; or else it finds itself starting with miserable little unimportant syllables, "buts" and "ands" and "ifs," which have to pretend to be strong. The trouble here comes from the trisyllabic foot. "But" and "if" are quite strong enough to bear the stress in a foot of two syllables, but not in one of three.

> Ín the stormy east wind straining,
> Thé pale yellow woods were waning.

Here the very weak syllables "in" and "the" are nevertheless sufficient for the trochaic effect. But take a trisyllabic metre:

> Bút in the interval here the boiling pent-up water,

or

> Ánd of the older twain the elder was telling the younger.

[4] The following discussion may be compared with the writer's remarks on "What English Poetry may still learn from Greek" in *Essays and Studies by Members of the English Association*, vol. 3 (1912).

"But" and "and" are not strong enough for their work. And it seems that English hexameter verse is always wanting to begin on one of these weakish syllables.

Secondly, the hexameter has a dissyllabic ending, trochee or spondee, and in a predominantly monosyllabic language like English this becomes painfully monotonous.

Thirdly, and most important of all, in an uninflected language, or a language which has few inflexions and therefore is not carefully pronounced, there is great difficulty in keeping the unstressed parts of the feet sufficiently clear and long. One is always finding a trochee where there ought to be a spondee or dactyl: that is, a short syllable where there ought to be either a long or two short. For example:

Bright October was come, thĕ mistў-bright Ŏctober,
Bright October was come tŏ burn ănd glen ănd cottage,
Bŭt the cottage was empty, the Matutine dĕserted.

In elegiacs there is a fourth difficulty: the clash of the strong syllable at the end of the first half-line with the strong syllable at the beginning of the second needs great care. It goes rightly in

When from Janiculan heíghts thúndered the cannon of
    France,

but less well in

Therefore farewell, we depárt, bút to behold you again.

Consequently more success has attended a modification of the ancient dactylic hexameter which admits an anacrusis at the beginning and knocks off the unstressed syllable at the end—one might say, takes off an unstressed syllable at the end and puts it on at the beginning. This gives one something like the metre of Sigurd the Volsung:

93

And Gudrun came in the sunrise, on the edge of the sea
    she stood,
And she looked o'er the shining waters and cried out o'er
    the measureless flood:
"O Sea, I stand before thee, and I, that was Sigurd's wife,
By his brightness unforgotten I charge thee deliver my life
From the grief and the passing of days and the lack I
    have won from the earth,
And the wrong amended by wrong, and the bitter wrong
    of my birth."

But it is worth observing that this modified hexameter,
fine as it is, is still embarrassed by the uncertainty of
the unstressed syllables. Syllables that ought to be long
are left short, trochees take the place of dactyls, hypermetric syllables are freely admitted after the caesura, and
the whole character of the line fluctuates between a six-
foot dactylic measure and a ballad metre of the eight-and-
six type (mostly with $\smile - \smile$ for $\smile - \smile -$ in the middle), as in

Ye have heard of the Cloudy People and | the dimming
    of the day,
And the latter world's confusion, | and Sigurd gone away.

Of course it may fairly be answered that these "irregularities" are not irregularities at all; they are within
the rules of the metre as Morris deliberately writes it. But
I think it remains true that this metre does not quite
attain the power of variety in unity possessed by the
Latin hexameter or by English blank verse. It loses unity
in *Sigurd*; and when it attains unity, as it does in the
hands of Swinburne, it becomes monotonous.

Take the *Hymn to Proserpine:*

I have lived long enough, having seen one thing, that
    Love hath an end:
Goddess and Maiden and Queen, be near me now and be-
    friend.

Thou art more than the day and the morrow, the seasons
    that laugh and that weep:
For these bring joy or sorrow, but thou, Proserpina, sleep.

. . . .

Thou art more than the Gods who number the days of
    our temporal breath,
For these bring labour and slumber, but thou, Proserpina,
    death.

These lines have both a texture and a resonance that can
quite stand beside Homer or Dante. But one can hardly
imagine them used successfully for a long narrative poem.
They remain, according to English standards, exotic and
exquisite. The truth is that they are lyrical, not epic.[5]

If I am asked why I call these passages lyrical, I think
I shall boldly say, "Because they possess the quality of
metrical construction or architecture." I hope to speak
of this quality more in detail in a later chapter. For the
present let it be defined as the arrangement of a complex form in such a way that no part stands alone but
each contributes to the value of other parts and to the
main effect of the whole. It is a quality that eminently
belongs to the classical style in narrative or drama, and
in both Latin and Greek poetry it seems to me to be applied brilliantly to the treatment of the metre.

---

[5] Still more striking, but also more monotonous, are the quasi-
elegiacs of *Hesperia*. These are "correct," except that anacrusis (a
connecting syllable or syllables) is admitted both before the hexameter and before both halves of the pentameter. I enclose the anacruses
in parentheses.

Fair as a rose is on earth, as a rose under water in prison
    (That) stretches and swings to the slow passionate pulse of the sea,
(Closed) up from the air and the sun, but alive, as a ghost re-arisen,
    Pale as the love that revives (as a) ghost re-arisen in me.
(From the) bountiful infinite West, from the happy memorial places
    Full of the stately repose (and the) lordly delight of the dead,
(Where the) Fortunate Islands are lit with the light of ineffable faces,
    (And the) sound of a sea without wind (is a)bout them, and
    sunset is red.

95

Of course there can be no metre, as there can be no pattern, without repetition. It is the repetition of feet that makes a metre, the repetition of dots or lines or curves that makes a pattern. An ordinary piece of blank verse or heroic couplets or a rhyming ballad consists of symmetrical repetitions. But in Greek or Latin verse there is generally architecture as well, and this gives much of it a lyrical quality.

In English an ordinary ballad in the metre called eight-and-six (that is, eight syllables followed by six, or four iambics followed by three) has architecture:

A slumber did my spirit seal, | I had no human fears,
She seemed a thing that could not feel | The touch of earthly years.

John Gilpin was a citizen | Of credit and renown,
A train-band captain eke was he | Of famous London town.

Each couplet consists of four syllables balanced by four and the whole held together by six. Or of two feet, two feet, three feet. The three-foot line gets a special value, and gives a special satisfaction to the ear, because it follows a four-foot line. We shall find a similar special satisfaction to the ear in all the varieties of what one may roughly call a 4 + 3 metre, whether in iambics, trochees, anapaests, or what not. I call it 4 + 3, but the best way to analyze this metre is to treat it not as 4,3, but as 2,2,2,1:

John Gilpin was | a citizen | of credit and | renown;
Or leave a kiss | within the cup | And I'll not ask | for wine;

or more generally, as x, x, x, (x — Y).

There is, I think, no formula of metrical construction so simple and easily recognized as x, x, x, (x — Y). It can be applied to almost any metrical unit:

If x is a single iambic and Y one syllable, we get:

And spring | and seed | and swal|low.

If x is a trochee and y one syllable:

> Home they | brought her | warrior | dead.

If x is a double iambic and y an iambic, we get the eight-and-six ballad metre quoted above.

If x is a double iambic and y is one syllable:

A Captain bold | of Halifax | who lived in coun|try quar-ters.

If x is three iambics and y one:

> O world, O life, O time |
> On whose last steps I climb |
> Trembling at that where I | had stood before.

If x is a double trochee, with y one syllable:

'Tis the place and | all around it | as of old the | curlews call.

If x is an anapaest and y one syllable or, say, a half-foot:

> But of old | in the sea|son of ro|ses.

If x is a double anapaest, and y one foot:

Now hush, oh hush, | for our song begins; | let everyone stand | aside
Who owns an in|tellect muddled with sins, | or in arts like these | untried.

If x is a double anapaest, and y a half-foot:

> In Westminster Hall | I danced a dance |
> Like a semi-despon|dent fury,
> For I thought I ne|ver should hit on a chance |
> Of addressing a Brit|ish jury.

We can consider some more subtle effects later. I take these for the present, clear and jingly as they are, in order to illustrate what I mean by construction or lyrical quality. The latter part of these lines gets an

97

impetus from the earlier part; the ear acquires an irresistible expectation of what is to come.[6]

But in Greek and even in Latin metre, this process of construction is carried much further. In elegiac verse, the unit is a couplet; and the couplet not only consists of two lines divided into symmetrical halves—that is sym-

---

[6] Perhaps this leaves the impression that I am making an idol of mere regularity or even of mere "swing." The subtler English writers often prefer a broken rhythm to one that swings uninterrupted to its goal. They deliberately seek such effects as:

> From cloud and from crag
> With many a jag
> Shepherding her bright fountains,   (Shelley)

or

> Building a sorrowful loveliness
> Out of the battles of old times,   (Yeats)

where the weak syllables "her" and "of" are put where the ear expects the metrical stress. Is there nothing like that in Greek?

On the contrary, that is what is called in Greek a "scazon" or "limping" effect. It is very common in lyric metres and has its place in iambics and hexameters. In lyric metres it is characteristic of tragedy as opposed to comedy. Comedy likes a rattling swing: it is not afraid of

Ἄγε δὴ φύσιν ἄνδρες ἀμαυρόβιοι, φύλλων γενεᾷ προσόμοιοι.

Tragedy will generally prevent that rush of sound either by inserting a half-line before the clausula or by putting a dactyl amid the anapaests:

οὓς αὐτὸς ἄναξ Ξέρξης βασιλεὺς
Δαρειογένης,
εἵλετο χώρας ἐφορεύειν.

In iambics the "limp" is produced by putting a trochee or spondee in the sixth foot; in hexameters, by putting an iambic there. The former produces a harsh effect suitable for satire or puritan moralizing, the latter a feeling of weakness or disappointment. For example, a charming Omar-Khayyam-like poem recently found on a papyrus * has the following metrical form:

Proud was Croesus of old, and proud King Cyrus in | hĭs hour:

Now their chambers are empty, the sceptre of ivory | forgot,

where a normal hexameter would require, e.g., "Cyrus aforetime," "ivory broken." A discussion of ancient "limps" would take us too far afield; but in general one may notice that ancient poetry when it intends to break a rule breaks it regularly. It never breaks rules chaotically or by mistake.

* Cf. J. U. Powell's *Collectanea Alexandrina*, p. 199.

metry: it also ends on a rhythm which would be un-interesting to the ear unless it were led up to by a series of rhythms which do not receive their full explanation until it comes—that is architecture. Take a couplet like:

> Hospita Demophoön | tua te Rhodopeia Phyllis
> Ultra promissum | tempus abesse queror;

or

> Et flesti, et nostros | vidisti flentis ocellos:
> Miscuimus lacrimas | maestus uterque suas;

or

> Βοῦς ἐπί μοι γλώσσῃ | κρατερῷ ποδὶ λὰξ ἐπιβαίνων
> Ἴσχει κωτίλλειν | καίπερ ἐπιστάμενον.

It divides into four; and each member is an attempt, and a different attempt, at the rhythm which is at last perfected in the fourth member. The first and third attempts diverge by admitting spondees and avoiding the dissyllabic close; the second is hypermetric at both ends. The exquisite smoothness of the last member, with its regular unvarying dactyls and its dissyllabic or polysyllabic close, would have nothing like the same value if it had not been led up to by the three others. A poem in continuous pentameters would be tedious; in continuous dactylic pentameters, intolerable.[7]

---

[7] It is interesting to see how the compromise or harmony between metre and normal speech is attained in the Latin hexameter and pentameter. Given the general metrical scheme, we find that there are certain secondary rules:

(1) The hexameter must end with a dissyllable or trisyllable (moénia Trójae, ploravit Achillem). This ensures that the end of the verse shall be clear and the speech-stress coincide with the metrical stress.

(2) Similarly, the pentameter (in Ovid and after) must end with a dissyllable: this at first sight might seem to spoil the harmony of speech-stress and metrical stress, since such dissyllables (erat, amor) have normally a slight stress on the penultimate. But in reality the object of the rule is not the final dissyllable but the pause before it: the dissyllable has to be preceded by a member like praetereúntis, saéva puélla, trístia fácta, which have an unmistakable speech-rhythm exactly according with the metrical rhythm. Praetereuntis aquae, saeva

99

Again, take any of the Lesbian four-line strophes, sapphic or alcaic or asclepiad: the sapphic has obviously the form x, x, x, (x–y), and so have some of the asclepiads. But something similar is true of the alcaic also.

> Eheu fugaces, Postume, Postume,
> Labuntur anni, nec pietas moram
> Rugis et instanti senectae
> Afferet, indomitaeque morti.

There is symmetry between 1 and 2, symmetry between

puella dedit, tristia facta deas, accord much more closely with the metre than would, e.g., *ludibrium capitis* or *saepe bibunt cyathos.* (A quadrisyllabic ending, *vivere consilio,* is half-way between, both in rhythm and in legitimacy.)

(3) Then, the general harmony being safe, the next requirement is a more subtle one. It is to secure that the spondees shall really be spondees and not trail off into mere trochees, as they are so apt to do. Words like *Trojae, fato,* and—still more exposed to danger—*dicit* followed by a consonant, must be so treated as to have both their long syllables enunciated clearly. This end was attained by changing the more obvious or Lucretian order

> qui | Trojae | primus ab oris

into the characteristic Vergilian

> Tro|jae qui | primus ab oris.

The first puts both speech-stress and metrical stress on the first syllable of *Trojae* making that syllable over-emphatic and leaving the syllable *-jae* unprotected; the Vergilian order puts the metrical stress on *-jae* while leaving the speech-stress on *Tro-*, and thus protects both syllables.

A consequence of this treatment of the higher style of Latin verse —Plautus is quite different—is a lessening of stress and an increase of distinct articulation. Thus the word *fato* was presumably in ordinary speech stressed on the first syllable, *fáto.* But Latin has no difficulty in a line like

> Fato Deucalion, fato servatus Ulixes,

where the second *fato* has the metrical stress on the second syllable. One might compare a line suitable for Daphnis the cowherd:

> Shórthorn under the hill, Shorthórn from slumber awaken'd;

or

> Farewéll, home of the proud, farewéll, thou Castle accursed.

But English of course has few spondaic words, like *shorthorn* or *farewell.*

3 and 4; but 4 is the perfect rhythm, smooth and untroubled, at which 3 is an approximation or "attempt," and to which all three verses lead by a kind of progress. The last verse of an alcaic is extraordinarily delightful in rhythm; but it would be nothing in particular if it were not reached by a struggle—and just the right kind of struggle. Much the same can be said, though to a lesser degree, of the other four-line stanzas. They are not mere repetitions of a pattern; they are constructed wholes.

I use Latin for purposes of illustration as being more generally familiar; but these metres are of course all Greek. In Greek choral lyrics we have the principles of symmetry and architecture carried very far. The poems are composed in stanzas which metrically correspond: that is, each strophe is followed—sometimes immediately, sometimes after a longer interval—by an antistrophe of exactly the same form. It may be said that that is the case with any ballad; one verse is metrically like another. But the ballad is a mere string of equal verses. In the Greek lyric, there are two differences. First, each strophe consists, not of a row of identical lines, but of a more or less elaborate construction of lines which are similar but not identical, and which lead up, first, to one or more minor rests, and eventually to a final "clausula." The point is difficult to illustrate shortly, and one must admit that often a modern ear cannot hold the rhythm long enough to feel the pattern. But, to take one instance, there is a chorus in Euripides' *Andromache* (lines 274–308) in which each strophe ends on a simple rhythm like "Wind across the marshes"—really two syncopated iambic metra, − ∪ − | ∪ − −. The rest of the strophe is mostly written in a metre (syncopated iambic) to which this rhythm would come very easily, but it is always avoided until the very end, and is preceded in each strophe by a short retardation of the metre, so that when it comes it is the more welcome. Thus in this chorus it is (1) − ∪ ∪ − | − ∪ − ∪ − ⌣: "Wind of the North, wind across the marshes"; or (2) ∪ − − | − ∪ − ∪ − ⌣:

"A cold wind | Blows across the marshes." In a later chorus in the same play this idea is repeated in the form $- \cup - | - \cup - | - \cup - \cup - \cup$: "Wind that blows, | Wind that blows | Cold across the marshes." Again, in the most complete form of choral lyric, besides the strophe and antistrophe we have a third stanza, or *Epodos*, which puts a crown on the pair, much as the central figure in the pediment puts a crown on the two sides. Thus, for example, in Pindar's fourth Pythian we have, first, a strophe of eight lines, antistrophe of eight, epode of seven, many times repeated; secondly, inside each stanza there is a further construction, with balance, symmetry, and climax; and, thirdly, there is a relation between the rhythms in the strophe and antistrophe and those in the epode. For example: each strophe ends with a slow, trochaic movement, which goes forward twice, is held back twice, and then moves uninterrupted to its close:

$$- \cup - - | - \cup - - | - \cup - | - \cup - |$$
$$\cup \cup \cup - - | - \cup - -$$

ἐστάθη γνώ— μας ἀταρβά— τοιο πει— ρώμενος
ἐν ἀγορᾷ πλή— θοντος ὄχλου.
ἂν περὶ ψυ— χὰν ἐπεὶ γά— θασεν ἐξ— αίρετον
γόνον ἰδὼν κάλ— λιστον ἀνδρῶν.[8]

First, two trochaic metra, then the same with syncope, then the same with a resolution of the first long syllable, giving a ripple in the swell of the wave. The haunting rhythm of this last clause depends mainly on the movement, the check, and the burst through.

The epode also ends with two trochaic metra, though without any resolution; but the leading up is different.

There is, as far as I know, nothing approaching this in modern metre.

Yet of course there is, especially in the poetry of the nineteenth century, a great deal of very fine metrical

---

[8] The metre is roughly like:

Misty cloudlands | rose before him, | lines of light | marked the dim | Perilous edge of old Avernus.

structure, made both more emphatic to the ear, and also more difficult to write, by the presence of rhyme. One sees the effect most clearly in poems which are written in regular stanzas, but have an internal structure—as distinguished from a repeated pattern—inside each stanza.

> O what can ail thee, knight at arms,
>> So haggard and so woe-begone;
> The squirrel's granary is full,
>> And the harvest's done.

The first couplet is 2, 2: 2, 2; the second is 2, 2: 2 + ? The shorter and slower fourth line gets great emphasis and weight from its position. It is a two-beat line, but a little slower or longer than ordinary. If it were four-beat it would be merely uniform; if it were three-beat, it would be hurried, as the ear would fall into the ordinary eight-and-six hymn verse. As it is, there is an expectation produced by the previous four-beat lines; there is a large space, and a waiting ear, and some checked and slow words which do not quite fill it, and which make us think. That is construction.

Take another example:

> Thy brother Death came, and cried,
>> Wouldst thou me?
> Thy sweet child Sleep, the filmy-eyed,
> Murmured like a noon–tide bee,
> Shall I nestle near thy side?
> Wouldst thou me?—And I replied,
>> No, not thee!

What a wonderful effect, both in rhythm and emphasis, is produced by the last three words in their present position as a "clausula," or ending! In another position they would be uninteresting. It is impertinent to attempt to explain the whole secret of so great a craftsman as Shelley, but one may point out three elements in the effect. First, the second line, "Wouldst thou me?" with its three long syllables prepares one for a similar rhythm later; next, the line which rhymes with that, and which might naturally have had the same form of three long syllables, has not; it remains a regular seven-syllable trochaic; this shakes our expectation. Perhaps it is not coming after all? The next verse comes and the next, and there is still no sign of our rhythm; the suspense becomes great: at last, and just in a place where it makes a peculiarly satisfying effect, it comes. This particular analysis of the metrical construction may be wrong, and is certainly imperfect; but construction is there.

Throughout the above discussion it will be noticed—by some, I fear, with indignation—that I have not raised the distinction between stress and quantity, but have used the terms iambic, dactyl, and the rest as if short-long meant the same thing as weak-strong, and long-short-short the same as strong-weak-weak. I do this partly because the classical metrical terms are so vastly more complete and better developed, and still perhaps on the whole better known among educated people, than any modern equivalents; partly because I cannot help believing that what the ancients called "length," and what we call "stress," and what some Far Eastern nations, I believe, call "tone," are psychologically all subdivisions of "importance," or "the quality attended to." It may be that, in the matter of pure length, "merry," "never," "river," are pyrrhics; it may be that "meadow" and "shadow" are iambics. The Poet Laureate says so, and the kymograph, I believe, confirms him. But I venture to treat them all as trochees, because as used in English verse they consist of an important syllable followed by an unimportant, a syllable attended to followed by one less attended to, just as a trochee did in Latin or Greek. If there is a language which attends chiefly to musical tone in its verse and treats, for instance, bass notes as Greek treats long syllables, I think there would probably be no harm in using the marks $-\ \smile\ \smile$ to denote bass-treble-treble.

But, further, it has been pointed out in a most interesting way by Dr. Sonnenschein in his book on Rhythm, that English verse, though chiefly attending to differences of stress, does pay considerable attention also to differences of quantity. It is not difficult in the more elevated and carefully written verse to find endings like "in ex̄treme need," "Ye shall not ēscape now," or even "We meet in ā strange hour." [9] I suspect that the more carefully and exactly we speak our words, the more will the element of quantity or duration become important as compared with the element of stress.

It is difficult in any circumstances to predict what one literature can learn from another. And the classical literatures, it might plausibly be argued, have long since taught English quite as much as can be considered desirable, and in some matters a great deal more. Still, as Shelley says, poetry is infinite. And a man must, I think, be in a state of "savage torpor" who imagines that he has no more to learn from Homer or Vergil.

The ancients seem to have advantage over us in three points affecting technique: the sonority and smoothness of their language, the keenness of their sense of quantity, and their rich and exquisite metres. As to the first, I fear, we must admit the improbability that any language that we or our descendants are likely to speak will ever produce such sonorous words and phrases as came easily to Aeschylus and Homer, Lucretius and Vergil. Even if we could devise such sonority, the result would be something exotic and artificial. We must content ourselves with a thinner stream of sound, and try to find our music in other ways.

As for quantity, the attempt to substitute duration of sound for stress-accent in English verse has often been made. The Elizabethans tried it, with rather grotesque

[9] Some of these may be due to tradition. In Spenser and Milton such words as *obscure, supreme, future, prostrate, complete, oblique, congeal'd* were accented on either syllable to suit the poet's purpose. Todd, *Milton*, ii, p. cviii. Perhaps also *fountain.*

results; and it has recently been carried out with greater skill than ever before by one who is a past master of metrical technique in English. Yet even Robert Bridges has not made many converts to his quantitative verse. And I incline to the view that our metrical progress here will be on less revolutionary lines. Those poets who have a good ear are growing increasingly sensitive to the length of unstressed syllables, and more skilled in working into the texture of their accentual verse a more subtle regard for time.

In a similar way, though I doubt the likelihood of a great future for English hexameters or alcaics, there is no doubt that our ear is being haunted by some of these metres, and is feeling them to be richer and fuller and more exact than those which are native to us. Some of Tennyson's alcaics and quasi-alcaics, Swinburne's hendecasyllabics and quasi-elegiacs, attain the real and vital beauty of poetry. And I have seen recent editors accept into anthologies poems whose chief merit was a scrupulous observation and development of the rules of Greek *ionic-a-minore*.

Of course, there is a strong spirit abroad which tries to throw off rules and exactitude. It is proud of trusting not to measured feet, but merely to its ear, which is perfectly sound doctrine if the ear is correct, but not otherwise. Unfortunately it hates a correct ear almost as much as a measured foot. Such a school, whether it makes merely for rough versification or definitely for *vers libre*, has its place and its justification in the progress of poetry; but the classical tradition will probably continue to look for advance by writing better and more carefully, not more carelessly and impatiently. No one can be sure that a method is wrong until it has been well tried; but it is difficult to expect good permanent results from one which is based predominantly on contempt for the practice of good poets, on self-assertion rather than worship, and on ennui rather than delight. Otherwise no one can prophesy or point the way. A poet must love the Tradition; otherwise he will not love poetry. He must love language and be tender and reverent with it, as well as bold; or he will never have mastery of its secrets. He must care enough for his work not to notice how much time and trouble he spends on it. He must, as Plutarch warns us, not be like those false lovers of Penelope who, when they found the Queen obdurate, contented themselves with the handmaids. It is along some such lines as these, and not by violent divergence from them, that I should expect to see the modern world find its way to some new Dante or Milton or Goethe, a *poietes-aoidos* who will bring back into our poetry the forgotten music of the lyre and the old sweep of the sea-bird.

V

POETIC DICTION

IS THERE IN THE CLASSICAL AND PERMANENT TRADITION
any essential difference between the language of verse
and ordinary prose speech when each is engaged on its
characteristic work? There has always been, among both
the despisers of poetry and the admirers, a feeling of im-
patience and rebellion against the robes and ornaments
in which she is swathed. "If poetry really means something," cry the Philistine and the realist poet alike, "surely
it can say what it means, and say it as truly and exactly
as possible! If it cannot, if it must always use poetic diction and ornamental phrases, and call things out of their
proper names, then surely it stands condemned. We want
the true, unveiled beauty of Nature, and we are given a
figure rouged and robed and bewigged and lime-lighted,
from a theatrical costumier."

Everyone at times feels something like this. Yet before
we yield to the feeling, we must bear in mind the enormous weight of authority against us. Homer, Vergil, Milton, Shakespeare—are they too classical and sophisticated?
Then think of the strangely artificial language of the
mediaeval poets, of the curious tortuousness of much of
Dante. Think of the great primitive Icelandic poems,
with their riddles and kennings, or equally of the early
Irish. It is quite indubitable that poetry, and primitive

poetry as much as any, does try to make its language different from that of ordinary life.

Aristotle, at any rate, had no doubts on the subject. Indeed, Greek practice in the matter was so clear-cut and unanimous that theory could hardly venture to contradict it. Greek had not only a different method of speech for prose and poetry, but different dialects for epic, lyric, and dramatic poetry, and different sub-dialects, as it were, in prose for history and oratory, and in verse for love-elegies and for philosophical rhapsodies, even if both were in the same metre. Aristotle does not even show any consciousness here, as he so often does, that other philosophers differ from him and have to be confuted. He simply says:

"The virtue of poetical diction is to be clear and not mean. The clearest is that which is made up of the 'regular' or 'proper' words for things (κύρια ὀνόματα), but it is mean, as is shown by the poetry of Cleophon and Sthenelus. [We might perhaps think of Crabbe or parts of Wordsworth.] To be impressive and avoid commonness (σεμνὴ καὶ ἐξαλλάττουσα τὸ ἰδιωτικόν), diction must use unfamiliar terms: by which I mean strange words, metaphors, lengthened forms, and everything out of the ordinary, though a style consisting entirely of such will result in riddles or barbarism. . . . A certain admixture is necessary.[1] . . .

"What helps most to make the diction clear and not common is the use of lengthened, curtailed, and altered forms."

Here, no doubt, Aristotle is expressing himself wrongly, as was inevitable at a time when the science of language was unborn. His own dialect, fourth-century Attic, differed from the Greek of Homer by a long period of historic growth, involving much contraction of vowels.

---

[1] E.g., a critic of one of Andrew Lang's translations unfairly parodied it by collecting the archaic words together: "What would Mr. Lang do if he found a redeless etin pilling in an almry? Eftsoons he would busk him a winsome mead."

When an Attic poet used the old, uncontracted form of some word which was traditional in epic, he seemed to Aristotle—and no doubt to himself—to be "lengthening" or "altering" the normal form (in rare cases, curtailing it). The nearest modern parallel would be the use of obsolete verbal terminations, and so forth, like "thou goest, he goeth."

"A too apparent use of these licenses has certainly a ludicrous effect . . . the rule of moderation applies everywhere. To realize the difference one should take an epic verse and see how it reads when ordinary words are used." [2]

"Ariphrades used to ridicule the tragedians for introducing expressions unknown to common life. . . . In reality the fact of their not being ordinary saves the language from commonness. But he never saw this."

A little later: "It is important to make proper use of these poetical forms . . . but the greatest thing by far is to be master of metaphor. It is the one thing that cannot be learnt from others and it is also a sign of genius (εὐφυΐα), for to make good metaphors is to see similarity in things dissimilar.

"In heroic poetry all these varieties are useful. But iambic verse [that is, principally drama], which represents, as far as may be, familiar speech, prefers those words which can also be used in prose."

The last two statements will be generally accepted:

[2] Aristotle's examples illustrate, of course, only the effect of the Greek words, and cannot be translated. Polyphemus calls Odysseus

"Little and strengthless and of mean aspect."

Aristotle suggests an alternative consisting of prose words something like

"Quite short and plain and physically weak."

In English we might take the lines:

"Man comes and tills the field and lies beneath,
And after many a summer dies the swan."

To substitute "dies the duck" would—such is the injustice of the world—make the line ridiculous.

110

metaphor is a very important characteristic of the poetic style, and drama should keep generally closer to real speech than other poetry. But the main doctrine is both disputed by critics and not quite rightly stated by Aristotle himself. He saw indeed, what Ariphrades and perhaps Wordsworth failed to see, that the use of "expressions unknown to common life" somehow increases the dignity and beauty of poetry, but he did not fully see the reason why. He says that they "save the language from commonness." That is quite true: they keep it away from the associations of the shop, the newspaper, and the drinking saloon. They keep it free from infections that would spoil the poetry. So much Aristotle sees; but he does not perhaps see clearly that these "expressions unknown to common life" are good not merely because they are uncommon, but positively because they are poetical: that is, they carry with them the atmosphere and associations of poetry. A poet tends to use the language that is generally used in poetry: it comes natural to him, just because it is used in poetry, and it helps to produce the expectation of poetry in the reader or hearer for the same reason. This also explains why old words are generally poetical: not simply because they are old, but because it is chiefly through poetry or good literature that they are known. They bring to our mind Chaucer or Shakespeare, not their average vulgar contemporaries.

Observe also an interesting point of style. If a poet wants a particular passage to stand out with special effect from the body of his poem, he can equally well do two opposite things: he can either key up the poetical quality of his language, or he can drop suddenly into extreme prose-like simplicity. There is a time to say,

> Nay this my hand would rather
> The multitudinous seas incarnadine,

and a time to say, "Undo this button"; a time in Greek tragedy to say,

$$\phi \alpha \iota o \chi \acute{\iota} \tau \omega \nu \epsilon \varsigma \ \kappa \alpha \grave{\iota} \ \pi \epsilon \pi \lambda \epsilon \kappa \tau \alpha \nu \eta \mu \acute{\epsilon} \nu \alpha \iota,$$

and a time to say, "Οὖτος ἐστὶν Ἀγαμέμνων ἐμὸς πόσις."
Both the gorgeousness and the plainness stand out against
the background of normal poetical speech.

Now suppose we take the opening of Book II of *Paradise Lost*:

> High on a throne of royal state, which far
> Outshone the wealth of Ormuz and of Ind,
> Satan exalted sate;

and rewrite it: "His Excellency was on a raised daïs,
seated on a state chair carved in a style suggestive of the
Persian Gulf or India, but far more brilliant and expensive than can be found in the possession of any of the
native rulers." The information conveyed is, as far as
possible, the same, though slightly more explicit; the
whole change is a change of atmosphere, from poetry to
prose. To say that the throne outshone the wealth of
Ormuz and of Ind is poetry; to say that it was far more
expensive and brilliant than is usual in the Persian Gulf
is prose, though the objective fact stated may be the
same. Any detailed analysis will probably be deceptive,
but we may notice that in the first place the order of the
words has an effect:

> High on a throne of royal state . . .

The mind is filled with a conception of loftiness and
majesty: "height," "throne," "royal state," with no details added; then a great brilliance. Further, when "wealth"
—generally a most unpoetical subject—is mentioned, it
is a vague splendour, like wealth in dreams, with no
suggestion of expenses and bills and sums. The wealth
"of Ormuz and of Ind" forms an undefined impression in
our minds, coloured by old poetical memories. If we
substitute "the wealth of the Rockefeller Foundation,"
the phrase is stronger and more precise, and therefore
according to some critics altogether better; but the associations are wrong.

This is, briefly and simply, the case for the Aristotelian or classical view that there is such a thing as "poetic diction," and that the language of poetry is essentially somewhat different from that of prose. But let us hear the objectors. I remember a modern rhapsody in which the writer enthusiastically argued that the true ideal of style was to utter the most elevated and profound thoughts in the most common and colloquial language, by no means avoiding slang. The difficulty is that colloquial language consists of a small number of words used by common men on common occasions; while slang, though no doubt it has its place and its uses, consists mostly of unnecessary and ill-thought-out words used, I will not say by ignoble people, but by people in ignoble states of mind on ignoble occasions. There is generally a grumble, a snarl, or at best some affectionate derision, latent at the heart of slang. And how "the most elevated thoughts" are to be uttered in a medium invented for a quite different and almost contrary purpose is a problem that would, I think, tax the ingenuity of the poet beyond its limits.

What a poet can do, of course, is to use dialect or slang for the sake of contrast, and so get a poignant, though perhaps sometimes rather a cheap, effect. But the effect depends on the deliberate unsuitability of the medium chosen: just as when a fool in Shakespeare, or a drunken man in Ibsen, is made to utter words of wisdom, or the thief gives back the money, or the executioner weeps. These are effects of shock or paradox. You cannot construct a consistent world of wise fools and scrupulously honest thieves.

But let us consider the arguments of the greatest poet who ever maintained that poetry should speak exactly the same language as prose. Wordsworth in the preface to the second edition of *Lyrical Ballads* claims—or admits—that, in so far as he is carrying out his own theory, he is making "an experiment," and that, if his example is followed, "a class of poetry will be produced well adapted to interest mankind permanently." It is clear that he conceives it to be a new kind; that is, that on the whole he recognizes that the tradition of poetry is against him.

The experiment consists in "fitting to metrical arrangement a selection of the real language of men in a state of vivid sensation." The phrase occurs repeatedly: "to imitate and, as far as possible, adopt the very language of men." He will "choose incidents and situations from common life, and relate or describe them throughout, as far as is possible, in a selection of the language really used by men."

In one place he gives a quasi-historical explanation. "The earliest poets of all nations generally wrote from passion excited by real events: they wrote naturally and as men: feeling powerfully, as they did, their language was daring and figurative.

"In succeeding times poets, and men ambitious of the fame of poets, perceiving the influence of such language and desirous of producing the same effect without being animated by the same passion, set themselves to a mechanical adoption of these figures of speech. . . . A language was thus produced differing materially from the real language of men in any situation.

"This language was received as the natural language of poetry; and at length, by the influence of books upon men, did to a certain degree really become so. Abuses of this kind were imported from one nation to another."

"Poetry is the spontaneous overflow of powerful feelings."

"The object of Poetry is truth, not individual and local, but general and operative."

"There neither is nor can be any essential difference between the language of prose and metrical composition."

Let us observe first the complete doctrine which seems to lie behind these various utterances, and then make allowance for the compromises and qualifications which the wise poet has been careful to admit.

The doctrine is the old fallacy of realism or naturalism, so often slain and reborn. It holds that the beauty of poetry is in the real facts of life, and more or less equally in all of them. The object of poetry is truth. A passion and a tree and a dead pig are all facts of life, and the poet can either describe them objectively—and if so must describe them correctly—or, in the case of the passion, can let the fact express itself. (Strictly speaking, he should do the same by the tree and the pig, also.) Poetry is then "the spontaneous overflow of strong feeling." And that is the only true poetry.

Many questions will then arise, and it will be seen that Wordsworth takes a position quite different from that of the true realist. He makes concessions. He says that a poet "writes under one restriction only, that of giving immediate pleasure to a human being." Why in the world, asks the orthodox realist, should the poet seek to give pleasure—and immediate pleasure—to a human being if his real object is truth? Why should he yield to the wish to be agreeable, a notorious and not very interesting source of mendacity?

Again, Wordsworth strongly insists on the need of metre. But real men do not naturally speak in metre. Why mar the exact truthfulness of your picture by an obvious falsity?

Lastly, Wordsworth always speaks of "selection." He gives a "selection of the real language of men," and the like. He also selects the subjects of his poems, preferring common life and rustic scenes to the pursuits of the idle rich. But if mere truth is the object, if beauty is present in all life and only needs to be expressed, why make a selection? All life is beautiful; let it speak. And let it speak its natural language. It is of little use to answer that the poet is not trying to represent concrete facts but the inner spirit of life, because on the realist theory this inner spirit is necessarily existent everywhere. The purpose of God—to use theological language—is just as truly present in a General Purposes Committee or a rubbish-heap or a Newport dinner-party, as in the Aphrodite of Melos or in Socrates or in a peasant woman weeping for her son. To select one aspect of life rather than another is a sort of blasphemy. The poet, in fact, has nothing to do, except to express the overflow of his feelings. And he need not really trouble about that, because in so far as they are real they will express themselves; and that is all that is wanted. If he thinks about them and adds something of his own, he makes them artificial, and ruins everything. In fact, the best thing the poet, *qua* poet, can do is to "shut up." The theory of pure Realism or Naturalism destroys itself by its own contradictions in the realm of aesthetic, as well as in the realms of ethics and of logic.

This means, if I am not mistaken, that, exquisite as Wordsworth's style is at its best, the speculative foundation on which his theory rests is completely unsound. Poetry is not a representation of an objective fact, nor yet a series of propositions whose merit is to be true. Poetry is creation or mimesis; and the poem an "artifact," whose merit is to be beautiful. And the beauty of the poem is in the poem itself, not in the thing described by the poem. How the poem can best attain its end— by simple prose-like language or by elaborate and exquisite language—is purely a question of technique.

As for Truth, the furthest Aristotle will go is to say that the poem must not be so untrue as to be improbable "Better to write plausible impossibilities than things improbable and yet true." Similarly, Wordsworth himself admits—though he thinks the admission dangerous—that poetry is concerned with appearance, not with reality "Poetry's appropriate employment, her privilege and her duty, is to treat of things not as they are, but as they appear; not as they exist in themselves, but as they seem to exist to the sense and the passions." If this is true, the aim of poetry is illusion; what, then, do people mean by claiming with Wordsworth and Shelley that its object is truth, and that it is really a higher kind of knowledge?[3]

I believe that there are two distinct meanings in this claim.

There is, first of all, Aristotle's famous and much-mis-understood dictum that poetry is "more philosophic and higher than history," because history merely narrates what happened, poetry narrates "the sort of thing that would happen—probably or inevitably—under given conditions."[4] That is, a chronicle simply narrates in order of time a number of things which happened to happen; poetry, taking a given situation as a datum, shows the sort of thing that would result from that situation by a process of modified deduction—a deduction which admits the probable as well as the necessary consequence. Poetry is thus nearer to philosophy, which, given certain premisses, shows by strict deduction the necessary conclusions.

Thus it is "history" to write:

> 1639. Charles marches north to punish the Scots. The East India Company buys land on which it builds Madras. Wroth, Erbery, and Cradock, Welsh clergymen, are deprived of their livings. Horrocks observes the transit of Venus.

Every statement here is true; but they are not casually connected—at least, not within the sphere of the narrative.

Poetry tells us how Pyramus and Thisbe, young lovers living next door to one another in Babylon, were forbidden by their parents to meet, and how they found a crack in the mud wall to whisper through, and what other

---

[3] "Poetry is the first and last of all knowledge."—Wordsworth. Poetry "is at once the centre and the circumference of knowledge."—Shelley, *Defence of Poetry*.

[4] It is worth noticing that the proper meaning of οἷα ἄν γένοιτο is 'the sort of thing that would happen, if . . .' rather than simply 'the sort of thing that might happen.' The distinction is not always kept clear, even by Aristotle himself, but it is important.

things they did and suffered in consequence. Every statement is untrue, but all are casually connected, and all represent "the sort of thing that would" result, or be quite likely to result, from that situation.

Thus poetry implies knowledge of human nature and power of generalization. It is "more philosophic" than a mere historical narrative, though Aristotle never for a moment says it is more "true."

It may, however, show truths and teach truths about life which a plain prose record would miss. Poetry, or, as we should say, fiction, kindles the imagination; and that kindling of the imagination certainly does reveal, or bring to light, facts in life and elements in human nature which the dull eye of ordinary prose does not see. Impassioned scenes of tragedy often strike one, not merely as "true to life," but as revealing details or elements ordinarily hidden. Take a very simple Old Testament narrative. When Hagar and Ishmael were driven out into the wilderness, "The water was spent in the bottle, and she cast the child under one of the shrubs. And she went and sat her down over against him a good way off, as it were a bow-shot; for she said, 'Let me not see the death of the child.' And she sat over against him, and lift up her voice and wept."

That is impassioned imaginative narrative. The story may be history or myth or fiction; but whichever it is, there is in it an imaginative or poetical quality which makes one realize more exactly and fully how Hagar felt and acted, or how a woman in Hagar's position would feel and act. The essential poetry, or use of the imagination, in the narrative makes us see more truth, and so gives us more knowledge. Indeed, the plain fact is that without a lively use of the imagination people understand nothing.

So far there is nothing in the least mystical in our discussion. Poetry aims at illusion or credibility; it must therefore know the sort of thing that people will believe. It makes people use their imagination and observation, and so educates them to see more than they saw before. In this sense, poetry can be said to see and reveal truth.

But there is another sense in which this claim is made, which is stated more clearly and with more philosophic power by Shelley than by Wordsworth, though Wordsworth, I think, meant much the same. We noticed that in the ancient mimetic dances and other forms of ecstatic worship there came a climax in which the worshipper felt himself to be transfigured: his long prayer and effort had borne fruit and he had become identified with his god. Expressions such as, "From man I am become god," "Thou in me and I in thee," are typical of this phase. It was accompanied, of course, by other revelations or illusions; and in the result the whole of the worshipper's life and surroundings were equally transfigured. This ecstasy, or a state of mind resembling this ecstasy, is well known, in one degree or another, to most lovers of poetry and people of keen sensibility. Indeed, most people who are honest with themselves would admit the general truth of Shelley's description:

"We are aware of evanescent visitations of thought and feeling . . . elevating and delightful beyond all expression. . . . It is, as it were, the interpenetration of a diviner nature through our own. Poets are not only subject to these experiences as spirits of the most refined organization, but they can colour all that they combine [that is, all the "combinations" or "compositions" they make] with the evanescent hues of this ethereal world. . . . Poetry thus makes immortal all that is best and most beautiful in the world. . . . Poetry redeems from decay the visitations of the divinity in man."

So much we can all accept: we recognize, in various degrees, this kind of experience, and admit that great poetry perpetuates it. The question then becomes simply this: is the experience in question an illusion—a subjective experience no less real, but also no more true, than the visions produced by hashish or opium, or any other illusion or dream? Or is it a sort of revelation of the true world of being, of which this ordinary world of phenomena is only a transitory and inadequate image? This last is what Shelley, under the influence of Plato, believed about the world as a whole, and what Wordsworth believed at least in respect of the "spirit of Nature." Both poets thought that, by poetic ecstasy, they could really discover truth.

Shelley expresses himself clearly on this point: "Poetry strips the veil of familiarity from the world, and lays bare the naked and sleeping beauty which is the spirit of all its forms." And again: "Poetry lifts the veil from the hidden beauty of the world, and makes familiar objects to be as they were not familiar." Thus: "Poetry is the very image of life expressed in its eternal truth." The doctrine is really a form of Platonism. Are material objects the only reality, and consequently mathematical or scientific laws only so many imperfect generalizations about them? Or is the mathematical law the real, permanent truth, and the various round and square and angular objects which we sit upon and knock against, so many transient and faulty "images" or representations of it? The plain man assumes the first; Plato has convinced himself of the second. If you agree with Plato, it is not difficult to take a further step and agree with Wordsworth and Shelley.

Neither of these great poets could possibly have known the importance which the Molpê, or ancient communal dance, would eventually acquire in this connexion through the advances of anthropology; but both make use of it to explain the essence of poetry. "The poet, singing a song in which all human beings join him, rejoices in the presence of Truth as our visible friend and hourly companion." An ancient mystic might say "Dionysus" or 'Hermes" instead of "Truth"; but otherwise the statement would suit him admirably.

Shelley says more simply: "In the youth of the world men dance and sing and imitate natural objects, observing in these actions . . . a certain rhythm or order." He goes on to explain that there is one rhythm or order, in each case, which would produce an intenser and purer pleasure than any other. The effort of the dance is to attain this rhythm; it is an effort of "approximation to the beautiful," and those in whom the faculty of such approximation exists in excess are poets. This is exactly stated; and no one can well deny two other claims that Shelley makes for poetry: that "it makes us the inhabitants of a world to which the familiar world is a chaos," and that it "defeats the curse which binds us to be subjected to the accident of surrounding impressions." It breaks, as I have put it elsewhere, the prison walls of the immediate material present.

It may be said that the question which we have just raised, and slurred over, is of vital interest. It makes all the difference whether the poet's or dancer's ecstasy is an illusion or a revelation, and a critic has no right to pass the question by. I shall come back to it in a later chapter. For the present, I can only say that the Classical Tradition has never pronounced itself: both views are in the canon of great poetry. The question itself, apart from its metaphysical side, takes one straight into the most obscure and debated provinces of psychology and the problem of the control of matter by mind. One may perhaps acquiesce in Shelley's own words about the Poet:

> He will watch, from dawn to gloom,
> The lake-reflected sun illume
> The yellow bees in the ivy bloom;
> Nor heed nor see what things they be:
> Yet out of these create he can
> Forms more real than living man,
> Nurslings of immortality.

The poet in his vision creates something that is real, even if he does not discover something that is true.

But in either case, whether he finds a new and different world already existing under the veil of phenomena, or whether he himself creates the new and different world by his imagination, it seems only natural and inevitable that the language of that world should be somewhat different from this. Poetry must have its own style of speech. The singers of the Molpê were right.[5]

The character of that speech, as we have seen, is to a very slight extent a matter of euphony; much more it is a matter of appeal to the senses and the imagination rather than to intellect and calculation; most of all it is a matter of association, and therefore of tradition. Consequently the attitude of the poet toward the general tradition of poetry is often very instructive. One thinks of Shelley as a revolutionary and Wordsworth as the reverse. But in regard to the poetical tradition the rôles are changed. Shelley feels nothing but admiration and love for the poets of the past; he likes to think that he is following them and coöperating with them. As Milton reached out through the darkness for the sympathy of

> Blind Thamyris and blind Maeonides,
> And Teiresias and Phineus, prophets old,

so Shelley, in that inspired self-forgetfulness which sometimes makes him so adorable, idealizes other poets—and not only his predecessors, but even his contemporaries. Wordsworth thinks that other poets have all gone badly astray and that he himself has found out, or at least recovered, the proper way to write poetry. "The first poets of all nations wrote from passion excited by real events." It is only all the intervening poets who have gone wrong, by setting themselves to imitate the manner and language of their predecessors, and so inventing "poetical diction."

Now, as a historical statement this account is completely fallacious. It belongs to the idyll of Romanticism: "*Le monde naît, Homère chante,*" and the rest. So far as classical literature is concerned, the element of tradition or convention is just as strong in Homer and Hesiod

[5] Cf. pp. 37, 38 above.

as in the later forms of poetry. The epic language is demonstrably traditional; it is full of extremely ancient and obscure words, some of which are used wrongly in the actual poems;[6] it is full of highly varied metrical formulae for the same thing. It shows at every turn the effect of a long and exquisitely studied tradition. In Hebrew literature, again, the oldest books, such as Judges or Genesis, already show both marked conventions and a knowledge of previous literature. And I am told that one of the very earliest poems unearthed in Babylonia contains a lament that all reasonable subjects for literature are already exhausted. The imaginary primitive poet, whose utterance is the unspoiled utterance of Nature, must go the way of the "simple, primitive language" and Rousseau's natural Man. The process which Wordsworth condemns as vicious, that is, the loving discipleship of poet to poet, and the long bond of influence and association uniting the oldest to the newest, is the normal and healthy method for the progress of poesy, and was more dominant in primitive times than it is now.

Ancient society, being always insecure, laid great stress on the duty of the individual to his city and his gods, on tradition, obedience, and piety, and it looks as if the dangers threatening civilization since the outbreak of the Great War might well produce a similar state of public feeling in the near future. But in general, modern society since the middle of the nineteenth century being, in its own opinion, unshakeably secure, has liked to emphasize and encourage the emancipation of the individual and his right to please himself. Indeed, a certain amount of self-assertion and egotism became almost obligatory in literature, just as girls and schoolboys were almost forced by their own public opinion to smoke tobacco, whether they liked it or not. Not to do something which some imagined authorities condemned seemed like confessing a lack of personality.

This supposed duty of self-assertion has, of course, been

[6] E.g., δεδουπότος Ὀιδιπόδαο, στεῦτο, ἔεδνα.

particularly prevalent in the arts. Self-assertion is not as a rule disagreeable to the assertor, whatever it may be to his neighbours; and it looks as if many causes had coöperated to put a premium upon it during the last few generations. First, there is the analogy—so fatal in many spheres—of the mechanical arts in an age of invention. We expect every year a new and improved method in window-catches or steam-ploughs or motor engines; and consequently, by false analogy, we expect a new and improved method in music or painting or literature or even morals. This error sometimes approaches the idiotic. People actually cannot accommodate themselves to the fact that there is better poetry in Isaiah than in the New York *Evening Post*. Next, there is the great prevalence of competition and advertisement. A work of art has to attract attention in order to be noticed. Most artists have to sell their work in order to live; all artists have the natural desire to be recognized; and it is increasingly difficult in the enormously large societies of the present day for an artist either to be recognized or to sell except by exhibiting some marked diversity from his predecessors and colleagues. Thirdly, there is the critical incompetence of the general public and their advisers, a fact by no means peculiar to this age, but perhaps peculiarly influential in it. The reason for this is very simple. To distinguish really good work from bad is often a delicate and difficult task, demanding in the critic such qualities as taste and knowledge, and, above all, a fresh and interested mind. But to distinguish something startlingly unusual is not at all difficult. The most jaded and incompetent critic can see that a cubist picture—or even, as in one famous instance, a picture painted by the well-directed sweeps of a donkey's tail—is different from a Reynolds. It is far easier to form the judgement, "This is odd," or "This will make them sit up," and then decide for or against it according to your *parti pris*, than to decide by your unaided aesthetic judgement whether you really think it good or bad.

Lastly, though one hesitates to form judgements about one's own environment, it looks as if the present age was more exposed to one paralyzing influence than the ages which preceded the Industrial Revolution. I mean the influence of ennui. A process began at that period, and has probably increased in intensity since, which doubtless has some good points but does seem to involve over-stimulation and its natural consequences. Wordsworth at the beginning of the Industrial Revolution cries passionately: "A multitude of causes, unknown to former times, are now acting with combined force to blunt the discriminating powers of the mind, and, unfitting it for voluntary exertion, to reduce it to a state of almost savage torpor. The most effective of these causes are the great national events which are daily taking place, and the increasing accumulation of men in cities, where the uniformity of their occupations produces a craving for extraordinary incident which the rapid communication of intelligence hourly gratifies." A little later he speaks of "this degrading thirst for outrageous stimulation."

Now the time in which Wordsworth wrote was not in general a time of "torpor" or feebleness. It was a great period of artistic creation and of speculative achievement. Yet the poet's analysis may be true all the same. Excessive stimulus may well produce extraordinary energy, but it does, probably, produce ennui as well, and with ennui "a degrading thirst for outrageous stimulation." A man accustomed to the constant stream of external stimuli which are characteristic of modern city life, "amusements" mechanically laid on from outside, and "news" flung at him by the sensational newspapers which form his principal reading, is probably less able to appreciate beauty in literature or art than one who lives more quietly. His jaded nerves cry not for beauty, but for novelty; and the analogy of the mechanical arts steps in to assure him that novelty is the real mark of genius. Novelty is mistaken for "originality" or "individuality."

It seems strange to us moderns when we read Plato's

argument in the first book of the *Republic* (pp. 349 f.) that as the just man will not try to surpass the just man in justice, so the musician tuning a lyre will not try to "outdo" another musician, nor a physician, in prescribing for a complaint, wish to "go beyond" another physician or beyond the science of medicine. He means, of course, in each case to speak of the artist *qua* artist: if an artist has made a mistake and has to be corrected, then, in so far as he goes wrong, he is not an artist. And, given that explanation, we should not differ from Plato. But it is significant of a profound difference of outlook that Plato thinks of the art as something in itself perfect; something which a man has to learn and study and practise as well as he can, in order to "approximate to the beautiful." He never thinks of it as a thing which an individual can modify and alter as he thinks fit, or a vehicle by which he can "assert his personality." With him the artist serves his art; with the egotistic or rebellious modern, the art has to serve the artist.

Of course, there must always have been ennui; always men could have too much of a good thing, and when they had, they demanded change, though it were a change to something worse. Even the Odyssey complains that people always rush for the newest story. And Wordsworth himself was in some respects a victim of this ennui which he reviles. He hates the poetical style of his own day, and comes near to denouncing all poetic style whatsoever. He proudly avoids the "personifications of abstract terms," a trope which had become grossly common; he has even "abstained from the use of many expressions, in themselves proper and beautiful, but which have been foolishly repeated by bad poets until feelings of disgust are connected with them." That is the working of ennui. It is pardonable enough, but I doubt if Shelley or Milton or Vergil would have avoided an expression which seemed to them proper and beautiful just because they were "disgusted" by the "bad poets" who had used it.

The acme of this modern rebellion against the Tradition may be found in a man of some genius, whose sensitive and jealous egotism sometimes passed the bounds of the normal—Samuel Butler. "Blake was no good because he learned Italian at over sixty in order to read Dante. Dante was no good because he was fond of Vergil. Vergil was no good because Tennyson ran him, and as for Tennyson—well, he goes without saying." This was a jest, no doubt, in the sense that Butler knew it was funny; I cannot believe it was a jest, in the sense that he did not mean it. He did.

Against that outburst we may set the spirit of those poets, certainly great and perhaps the greatest, who have built up almost the major part of their marvellous fabric of poetry out of memories and reminiscences, at the head of them probably "Homer," undoubtedly Vergil and Milton. Critics sometimes sneer at the two latter for making their poems "out of books and not out of life"; but the sneer is a shallow one. No artist builds his work out of mere life; only a newspaper reporter does that, and not the most intelligent kind of reporter. A poet builds out of life interpreted; out of life seen through transfiguring and illuminating media of emotion and memory and imagination. To make up his experience, both at the moment of emotion and still more when the emotion is "remembered in tranquillity," there go elements from all his knowledge of life, all things remembered or imagined, all the experiences of other poets through which he has imaginatively lived, all the old poetry which has become a part of his being. The Iliad and Odyssey are full of traditions and formulae and similes which were certainly not first invented for the places where they now stand. Vergil's great poem is haunted in every line by memories of Greek or old Latin poets—Homer, Apollonius, Hesiod, Ennius, Lucretius—and perhaps most markedly so in his most magical parts. Yet he is utterly different in style and imagination from any one of them, and it needs a fairly tough ear and mind to deny his immense originality. He transmutes all he touches, and the

127

effect of his being so steeped to the lips in the tradition of poetry is not to take away anything that is his own but to add to all he writes a peculiar richness and depth of meaning. Vergil was regarded in the Middle Ages as a magician, and his book was used as a collection of oracles or *sortes*. And it has been well remarked that this was not a mere accident. Vergil at his best does write in such a way that almost every verse, if you think it over, seems to have some meaning beyond its immediate meaning. There is so much of reflection and memory, so much association behind association, in each line of his great passages, that readers of the most diverse characters and periods have felt as if the words had a special personal meaning to themselves. And it is almost the same in Milton; almost the same in much of the greatest work of the poets. For as Shelley puts it, "All high poetry is infinite. . . . Veil after veil may be withdrawn, and the inmost naked beauty of the meaning never exposed." It is this quality of infinitude that is specially produced by real love of the tradition. There is not only the thing said; the thing said is mostly a type or symbol, pointing beyond itself; and some word in which it is phrased, or some image or some turn of rhythm, carries with it, beyond the statement itself and beyond the direct meaning of the symbol, fragrances from that great garden which all the poets of the past have planted and watered and bequeathed to us. This does not mean that a check should be placed in the way of progress or of variety. It means that the future poet will naturally, if he cares for poetry, feed on the poetry of the past. That poetry will help to form his vision of the world; and it is that vision that he will express in his own writings. I do not, of course, dream of saying to the future poet that he should "imitate" or "mould himself upon" this or that great writer. I would only say to him: "Remember you are not the first human being to have seen the poetic vision. Millions have seen it before you, and seen it in innumerable different ways. A few hundred of them happen to have had their words preserved, and are there waiting for you, your brothers, comforters, leaders, if you care to listen to their voices, who can show you things you have never seen and make you feel what you have never felt. What you ultimately express will of course be your own vision of the world, but it will then come to you enriched by the imaginative experience of many great minds."

Nor, lastly, do I urge you to try to be learned, or to read everything that anyone else has read. That way lies despair. Try to read good things. Read them over and over. Make them a part of you: and do not imagine you are wasting time, because you are not. Read the books that you like best. And if there are famous books, generally praised by good judges, which you do not appreciate, give them a fair chance. Try them from time to time, to see if you enjoy them or understand them better. For remember that in that inner world to which great literature belongs, a man may go on all his life learning to see, but he can never see all that is there; he can only hope to see deeper and deeper, more and more, and as he sees, to understand and to love.

VI

UNITY AND ORGANIC CONSTRUCTION

TO BE CLASSICAL, AS WE ALL KNOW, A DRAMA OR POEM
must have unity, and Aristotle took unusual pains to explain what he meant by this unity. It was not enough for
the story to be about one person: that is obvious. A
complete biography contains masses of incidents only
accidentally connected. Nor on the other hand, though
Aristotle does not expressly say this, is it absolutely necessary that it be about one person. It might be about a
group of people like the *Heraclidae* or the *Trojan Women*
of Euripides, or the *Eumenides* of Aeschylus; or, again, it
might be about a process affecting a number of different
persons, like Hauptmann's *Die Weber* or Mr. Arnold
Bennett's *Milestones*. Unity of place is not mentioned by
Aristotle, though as a matter of fact changes of scene are
not common on the Greek stage. As to unity of time, he
merely remarks that tragedies as a rule "tend" ($\beta o \acute{u} \lambda o \nu \tau a \iota$)
to confine themselves "to a single revolution of the sun,
or exceed it but slightly," whereas the epic action is unlimited in time. This is true as a rule of Greek tragedies,
though there are many exceptions,[1] and the Greek stage
possessed in its Chorus an instrument for denoting an
unspecified interval of time, just like our curtain. The

[1] *Prometheus*, ages; *Agamemnon*, some days; *Eumenides*, some years
at least; *Trachiniae*, some weeks(?).

truth is that time, place, person, are all accidents; the thing that must have unity is the real object of the representation, the *praxis*.

Unfortunately we have no word for *praxis*. It is translated "action," and the verb πράττω often means to "act" or "do." But it is also used intransitively, meaning to "fare" or to "do" in the intransitive sense, as when we say, "The patient is doing well." Aristotle seems to waver a little between the two senses. He says, for instance, that it depends on "how they are doing" (κατὰ τὰς πράξεις) that people are called "happy" or "unhappy." And he says explicitly in the *Politics*[2] that *praxis* includes such mental activities as understanding and speculation. On the other hand, he sometimes uses instead of πράττειν the word δρᾶν, which definitely means to "do" in the transitive sense. A play is called δρᾶμα ("drama") "because the players represent by doing things" (ὅτι μιμοῦνται δρῶντες).

I have no better word to suggest in place of "action." Neither "experience" nor "faring" nor Professor Margoliouth's phrase, "chapter of life," is quite satisfactory. So we may keep the term "action," while realizing that it is used in a very broad sense, covering the way the people fare, the things they do, and the inner life they lead. Then Aristotle's doctrine is clear. "The chief thing is the putting together of the *praxis*. . . . The story is the first principle and, as it were, the soul of the tragedy." And of epic: "The story ought obviously to be constructed dramatically, and be about a single action complete in itself, with a beginning, middle, and end, so that it may produce its own proper pleasure, as if it were one complete living creature." This last sentence is vital.

The view which Aristotle is combatting is the view that character is more important than story, a heresy which has always had its adherents. Aristotle gives many arguments; among them, he points out that tragedy does not "imitate" human beings—that would be a mime; it

<hr />

[2] *Politics*, 1325b, 16.

"imitates" living, or action. Also, it is through the things they do that people show their characters. The gallery hisses the villain because of things he does or intends to do. Finally, a coherent story is at least like a pencil drawing, an intelligible constructed whole; a mass of characters —even with fine speeches added—would be like a mass of colours flung out on the paper.

This seems true. It is not merely that the average mass of mankind is more interested in story than in character, or at least primarily interested in the story, and through the story in the character. It is something more fundamental. The primary importance of the *praxis*, or action, results at once from the principle of unity or coherence. It is the artistic creation itself—the poem or play or whatever it is—that must have unity, and this cannot be attained merely by the description of so many different characters. It is their *praxis*, the story you have to tell about them, that must be one. Of course, you might make your subject, your *praxis*, something intimately dependent on character: for example, how a character can be transformed by success or by failure, as in *The Rise of Silas Lapham*, or by bad treatment, as in Euripides' *Hecuba*. Then the change of character is the story. Or you might take the effect in life of certain weaknesses of character in one person or many, as in the "Tartarin" series, or Tchekhov's *Cherry Orchard*. In all such cases the story remains the essential thing, but it happens to be about human character, as it might be about a passion or a vendetta or the development of a railroad. It is always the *praxis* itself—the action or experience, the "faring" or "doing" represented in the work of art—that must have unity and coherence.

Why then does the other view maintain its vitality among the cultured? I think it is partly through a misunderstanding. People think of "story" or "action" as meaning something external, and they know that they are more interested in something internal or spiritual. If they realized that Aristotle's *praxis*, or story, covers the internal as well as the external, they would withdraw much of their objection. The essential point, it seems to me, is that the subject of *Romeo and Juliet* is "the tragic history of Romeo and Juliet": it is not a study of Romeo plus Juliet plus Mercutio plus the Nurse plus Friar Laurence, and so on, though it must contain studies or at least sketches of all of them.

It seems that in the present generation there is still a reaction against the over-ingenious and artificial plots invented in the latter part of the nineteenth century, especially on the French stage. Hence clever dramatists are "bored" by plots of the old sort, while most of them have not yet found out how to make really good plots of a more exacting sort. And secondly, there is no doubt that the last fifty years have seen an immense increase of interest in the study of character and increase of skill in analyzing or depicting it. The artist naturally likes the thing he can do and depreciates what he has no taste for.

We can see, therefore, what Aristotle means by insisting on the primacy of the "story" or the *praxis*, and the need of its being "one and complete." But it does not follow that the ancient Greek and Latin poets really did what Aristotle thought they ought to do. Let us consider the point.

First, there can be no doubt whatever of the artistic unity and admirable construction of the Iliad and the Odyssey. (The point has, of course, nothing to do with the supposed single authorship of a person called "Homer.") They are almost the only epics in the world which are still read with pleasure in prose translations, though these, of course, give little of the charm of the original except the story. They are read in full translations; they are read in abbreviated forms. They are read both by boys and by girls. They sell. And the reason is not so much any inherent magnificence in the actual incidents, as the skill of the story-telling. Vergil's Aeneid again has unity of a sort, and considerable variety, apart from its exquisite beauty in detail; but few would read it for the story. The *Nibelungenlied* and the *Chanson de Roland* in their extant forms are both diffuse and shapeless, however fine the underlying story of the first and the language of the second. *Paradise Lost* has unity, but not much human interest, and rather a limited range of incident. But think of most other epics! What is the story of the *Faery Queene*, or *Endymion*, or *The Revolt of Islam*? Few indeed could say. One cannot remember the stories, they are so shapeless and ill constructed. And consequently these epics, in spite of the beauty of individual parts, are difficult to read through. Chaucer, of course, has the power of seeing his story as a whole and consequently of telling it, but he is hardly an epic writer. *Don Juan*, *Orlando Furioso*, are entertaining or brilliant in episodes, but the plots of both wander helplessly. Even Dante's *Divina Commedia*, though a great continuous stretch, is hardly an organic unity. He chose a theme which enabled him to add incidents here and there as the mood took him. He can hardly stand up to Aristotle's dictum: "A thing whose presence or absence makes no difference to a whole is not a part of that whole." The truth is that few poets since the beginning of literature have had the strength both of will and of intellect to grasp a great continuous theme and work it out organically with an eye to the whole.

Outside the epic this rule of unity or construction has had far more influence. The modern counterpart of the epic is no doubt the novel; and most good novels have, allowing for the loose form in which they are written, a fairly definite and complete story, with a "beginning, middle, and end." They are markedly better in this respect than the ancient Greek novels, from Chariton to Heliodorus. The lesson seems also to have been learnt by the average modern dramatist. But there are considerable varieties in degree.

If we take Sophocles' *Oedipus Tyrannus* or *Electra*, or Euripides' *Hippolytus* or *Medea* as a model Greek play, we shall find that there is not a single scene that is not strictly relevant or does not directly contribute to the climax.[3] Compared with these, the Odyssey is full of digressions and retardations, and even anecdotes; and there are parts of the Iliad which are not strictly business. But these are not really derogations from unity, or faults in construction. The epic is a looser form than tragedy, and is also much longer. Consequently, in order to get the maximum of concentrated interest in the poem as a whole, there is actually an advantage in admitting digressions and retardations. The only rule is that the whole must be stronger as well as larger than the part. The digression must give the hearer a rest in his main interest, not so excite him as to divert him from it. The retardation must add to the reader's suspense, not make him lose the thread of the story. Thus, the first four books of the Odyssey, in which the hero never appears but everyone is thinking about him and being affected one way or another by his absence, add immensely to the effect of his first appearance on the isle of Calypso in the fifth book. And the slow building-up of preparations in the later books, the testing of Eumaeus and Telemachus and Penelope and Eurycleia, increase the weight and volume, as it were, of the culminating moment when Odysseus leaps up on the threshold and draws his bow.

Again, a Shakespearean play is apt to be about twice the length of a Greek tragedy, or more; it is much looser in texture and admits far more characters and changes of scene and incidents. Consequently it cannot be expected to keep so strictly to business as a Greek tragedy, though I do not say that it would be the worse for doing so. *Macbeth* has no serious digressions;[4] it is constructed with almost Aristotelian severity; it never leaves its main theme, and many people love it the best of Shakespeare's

---

[3] Possibly in the *Medea* there is one scene, that with Aigeus, which only serves to say what "happened afterwards," but even there perhaps the misery of the childless king is meant to suggest to Medea's mind the strange form that her revenge is to take.

[4] Nor has *Othello*; but its theme is un-Greek.

plays. But it would be pedantic to quarrel with Shakespeare for relaxing the tension and varying the atmosphere, from time to time, or to hold with Frederick the Great that his plays are "farces worthy of the savages of Canada," because they break rules which were not made for them, but for something else. The question really is, whether any particular digression or diversion serves the total effect, or no. A typical case would be Hamlet's longish conversation with the players. Does it serve a real purpose in the play—for example, to show what Hamlet was like in ordinary life, as one critic says; or to show how, like most young persons of high rank, he fancied that he could teach professional people their business, as another suggests? Or is it an irrelevant outburst of criticism on contemporary acting, which may be interesting, as coming from Shakespeare, but is no part of *Hamlet*? If so, by the classical canon, it is bad. Again, in the much-discussed scene of the comic Porter in *Macbeth*, the goodness or badness of the incident depends on whether it increases or merely interrupts the tragic value of the scenes among which it comes. To put it crudely, if the Porter's facetiae make you either forget the murder of Duncan, or want to laugh during the next scene, they are bad. If by contrast they enhance the effect of the next scene, they are good.

Similarly, in a modern novel of the long and leisurely type, such as Thackeray's, varieties and changes and digressions are part of the art-form. Yet the question always remains whether or no they carry more than their own weight, and so play their part in the main structure. For instance, it might be held that in *Vanity Fair* there was practically not a stroke that did not help in making up the great picture of the vanity of human wishes; while in *Pendennis* most people would agree that there was a lot of "dead wood." Curiously enough, the average modern reader is apt to think of classical literature, from Homer to Scott, as containing too much "dead wood," because it often moves more leisurely and prepares its effects more fully. There is, no doubt, in modern readers a greater expectation of speed, and possibly a greater capacity for rapid apprehension. But that is largely a matter of fashion. In reality it is dead wood that the classical tradition hates; and dead wood that shines and rattles and attracts attention it hates rather more than that which is merely dull, because it does more to dissipate the interest and spoil the main effect.

Here the so-called Gothic tradition, still on the whole prevailing in England and northern Europe, and in popular taste almost everywhere, enters its protest. It points to a great deal of modern and mediaeval literature, and even to some parts of Shakespeare. Above all, it points triumphantly to its cathedrals. It says: "Why should I be the slave of rules? This morning, while I was writing my tragedy about the Archangel Michael, I saw a blind man take off his hat to a horse and ask it the way, and this gave me an idea which made me laugh consumedly. So I have put it in. Why lose a good laugh?"

Or again: "While pegging away, month in month out, at my old cathedral, I suddenly conceived the idea of a peculiarly disgusting kind of devil, so I have stuck him in where there was a good vacant space, just over the Virgin Mary. Also, I have heard so much about the richly carved porch that those idiots at P—— have just had built, that I have determined to stick in an extra porch somewhere which shall be twice as richly carved. It may not exactly be necessary to the plan; but it will be one more beautiful thing to look at. And, furthermore, if you talk high doctrine to me and say that I should treat my art seriously, I answer that in real life the tragic and the ridiculous, the beautiful and the ugly, are always apt to be mixed up like that. And as for symmetry and order, that is just what you do not get in life. You get lots of beautiful and interesting things, mostly muddled together and fighting one another. So I consider my methods both freer and truer to life than yours."

This doctrine is without doubt very popular. The newspaper and the music-hall are both built upon it. Quite serious critics support it, and even Dr. Johnson, in an unguarded moment, has uttered an apparent defence of it.[5] It consists essentially in a denial of Aristotle's principle, "Tragedy should not be expected to produce every kind of pleasure, but the kind proper to it."

The popular love of it, I think, rests on laziness and on a lack of real interest in art. The sort of being who is, I believe, happily described in America as "the tired business man" is not prepared to make the mental effort necessary for grasping a great artistic climax; his attention wanders and he likes it to wander; consequently he likes to be amused from moment to moment. He cannot exercise the self-restraint or make the temporary sacrifice necessary for good art.

The theoretic defence is that, since real life is a confused mixture of things and not a unity, therefore art should also be a confused mixture of things. This, I think, is a patent fallacy. If you wish to depict the confusion of life, by all means do so; but you will not do it by confused art. That will only produce muddle. You must do it by careful construction and arrangement so

[5] *Poetics*, 1453b, 11. Contrast *The Rambler*, No. 156:
"What is there in the mingled drama which impartial reason can condemn? The connexion of important with trivial incidents, since it is not only common but perpetual in the world, may surely be allowed upon the stage which pretends only to be the mirror of life. The impropriety of suppressing passions before we have raised them to the intended agitation, and of diverting the expectation from an event which we keep suspended only to raise it, may be speciously urged. But will not experience show this objection to be rather subtle than just? Is it not certain that the tragic and comic affections have been moved alternately with equal force, and that no plays have oftener filled the eye with tears . . . than those which are variegated with interludes of mirth? I do not, however, think it safe to judge of works of genius merely by the event; . . . and instead of vindicating tragicomedy by the success of Shakespeare, we ought perhaps to pay new honours to that transcendant and unbounded genius that could preside over the passions in sport; who, to actuate the affections, needed not the slow gradation of common means, but could fill the heart with instantaneous jollity or sorrow, and vary our disposition as he changed his scenes."

as to produce the effect of confusion, as Thackeray does in *Vanity Fair*, or Tolstoy in *War and Peace*. A picture of Chaos must be as carefully planned and thought out as a picture of anything else, and must have as much unity of purpose. It cannot be made by flinging tubes of paint at a canvas. Putting the case more generally, if you want to enjoy the Parthenon, though there will be great beauty of detail, which you will study at your leisure, the main artistic enjoyment will lie in the contemplation of the whole as a whole, in its full symmetry. If you want to enjoy the Gothic cathedral, you will find your chief pleasure in walking round about, prying into curious and exciting details. As for the whole, it will probably not have been constructed on one plan, and if it has, the plan will probably have been lost through additions and digressions. And the ordinary man finds it far easier to be amused with curious details than to stand in contemplation of a great, serious, and complex whole.

Let us, then, try to see exactly what advantage there is in "unity" or "congruity," and what is meant by the classical insistence on unity of construction, or the need that a work of art should be, in Aristotle's phrase, "seen as a whole," or "grasped as one by the memory" (εὐ-σύνοπτον, εὐμνημόνευτον).

First, an isolated incident is not interesting. I see in the paper that in such-and-such a city a man was choked by swallowing a fishbone; I can hardly imagine anything much less interesting. Except to a reader already interested in fishbones, this information possesses what one might almost call the very minimum of interest. But let us reduce it still further: say the man only coughed and recovered. But, at the same time, suppose you look further and see that the victim of the accident was some one whom you know: the interest will be doubled immediately.

Thirdly, suppose that your friend who swallowed the fishbone turns out to have been gambling heavily, and suppose that you dimly remember a doctor having told you that swallowing a fishbone was a good way of committing suicide without exciting suspicion; that you remember, now you think of it, that your friend was in the room at the time. (Did he or did he not, ask the doctor some question? And what question was it?) Each new item does not merely add to the story its own small amount of interest: it multiplies the interest of each item that has gone before and contributes to a whole which begins to emerge out of them.

I have tried to put the matter in a crude and obvious form, since in talking of aesthetics there is always a danger of using the terms abstractly and without immediate reference to fact. The whole essence of construction is to increase the value of scenes or acts or words by the surroundings in which they are put, or the way in which they are led up to. Aristotle is very clear, and very clear-sighted, about this. The word he uses for the "construction" or "fitting together" of a story is the same that he uses for the biological or "organic" construction of live animals ($\sigma\acute{u}\sigma\tau\alpha\sigma\iota\varsigma$). As the different muscles or bones work together in the physical organism, each serving the other or enabling the other to operate, so should the different "parts" of a story. This coöperation of "parts" is a delicate and elaborate business, and any brief illustration cannot avoid being rather coarse and obvious.

Take what is practically an identical scene in the two Greek tragedies about Electra. In Sophocles' play the heroine is alone with the Chorus, and makes a moving speech about the horrors of her life, culminating in a description of Aegisthus in her father's bed, with her mother in his arms. In Euripides' *Electra*, she makes a very similar speech, but with this, the most poignant part, left out. Why? Because she is telling it to a strange man, and there are things which a woman does not say to a strange man. But the value of every word is doubled because we know, though she does not, that the strange man is Orestes himself. The construction doubles the value of the scene, and more than compensates for the effect omitted.

Again, in Aeschylus' play on the same subject, Orestes, when about to enter the palace to do his deed of vengeance, is met in the doorway by Clytemnestra, who greets him with dignified courtesy. The interest of every word spoken in the scene is multiplied for us by the fact that, the last time we saw her in just that position, she was standing triumphant over the dead bodies of her husband and Cassandra. One part of the play is helping another, and every word becomes thrilling.[6]

Take an instance on a larger scale. The hero, or quasi-hero, of *Vanity Fair*, George Osborne, is killed on the field of Waterloo. One would expect a fairly detailed and emphatic description of his death, his feelings, his last words, and so forth. All that we get is in the final sentence of a chapter describing the doings of quite other people in another place. "No more firing was heard at Brussels. The pursuit rolled miles away. Darkness came down on the field and city: and Amelia was praying for George, who was lying on his face, dead, with a bullet through his heart." That half-sentence is all that we hear about George's death. There are no details. It owes the whole of its effect to the setting in which it is placed. It is only one item in the *vanitas vanitatum*. All the pity and contempt and anger and sympathy and the various impressions of futility, which have been slowly piling up in scores of earlier chapters, are doing their work to deepen and enrich this particular stroke of tragedy. They are all in it; and it could not be what it is without them.

In contrast with this, one might take the last act of *The Merchant of Venice*, or one might take many instances from modern literature, and from almost all the long, shapeless, meandering romances of the Middle Ages, in which incident after incident and description after description trickle endlessly along. But it is less invidious

[6] S., *Electra*, 254 ff., E., *Electra*, 300 ff., Aesch., *Choephoroe*, 668 ff.

to take a case from a Greek tragedy. It is one of the rare mistakes of Euripides. In that poet's *Suppliant Women*, after the bodies of the champions slain at Thebes are brought back for burial, and the main conflict of the play is over, there suddenly appears a woman whom we have not seen before, who, after a lamentation, throws herself upon her husband's pyre. She is Evadne, the wife of Capaneus. There is no preparation; we knew nothing about Evadne beforehand. The incident, which ought to have been full of value, is ineffective just because there is no organic connexion between it and the rest of the play. With proper treatment from the beginning it might have produced various effects. We might have been made to feel long before how Evadne loved her husband, and to wonder what she would do when his body was brought home; or she might have said something ambiguous, to set us thinking; she might have shown indifference when the other wives were lamenting, and seemed callous because in her heart she was determined to join her husband so soon. It is also possible that we might—by careful preparation—have been made to receive the shock of horror and surprise which the incident would have caused in real life; and it may be that this surprise was what Euripides, with insufficient resources of technique, was aiming at. But as it is, the incident just happens "on the flat," with no accumulated suspense or tension.

The defect is not uncommon in ancient plays, and perhaps that is what makes Aristotle so emphatic in condemning it. Of all plays, he says, "the episodic are the worst." And by "episodic" he means those that depend for their appeal on mere episodes, or incidents without inner connexion or construction. The reason is not far to seek. The construction of a fully symmetrical work of art, with the parts subordinate to the whole, demands prolonged effort and faith and self-control, both in the artist and in the spectator. Both of them only get their reward when they have worked through to the end of the last scene. They must persevere, and have faith that the effort is worth making. They must be willing to dispense with little amusements and diversions and refreshments by the way. Self-restraint and faith go together: self-restraint is the renunciation of some immediate good for the sake of a greater good seen by the eye of faith. And this self-restraint is specially characteristic of classical art. It renounces the cheap and easy and immediate, in order to seek perfection.

We have so far been considering construction in what Aristotle calls poetry, and we should call fiction. But it is equally characteristic of classical art in other branches. This is clearest of all in architecture and the groups of sculpture associated with architecture. In such work no individual figure, however fine, lives to itself; it is always a counterpoise to some other figure, and the two are generally held together by some boundary or drawn together by some centre. The symmetry is essential and obvious; but, if I am not mistaken, it is seldom or never a mere equipoise of two similar and contrasted objects: there is usually something to which they both lead. The simplest case is the sculpture inside a pediment, where the two sets of balancing and contrasted figures all lead up to the towering central figure. The same consideration applies to the temple. There is not only balance: there is also climax and unity.

But now let us make a distinction. This quality of unity or organic construction is not the same as plot. A good ancient work of art has generally a certain artistic quality which, though it involves matters of plot, is more like symmetry or rhythm. Each element in the story contributes not only to the plot-interest of the whole, but to the symmetry or rhythm of the whole, so that, when you think the story over, it has the beauty that comes from form. It is, in Aristotle's phrase, εὐσύνοπτον; it is right when seen as a whole. You can reflect upon it and feel it as one thing. It is only a few of the best modern novels that satisfy this requirement.

Let us now consider again the meaning of organic

construction in verbal style, or, as the ancients would say, in rhetoric. Think of any Messenger's speech in Euripides. You will find almost always that the Messenger starts his speech on a quite low note. Then comes a rise, then a different rise, then a quickening, then a deepening, then a climax, then climax upon climax of excitement, and perhaps of horror; then, at much less length, a diminuendo effect, a lessening of strain, an increase of solemnity perhaps, and almost always an ending in something like resignation or calm. That calm ending is called in Greek "catastrophe"; and it is instructive to see how we have utterly changed the word's meaning. But how is it that the Messenger is able to start thus on the low note, and so build up all his varied effects? It is because the ground is prepared.

Let me take an instance from the scene where a Messenger comes to announce the death of Hippolytus, who has just gone to exile under his father's curse. You might have a Messenger simply bursting in with a cry and pouring out his tale in thunderous language. Instead, we have a short scene which, first, works up the suspense so that we are eager to hear the speech before it begins, and secondly brings out the conflicting emotions of the different characters so that, when it does begin, it is interesting not merely as a good story but because of the situation in which it is told and the people to whom it is told.[7] It would take too much space to illustrate the

---

[7] L. Look yonder. Surely from the prince 't is one
    That cometh, full of haste and woebegone.

                        (Enter Messenger.)

M. Ye women; whither shall I go to seek
    King Theseus? Is he in this dwelling? Speak.

L. Lo where he cometh thro' the castle gate.

                        (Enter Theseus.)

M. O King, I come with tidings of dire weight
    To thee, yea, and to every man, I ween,
    From Athens to the marches of Trozên.

Th. How? Some new stroke hath touched, unknown to me,
    The sister cities of my sovranty?

M. Hippolytus is . . . nay, not dead, but stark
    Outstretched, a hairsbreadth this side of the dark.

building up or rhythm of this speech, but I will take a short piece of Tennyson to illustrate, on a smaller scale, what I mean by construction in the realm of diction and metre. It is a passage in the *Idylls of the King*, where the "little maid" is "babbling" to Guinevere:

> My father said—and was himself a knight
> Of the great Table, at the founding of it,
> And rode thereto from Lyonnesse; and he said
> That, as he rode, an hour or maybe twain
> 5 After the sunset, down the coast, he heard
> Strange music; and he turned, and, turning, there—
> All down the lonely coast of Lyonnesse,
> Each with a beacon star upon his head,
> And with a wild sea-light about his feet,
> 10 He saw them, headland after headland, flare
> Far on into the rich heart of the West.

That is constructed so as to lead from "babble" to serious and mysterious beauty. Lines 1 to 3 babble: rhythm intentionally poor, but varied in each; 4, rather babbly, with its "hour or maybe twain after the sunset," but a growing interest in the tale, and firmness of metre; 6, firm metre, but much held back by pauses, to lead up to 7, perfectly firm and smooth; 8, 9 similar: increasing beauty of rhythm and tension of expectation, since we do not yet know what noun these descriptive lines are referring to; 10, tension resolved, "headland after headland," strong end on "flare"; 11, tension relaxed in musical distance.

Every line in this set of ten gets special value from those that precede. We may notice also that in line 10

Th. How slain? Was there some other man whose wife
    He had, like mine, defiled, who sought his life?
M. His own wild team destroyed him, and the dire
    Curse of thy lips. The boon of thy great sire
    Is granted thee, O King, and thy son slain.
Th. Ye gods, and thou Poseidon! Not in vain
    I called thee father. Thou hast heard my prayer. . . .
    How did he die? Speak on. How closed the snare
    Of heaven, to smite the shamer of my blood?

there is just a faint re-suggestion of "babble," in the insertion of "them." A realist would make the little maid say, "He saw them, he did."

Another field for construction is in the words themselves, the paragraph and the chapter, but particularly the sentence. In the construction of the larger wholes we have generally surpassed antiquity. The ancients worked without indices or pages, or even a clear and quickly read script, and were consequently thrown back upon their memory. But the critic can trace organic construction in a sentence just as the biologist can in a living cell. Indeed, the sentence raises interesting problems, affecting both the order of the words and the amount of sentence-architecture which a given language will comfortably and safely support. In both points there is a great difference between an inflected and an uninflected language, or, to speak more accurately, between a language that is rich in inflexion and one that is poor.

As to order, most languages have some order which they prefer, and uninflected languages generally have a more or less cast-iron order from which they depart at their peril. French, for example, has, like most of the Romance languages, a strong preference for what may be called a "descending order"—that is, the dependent word is put after the word that governs it, the weak after the strong. The order is subject–object, noun–adjective, verb–adverb.

$$\overset{1}{Le} \overset{2}{fils} \mid \overset{}{ainé} \mid \overset{3}{du} \overset{}{roi} \mid \overset{4}{a} \overset{}{donné} \mid \overset{5}{une} \overset{}{fête} \mid \overset{6}{aux} \overset{}{citoyens}.$$

If we take this descending order as a model, English will give: "The king's eldest son has given a feast to the citizens," that is, 3, 2, 1, 4, 5, 6; German: "*Des Königs ältester Sohn hat den Bürgern ein Fest gegeben,*" that is, 3, 2, 1, half-4, 6, 5, half-4. Turkish, so I read, has an absolutely fixed order which is the exact opposite of French. It is ascending: adjective before substantive, governed substantive before governing, complement before verb, "preposition" after the noun, subordinate clause before principal. The sentence, "We have seen that one finds consolation for many ills in devout prayer," will run: "Devout-prayer-in | many-ills'-consolation | to-be-found | we-have seen" (*"Piis precibus multorum malorum solacia inveniri vidimus"*).

Thus, languages with a poor system of inflections or with some other serious weakness (like the absence of relatives in Turkish) are generally driven to some one regular order. It often happens that it is only by the position of the word in the sentence that you can tell what case it is in and what part of speech it is. For example, "Him the Angel smote" is clear, because the pronoun "he" has an accusative form. "Satan the Angel smote" is ambiguous: to be clear you must say either, "Satan smote the Angel," or "The Angel smote Satan." The position shows the case. Similarly, "black" is an adjective in "a black deep" or "the black boots," a substantive in "a deep black," and a verb in "black the boots." More often the order is simply fixed, and to alter it would not make a different sense, but would merely produce faulty speech. ("One knows that by contemporaries unappreciated poets from the after-world a juster judgement await" would not be good English, though *"Man weiss dass von der Mitwelt verkannte Dichter von der Nachwelt ein gerechteres Urtheil erwarten,"* would be good German.) English is considerably freer than French in this matter, and perhaps a little freer than German. But English, too, has, on the whole, a fixed grammatical order in which it must speak. Now Greek and Latin have a free order. There are preferences, of course; Latin likes verbs at the end, prefers nouns to precede adjectives, and the like. But the order can at need be varied indefinitely.

Now unreflecting people naturally assume that the order in which they speak is the natural order of thought, the Turks thinking one order natural, the French the opposite order. But in reality the order of thought is quite a different thing from the order of grammar; that is certain. Let us take a simple English sentence: "Mr. B. went from Boston to Amherst by car." But put the sentence in the following context: "This brings us to Wednesday. That night Mr. B. and the prisoner remained in Boston. From Boston Mr. B. went on by car to Amherst, while the prisoner," and so forth. The regular grammatical order would be: "Mr. B. and the prisoner remained in Boston that night. Mr. B. went on from Boston to Amherst by car." But it would be less clear. The order of thought tends to make each new sentence start from the point already reached, or from the main object of thought at the end of the last sentence. We have got to "Wednesday"; we start, "That night." We have got to Boston; we start, "From Boston." Even in English the order can be so far changed.

However, the permissible variations in English are so slight that the point is better illustrated from Latin. The late Professor Weil[8] cites a passage in Livy about the brothers Aruns and Lucumo. Aruns had died, and his son fell into poverty: "*Lucumoni contra, omnium heredi bonorum, cum divitiae iam animos facerent, auxit ducta in matrimonium Tanaquil, summo loco nata, et quae haud facile iis in quibus nata erat humiliora sineret ea quae innupsisset. Spernentibus Etruscis Lucumonen . . .*" If you began this sentence with the grammatical subject, Tanaquil, you would have to wait till the end before the reader could know what it was about. He knows Aruns, he knows Lucumo; but Tanaquil he has never heard of. Sense demands that we start with Lucumo, and Livy's Latin has no difficulty in starting with him in the dative. The result is one clear sentence, proceeding from the known to the new. In English we should probably have to make several sentences. "Now Lucumo had inherited the whole property. His ambition was stirred by the possession of this wealth, and increased by his marriage with Tanaquil, a princess who was not

[8] *L'Ordre des Mots*, Paris, 1879.

disposed to let the conditions into which she married be inferior to those in which she had been born. The contempt shown for Lucumo by the Etruscans . . ." In general, it will be found that in sentences where Latin or Greek would begin a sentence with a noun in an oblique case followed by an active verb, English can keep the order by using either a passive or a causal verb (*"Tarquinio dat agrum"*—"Tarquin was presented with the farm"; *"Virtutum viri stupentibus barbaris"*—"His courage amazed the barbarians"), and this is the main reason why passive and causative verbs are so unnaturally abundant in most modern European languages, and abstract verbal substantives even more.[9] A looser and more unshapely way of obtaining the same result is to start with a phrase which takes the important word outside the syntax of the sentence. Thus the sentence taken above from Livy might start: "In the case of Lucumo, his marriage with Tanaquil," or, "With regard to Lucumo," or some other miserable makeshift. A final example may be taken from Dr. Weil: *"Il avait un beau-père; il l'obligea de se pendre. Il avait un beau-frère; il le fît étrangler"* (in Latin: *"Socerum ille ad suspendium adegit; affinem strangulari iussit"*). The Latin produces its epigrammatic effect with more neatness and less emphasis. It is a surprise to learn that the French is the original and comes from Voltaire.

Now in Greek and Latin poetry this power of arranging the words in whatever order best suits the speaker's purpose is exercised freely and with beautiful effect. The subject is well treated by Professor Naylor of Adelaide in his edition of Horace's *Odes*.[1] Horace is one of those poets, very few in number, who have been read and reread with delight by cultivated men of alien languages and civilizations for two thousand years, and that not

---

[9] Illustrations are hardly necessary: but I have seen "*quorum metu abiit*" represented in English by "Expectation of violence on the part of the barbarians caused his departure," *i.e.*, an abstraction of an abstraction caused an abstraction.

[1] Cambridge, 1922.

because he has anything very important to say, but simply for the beauty of his form. Beauty of form has made him immortal, and fully half of that beauty lies in the order of his words. This fact can be fully appreciated only after considerable familiarity with Horace, but the point can be illustrated. He writes:

> Nunc et latentis proditor intimo
> Gratus puellae risus ab angulo.[2]

Literally: "The delightful betraying laugh from a deep corner of a girl hiding there." If he had said, "*Ab intimo angulo risus proditor puellae latentis,*" there would be nothing in it. But we have together, "*latentis proditor*" —"betrayer of one hiding"; "*proditor intimo*"—"betrayer in the deep"; "*gratus puellae*"—"delightful, of a girl"; "*puellae risus*"—"girl's laugh"; "*risus ab angulo*"—"laugh from a corner." And I am not sure there is not something in "*intimo gratus*"—"delightful in the deep." The total result is magical.

Dr. Weil adduces and attempts to translate another famous and trite passage:

> Nihil est ab omni
> Parte beatum:
> Abstulit clarum cita mors Achillem,
> Longa Tithonum minuit senectus.

It is clear that a literal translation misses most of the meaning. "There is no perfect happiness. A quick death swept away glorious Achilles, a long old age wore down Tithonus." How can one get the series of contrasts? "Cut down in glory"—"glory, swift death"—"swift death Achilles"—"long life Tithonus"—"Tithonus dwindling" —"wasting age." A translator would be driven to a tiresome reduplication: "Achilles had glory, and quick death cut it off. Tithonus had long life, and age slowly wasted him." The sense, roughly speaking, would be kept, but the charm lost.

This "juxtaposition of opposites" is made easy in a

[2] *Odes*, I, ix, 21.

highly inflected language by the free order of the words; but, of course, it is much more than a juxtaposition of opposites. It is juxtaposition of those words which specially affect or explain or intensify one another, and so, without altering the intellectual meaning of the sentence, invest it with depths and shades of feeling, and knit it into a whole, like Aristotle's "live animal." It is, I think, the pursuit of this effect which leads Milton sometimes to repeat particular words or phrases, so as to associate them with first one idea and then another, since he cannot simply group all three together, as Horace does in "*latentis proditor intimo.*" Consider, for instance, the curious repetitions in Adam's speech in Book X of *Paradise Lost* (lines 720 ff.):

> O miserable of happie! is this the end
> Of this new *glorious* world, and mee so late
> The *Glory* of that *Glory*, who now become
> Accurst of blessed, hide me from the face
> Of God, whom to behold was then my highth
> Of happiness: yet well, if here would end
> The miserie, I *deserved* it and would bear
> My own *deservings*.

At other times it leads him to arrange the clauses of his sentence in a curious but effective order:

> Who from the Pit of Hell
> Roaming to seek their prey on Earth, durst fix
> Their Seats long after next the Seat of God,
> Their Altars by his Altar, Gods adored
> Among the nations round, and durst abide
> Jehovah thundering out of Sion, throned
> Between the Cherubim.

But how terribly this loses unity!

It is curious how the lucid eighteenth-century style, which considered itself classical, eschews almost entirely this delicate torsion of the threads of language, just as it eschews in general the qualities by which ancient literature achieved its richness of imaginative expression. In resolutely renouncing affectation and obscurity and all that it could not explain and defend, the eighteenth century lost so much besides.

At times a new effect is attained in English through some imitation of a Greek or Latin phrase which in itself would seem unjustified. "That forbidden Tree whose mortal tast brought death into the world" could certainly not be translated straight into Latin: *"cuius mortalis gustus"* would be more unintelligible than the English. In Greek, οὐ δὴ βροτεία γεῦσις would be possible, but would call for comment. When Shelley's Hermes says to Prometheus,

> Awful sufferer,
> To thee unwilling most unwillingly
> I come,

it is clear to any reader of Aeschylus' *Prometheus* that "unwilling" is accusative agreeing with "thee" (ἀκὼν πρὸς ἀκόντ'), and that "Awful sufferer" comes from Ὦ δεινὰ πάσχων ("O thou that sufferest awful things"). Yet, as a matter of fact, to most English readers, even Greek scholars, the words suggest something different. It is Prometheus himself rather than his suffering that is "awful" to us. And the same unintended enrichment of the original meaning results from many of the classicisms of Keats.

On the whole, it seems to me clear that, while the modern European languages, by the much wider experience which they embody and the much larger number of words, or at any rate of nouns, which they contain, can easily outstrip the ancient in variety and in particularity of definite meaning, the ancients, by means chiefly of their inflections, developed a degree of art in the use of language itself which we cannot emulate but from which we may possibly still learn. It is a little like the difference between modern English and the style of Hume or Adam Smith; or, better, between modern

French and the style of Pascal. Pascal used, I believe, a language which contained about half the number of words that are current in good modern French; yet he seems to be able to say whatever he wants to say, and he certainly produces an impression of clarity and of beauty. His organ has fewer stops, but he plays it better. Now the ancients had an organ, perhaps not with so many stops as ours, but certainly with different and subtler stops; an organ far more difficult to play at all, but, I think, more capable of response to a really exquisite artist.

The problem before us is not to imitate classical effects. It is simply impossible, for instance, to reproduce in English the free order of words in the sentence. Inversion of the order is a trope to be used sparingly in English and capable of being used only in a very simple way.

> Great praise the Duke of Marlborough won

and

> Of Nelson and the North
> Sing the glorious day's renown

are suitable and spirited phrases, but would not cause Horace to look interested; and if we put them forward as effective inversions, Catullus might indeed "make mouths at our speech."

> Flowers of all hue and without thorn the rose

is more interesting; or

> Adam first of men
> To first of women Eve.

There is poetry again in Keats's inversion in *La Belle Dame*:

> I saw pale kings and princes too,
> Pale warriors; death-pale were they all.

But the ancients would hesitate to repeat the same word

three times in a space of sixteen syllables, to attain no more effect than that.

The problem of learning from another language is not unlike the problem of translation. A translator finds an effect of style, of emphasis, of rhythm, of suggestion, of atmosphere, for which there exists no direct equivalent in his own language. In bald prose sometimes it can be ignored, provided you can state in your own language the facts stated in the other. In poetry or artistic prose sometimes it is the very thing that matters, far more than the statement of fact conveyed in the words. The translator may stand paralyzed before the particular problem how to turn into English the phrase of Tacitus describing what Rome felt about the death of Drusus: *"Breves et infaustos populi Romani amores,"* or the sinister impression produced at the public games by a prince, *"Quanquam vili sanguine nimis gaudens."* The English stylist will feel the stinging beauty of such a phrase and wonder how, in some totally different circumstances and material, he could make that sort of effect in English. And perhaps the greatest lesson to be learnt, next to those of self-control and exact expression, is the lesson of construction: the order of words in a sentence, of sentences in a chapter, or, it may be, of incidents in a poem or story, which will enable the whole to operate not like a series of disconnected pushes, but like Aristotle's living organism whose every muscle is helping in the main work, and thereby creating a beauty of form and rhythm in the whole, far beyond anything which the parts could attain by themselves.

I have tried to consider in this chapter the most central and characteristic doctrine of Aristotle, the doctrine of Unity of Action. We have seen that this unity implies construction. The work must have a beginning, middle, and end—a doctrine which seems to mean little and really means so vastly much. Furthermore, this construction must be organic, not merely mechanical. The whole must be like a live thing, an animal in which every organ serves a central purpose and coöperates with the rest.

Now, curiously enough, if we take the novel as the most characteristic form of modern imaginative work, we fulfill this demand in one sense much better than the ancients, while in another sense we generally neglect it. Aristotle was full of admiration for the plot of the *Oedipus*; but, as far as mere ingenuity of plot goes, dozens of modern writers of detective stories could give Sophocles a large handicap and beat him easily. We are extraordinarily good at ingenuity—better than any previous age of the world. But we use this ingenuity for a somewhat crude and trivial purpose, if not an utterly inartistic purpose. The detective story keeps us in a state of excitement till it is finished. When it is once finished, we have used it up. There is nothing left until we forget it sufficiently to read it again. The ingenuity of construction has not been used to create an object of permanent contemplation, a thing of beauty which will remain. The *Oedipus* is better to read the second time than the first, and better the twentieth time than the second. The Greek has not merely contrived a series of thrills, with a secret revealed in the last chapter but one. He has constructed a whole like the Parthenon, which you can look at from different angles, which you can explore and study, but which remains always *Eusunopton*, comprehensible as a whole and beautiful as a whole. The detective-story writer has constructed a maze, in which the fun is to find the way out, and when that is once found, the fun is over.

The reflection left in one's mind by this comparison is one that is often suggested by various phases of our incomparably rich and strong and ingenious modern civilization, typically perhaps by the inside works of a popular theatre or newspaper office. Immense outlay of wealth; immense energy and organization; marvellous machines and materials; the utilization of the great forests and natural forces and the labour of strong arms and the inventive power of ingenious brains, all formed into a vast complex engine devoted to the production of— Well, of what? Bewilderment as well as politeness makes me hesitate to finish the sentence. But it seems clear that our wisdom and our sense of beauty have not increased in proportion with our wealth and our mastery of nature.

VII

THE HEROIC AGE

HARDLY ANY OF THE BEST NARRATIVE POETRY KNOWN TO us deals with the age in which the poet himself lived. Its scene is set in some time long past, or in some strange and remote place, or, if not that, at least in some class of society that is strange to the poet and his readers. Byron, Kipling, and Masefield illustrate in different ways the same principle. Even if, like Dante's *Divina Commedia*, a great poem does treat of recent events about which the poet has direct and personal feelings, it treats them as objects seen from a great distance, or beyond some veil that separates.

This peculiarity is strongly marked in Greek poetry. Homer, indeed, not only tells the story of a past age, but deliberately uses the language of a past age, so that at first sight he seems to speak to us actually from out of the heroic period in which his characters lived, or at least from the confines of it. But it is not so. He sharply distinguishes his own times, with "men such as they now are," from the times of the Trojan War, and describes an age that is different and remote, not quite the actual Heroic Age as it was on earth, but at least a vision of that age seen through the mists of tradition and memory. The great lyrics of Pindar and Bacchylides, and, above all, the Attic tragedies, come from a definite and well-ascertained period in the fifth century B.C. But, with

157

rare exceptions, they set their scene in the heroic past. Written and acted in republican Athens, they are all about antique kings and queens. Written at a time when women lived in cloistered seclusion and took no part in public life, they are full of heroines of strong characters and passions, who generally dominate the stage more than the men. Written for a public keenly exercised in law and commerce, in democratic institutions and political intrigue, they practically never mention any of these subjects, but concentrate on passionate loves and deaths, curses and blood feuds, battles and deliverances. In their treatment of human character, indeed, they show a certain complexity. A keenly reflective and intellectual age had succeeded the heroic time and inherited its legends; and at times a cutting wind of criticism blows across the idyllic landscape. But in the main, the moral outlook is that of the older time: a certain contempt for statesmen and prophets and, in general, for persons of sedentary pursuits, and unquestioning admiration for the brave man of strong arm and generous passions, who keeps his honour clean, faces the enemy boldly, and never tells a lie. The old heroic rule holds good for them: "Hateful as the Gates of Hell is the man who hides one thing in his heart and speaks another."

Of course, not all poetry belongs to the grand style. There was always in Greece a certain amount of singing about personal and contemporary matters, love-songs and battle-songs, *stasiotica* or conspiracy-songs, elegies and idylls, and the like. But even in these the heroic background is never far from the poet's thoughts. His language will be more or less Homeric; his references to other stories will go back to Heracles and Priam. In the vulgarest and most modern Idyll of Theocritus, the two women at the show talk of Troy and the Achaeans, of Zeus and Cypris and Adonis.

The fascination of the legendary past of Greece was of long duration. Apollonius and the Alexandrian poets were still steeped in it, and from them the charm passed on to

Propertius and Ovid. Vergil, writing the great national epic of Rome, places his scene in the Heroic Age of Greece and chooses a Homeric hero for his protagonist. Statius writes about ancient Thebes; Valerius Flaccus, about the Argonauts. And when a poet does write a great poem about some recent event, as Aeschylus of the Persian Invasion or Lucan of the Roman Civil Wars, I think we shall find not only that they always choose a subject which has a touch of the superhuman about it, but that they treat it in the spirit of heroic tragedy. That is the spirit in which Lucan calls his hero not by his name, Pompey, but simply "Magnus" ("The Great"), and Aeschylus in the *Persae* makes the Great King, Darius, into a semi-divine being. It is significant, also, that the Greek poet never mentions, amid his superhuman incidents, the name of any individual Greek. Remote Persian satraps with strange names and titles appear and fight and die in large numbers, but a definite mention of Themistocles or Aristides would have brought the tragedy from the clouds to earth.

This tradition certainly continues. We all have a confused notion that there is something "poetical" in things connected with the Middle Ages, knights and dames and squires and armour and tournaments and the like. One can see the resentment of the modern man against this assumption in such books as Mark Twain's *A Connecticut Yankee in King Arthur's Court,* and its inferior progeny. "To be poetical is somehow to be superior; therefore these knights and squires and dames are supposed to be superior to us. But not to have a bathroom is to be inferior. Therefore"—the man in the street argues triumphantly—"they are not our superiors at all. They are only a fraud, like everything that claims to be better than me!"

The mediaeval convention itself was on the same lines as the ancient, though of course its heroic past was different in detail. The Middle Ages seem to have been bewildered and overburdened by a wealth of foreign tradition which they could not assimilate. The Norsemen, who were long left alone, had a great incipient epic, now wrecked and almost lost, and a magnificent saga literature, much of which is still extant. But the other West-European tribes, when they were whirled one after another into the vortex of the Roman–Christian tradition, with its vast literature both legendary and historical, its great though half-forgotten civilization, and its complex oriental religion, once despised but now backed by the whole prestige of the Roman Empire, became ashamed of their own poetry and tradition, as they were ashamed of their own gods. It is a curious historical coincidence that, as in her heyday Rome had killed the indigenous art and culture of almost every people she had absorbed into the Empire, so in her last decline she did much the same for the Franks and Goths, the Celts and the Germans. The native literatures were stifled before they reached maturity. Even in a true epic, like the *Chanson de Roland*, there are "omens" as the late Professor Ker put it, of the coming victory of mediaeval romance. What seems to go wrong in mediaeval poetry, from the twelfth century onward, is a loss of restraint and sincerity and constructive power. Amid all the ornamentation and exaggeration there is a "horror of infinite flatness" and a confused mixture of elements foreign to one another and tending nowhere. It is curious to reflect that these qualities, which are the very reverse of classical, came into the mediaeval romances from the imitation of Latin literature. The early Icelandic tradition, which knew nothing of the Roman world, remained uncorrupted, and in many important respects was in the true sense classical and even "Homeric." Still the romances do, in the main, place their scenes in some fabulous or mythological past, and though their conception of past history is so confused that one can hardly identify it with any particular time, it has at least the quality of remoteness.

Greek poetry, then, tends to draw its characters and its stories from the Greek Heroic Age; Roman poetry follows Greek; mediaeval romance, in a confused and vacillating way, does something more or less similar; while the modern world generally goes, for its epic themes, either to the Middle Ages or to one or other of the various heroic ages now known to us. For modern literature is enriched by new stores of tradition, both European and Asiatic, of which the most valuable in epic qualities is the Icelandic. And Iceland, like Greece, went for its poetry chiefly to its own heroic age.

It may be suspected that this merely means that narrative poetry deals with the past, as it needs must, since a story must be supposed to have happened before it can be told. But I think there is more in it than that. Poetry likes a past that is remote, at least remote enough to keep some little air of mystery and to leave the poet some freedom to invent and imagine. A past well dated and documented is always inconvenient, not merely because it hinders the poet's freedom, but even more because it loses most of the magic of memory. The memory that transmutes a man's own experience, and gives to some trivial word or scene a beauty that is often heart-rending in its poignancy, is always, I think, a memory that is free to create; it cannot without danger be too much checked and corrected. But, more important still, whether poetry seeks for the scene of its narrative a past time or a distant country, I think it almost always seeks for a state of society that is simpler and ruder than the poet's own. By simpler and ruder, I mean one in which the individual human soul is less protected, less standardized, more exposed to strain and peril, and more dependent on its own strength for its battle against the world. The modern city poet seeks the Middle Ages, or the wild west, or the various parts of the world in which Conrad delighted, for a quality which they all possess in common. In all of them life is dangerous; and the things which in civilized society are reduced to a more or less mechanical and harmless level there stand out in their full intensity—friend and foe, love and hate, truth and treachery, honour and dishonour, courage and cowardice. A man in danger there does not telephone to the police or consult his lawyer: he thinks for himself and, if necessary, fights for his life.

Now if we realize what, as a matter of history, the heroic ages of Greece and of Northern Europe really were, we can understand their importance to the poetry of the human race. In Greece the old safe and splendid Minoan empires—or at least the civilization of which the Minoan palaces are the only remaining witness—were overthrown root and branch by barbarian invaders: Achaioi, Northerners, Peoples of the Sea, outlaws and broken men from within the Minoan area, or whatever else they may have been. It was a time when almost all the social protections which man had devised for himself had been undermined or shattered; cities, customs, religious rules, tribes, and even the family itself, had broken down. The riches of a great civilisation, damaged no doubt but still vast and dazzling, lay open for the spoiler to seize, and, if he could, to keep. The dominant social organization consisted of a chief or king with a band of adventurers following his fortunes, who roamed abroad in the hope of winning perhaps a kingdom or a city, perhaps some armour and jewellery and slaves, perhaps merely a short life of abundant food and drink, or perhaps—for the wisest and most fortunate—some safe retreat where they could live once more like civilized and self-respecting men, and die, when the time came, without dishonour. And the same phenomenon was repeated on a larger scale when the Northern barbarians were engaged in breaking up the decaying civilization of Rome. It was a time, as Professor Chadwick says, "of Mars and the Muses": of Mars, because, unless a man was ready to fight, he found only too many people ready to fight him; of the Muses, because, while most of the arts require for their cultivation some continuous security, poetry does not. You cannot build temples or carve statues or paint pictures, you cannot make towns or gardens, grow vines and olives, or engage in regular trade or manufacture, without some assurance of the future and some fair safety for capital. But any fugitive or beggar or pirate can sing and tell stories if he has the gift. The people of the Heroic Age did so, and have been the cause of song and stories to others ever afterwards.[1]

It was a time evidently of intense experience and terrible ordeals. A time of "exultations, agonies," in some senses of "love," and, above all, "of man's unconquerable mind." Think of a child's sand castle, built slowly and carefully, with moats and battlements, and then of the great moment when the tide storms in, and the work of hours is swept away in as many minutes. Think of the slow laying and preparation of some elaborate fuse which is to set off a firework, and the moment when the fuse is touched and all goes up in flame. If it is true that, for poetry and romance, if for nothing else, "one crowded hour of glorious life" has a value not to be estimated in terms of ordinary experience, then one can see why the heroic ages, with all their misery and brutality and impoverishment, have been so intensely precious to later generations.

For what, after all, is great poetry about? There is poetry about drinking and feasting, and art, and pretty faces, and clothes and gardens and jewels and ornaments, and all kinds of pleasant things. There is poetry about dreams and fantasies, about enchanted princesses who fall in love with one, and magic swords with which one cuts off the legs of giants, and purses which are never empty, and the like. The Mediaeval and Celtic traditions were largely reared upon such fare. There is the poetry of allegory and mysticism, of theology and philosophy—even of social aspiration and political controversy. There may be beauty in all these things. But the great poetry of the world, especially the poetry of the classical tradition, is ultimately about the human soul; and not about its mere fortunes, but its doings. We

[1] Cf. Euripides, *Troades*, 1242 ff.

noticed above the subjects of the ancient communal Dance and Song, from which Greek poetry seems to be derived: Love, Strife, Death, and that which is beyond Death. These things, and the way in which man comports himself toward them, are the subjects which the Heroic Age provides for poetry; to these belong "the deeds of men of old," and, even more sharply perhaps, in contrast with tamer and happier ages, "the immortal gifts of the Gods and the endurances of men."

These facts are sometimes stated as if an age or society was poetical merely because it was lawless and full of crime; as if a noble life was a prosaic thing, and a selfish or licentious life beautiful. Any such conception is, I think, a mere muddle. The interesting thing is noble living; it is the only thing that really uplifts and thrills and stimulates. Nothing is so flat and boring to contemplate as the kind of man who cannot resist any temptation because he has no strength in him; who can never tell the truth or pay his debts or keep his promise or refrain from getting drunk or being envious or spiteful. He is not even comic. To get any value at all out of the bad man, you have to give him some startling goodness in the midst of his trumpery, so as to enjoy the effect of contrast. The cruel man shows some singular faithfulness or lovingkindness; the thief behaves with some keen sense of honour; the drunken rake remembers his mother and turns chivalrous; and out come all our pocket-handkerchiefs. The "goodness" may sometimes, no doubt, be of a superficial kind. There are some people who are so much interested in clothes that they will be thrilled by a Renaissance villain because he has one pink leg and one blue; but these are exceptions, and not important exceptions. As a rule, it is not wickedness that is interesting.

The real advantage of wickedness is that it puts goodness to the test. And the special advantage of a lawless and violent age is not merely that it gives scope to passion, but that it gives the real virtues a chance of proving their mettle. In a well-policed modern city there is generally no means of knowing whether a particular law-abiding man is really, as the Greeks would say, "Brave, wise, temperate, and just." He may be so, but he may be merely drifting along the line of least resistance and not daring to take risks. Whereas an Abdiel,

> faithful found,
> Among the faithless faithful only he,
> Among innumerable false unmoved,
> Unshaken, unseduced, unterrified,

owes much of his value to his bad companions.

So in the Iliad Achilles' sense of honour may be rather an unreasonable one, but still his defiance of Agamemnon in Book I, rejecting all worldly advantages rather than submit to dishonour, is stirring, and in its way noble. The refusal of the gifts in Book IX shows the same spirit intensified. The sending of Patroclus in Book XVI is a conflict between obstinacy and chivalry. The utter misery and self-reproach at Patroclus' death leads up to the fury of his revenge—a revenge, it must be remembered, which he knows will cost his own life, so that it is, amid all its cruelty, generous. But two scenes at the end have especially the full spirit of the Heroic Age in them. First the scene in which the mortally wounded Hector speaks to Achilles:

"I beseech thee by thy life and by thy knees and by thy parents leave me not for the dogs to eat beside the ships of the Achaeans, but take the store of bronze and gold that my parents will bring to thee, and give back my body that the Trojans and the wives of the Trojans may lay it upon the fire."

And swift-footed Achilles answered scowling: "Dog, talk not to me of knees nor parents! Would that my heart would let me hack thy flesh and eat thee raw, for the deed thou hast done to me. Not any one shall save thee from the dogs—not if they bring hither a ransom ten and twenty fold, and weigh it out, and promise more beside; no, not if Priam bade buy thee for thy weight in gold. Thy mother shall not lay thee in thy bed nor lament for her child. The dogs and the birds shall devour every part of thee."

And Hector of the glancing helm spake as he died: "I look upon thee, and I know thee well. I was not like to persuade thee, for the heart is iron in thy breast. Beware lest I be a wrath of god upon thee, on that day when Paris and Phoebus Apollo shall slay thee in all thy valour by the Scaean Gates."

The end of death encompassed him as he spake; and the soul went out from his limbs, and flew toward the House of Hades, wailing for her doom, leaving youth and manhood behind. And Achilles spake over the dead:

"Lie thou dead; I will accept my doom when Zeus sendeth it." [2]

Achilles tries for days to slake his rage and his misery by insults to the dead body. Afterwards Priam comes with the ransom, makes his way unseen into his enemy's tent, and suddenly kisses Achilles' hand and kneels before him:

"Forget not the Gods, Achilles, and have pity on me, remembering thine own father, for I am more miserable than he; and I have endured what no other mortal hath endured on earth, that I should put to my lips the hand of him who slew my son."

He spake, and waked in Achilles the desire of weeping. And he took the old man's hand and put him gently from him. And they wept together bitterly, as the old man sunken at Achilles' feet remembered red-handed Hector, and he thought of his own father, and again of Patroclus. And the noise of their weeping went through the room.

[2] *Iliad*, XXII, 337 ff.

It is not the rage and cruelty that move us; but if they were not there, we should not be moved so much. It is strength of will, and love and honour, and the independence of the individual soul. It would need very little change in the above scene to make it fit into the starkest parts of a tragic Icelandic saga. The language is more artistic in the Greek, and the tenderness more outspoken. But the incident and the passions might belong to any heroic age.

This imaginative dependence on the Heroic Age goes far, I would suggest, to explain one of the great characteristics of the classical style: that is, its reserve and truthfulness. A French critic has pungently said of the Romantic school that the characteristic of Romanticism, *"c'est le faux."* As contrasted with the classic style, Romanticism is never happy unless it exaggerates. Dumas's Antony, when annoyed, drives his dagger through an oaken table. Victor Hugo's Hernani offers people his head, but refuses to take his hat off. So certain Celtic heroes fight for thirty days on end, with no intervals for meals. Others are apt to have magic accoutrements, which enable them to do things never done on earth. The troubadour Rudel devotes his whole life to the Princess of Tripoli, whom he has never seen or spoken to, but loves desperately on the strength of a miniature and a verbal description.

I am not saying that these things do not produce very charming poetry; but I think they differ in one definite way from the manner of the Heroic Age. They are the inventions of people who either have no experience of the things they write about, or are not genuinely interested in them as real things. They are fantastic because the authors and audiences like dreaming; they describe impossible acts of valour because a lady in her bower, making up an imaginary hero, may just as well have one who routs a hundred antagonists as one who, like a real Northern hero, with difficulty baffles and escapes from three. The manner of the Heroic Age is that of poets who know what they are describing and audiences who know the thing that is being talked about. The battles in Homer, for instance, are numerous and detailed; the single combats and the exact wounds are fully described. Yet there is not a single "Aristeia" which is plainly impossible or fantastic; there is not a single Gargantuan blow or unnatural wound. It is all close to fact: as close, almost, as the Icelandic sagas. There are, of course, a few interventions of gods to explain how some one escaped when he really seemed done for, or how a beaten party inexplicably rallied. There are also in two places actual battles between the gods themselves. But even here there is nothing impossible or fantastic to a public which believed in the gods and thought it likely enough that, some generations back, they had intervened in human affairs more than they do now. Probably many a stout practical soldier in the fifth century B.C., and for a good two thousand years later, was quite disposed to think that the interference of gods or angels or the like afforded the only possible explanation of certain odd incidents within his own experience.

The same "sophrosynê," the same temperance and sobriety of invention, lasts on through the whole of classical Greek literature. Supernatural incidents occur in it, because people still believed that they occurred in real life. But while the gods, of course, behave like gods, the men and women behave like real men and women. The language is so free from bombast and exaggeration that it generally disappoints a modern reader, accustomed to the habitual over-emphasis of modern fiction, not to speak of newspapers and advertisements. The Roman writers indulge increasingly in exaggeration, but in Greek literature the fashion set by the poetry of the Heroic Age lasts on almost unbroken to the end.

Again, a great mark of early literatures and simple societies is the habit of telling a story with little or no moral comment or psychological explanation from the story-teller. Homer hardly ever comments on the behaviour of his actors. He describes their actions, and that is enough. It is the same in the sagas; and most of us, in our childhood, have felt a little puzzled by a similar absence of comment in the early books of the Bible. In origin, no doubt, this reticence may be due to the fact that primitive people have neither the necessary categories of thought nor the necessary vocabulary for making much ethical or psychological comment. They get their meaning across the footlights much more effectively and correctly by stating exactly what happened, and selecting among the things that happened those that are really important. To a modern reader, accustomed to the minute psychological interest of the contemporary novel and its crowded masses of small but significant detail, this habit of mentioning only facts, and only the great facts, gives to ancient literature an air of hardness and externality; he misses something that is warm and intimate and revealing.

It is like the difference between a crowded world in which a thousand interests jostle and obliterate one another, and a world in which a man's eyes see one landscape and his mind is filled by one or two main thoughts. Think of the methods which are necessary in the western world to heal some small misunderstanding between two modern governments, or bodies much less important than governments—the innumerable conversations and memoranda and minutes and diplomatic notes and banquets and polite phrases and cautious circumlocutions. And compare with them the following account, by an English eyewitness, of the renunciation of a long blood feud between two Arab tribes. "The two Sheikhs, each followed by his suite of tribesmen, advanced slowly, but without greeting, to meet one another. They stood still for some time, and then one Sheikh said: 'Is it enough?' The other looked back towards his followers and gathered an impression from their faces; then turned and said gravely, 'It is enough.'" As a matter of fact, the deaths on the two sides were just equal, so that honour was satisfied.

That thought was in every mind. And no doubt there were, in the minds of the two chiefs, as in those of various of their followers, all sorts of considerations and germs of feeling for which they simply had no words and did not feel that words were needed. They selected just the words which really mattered.

It is curious how this characteristic of the Heroic Age lingers on as a deliberate point of style even in fifth-century Athens, at a time when Socrates and Euripides were filling the city with eager disputants about the nature of righteousness and the real springs of human conduct. Drama, it is true, psychologizes; it would hardly be drama if it did not. But even drama in the fifth century was extremely sparing in its comments, and seldom labelled its characters "good" and "bad." Thucydides, who is not a poet but a historian, abstains so rigorously from comment on the actions of his characters that his real opinions are still subjects of doubt and discussion among critics. On the whole, it is in the essence of the classic tradition that the poet himself, though he tells you what his characters did and what they said, does not tell what he himself thinks; and similarly, even in producing effects of high emotion or ecstasy, he remains in command of his own feelings.

But there is another inheritance from the Heroic Age, or even from times more remote and primitive, which perhaps underlies this emphasizing of objective fact, and which certainly seems to characterize almost the whole tradition of higher poetry and imaginative fiction. It is that, whatever the personal views of life may be among the members of a given audience, in the main it is the heroic virtues that stir the imagination and not those of any later and more civilized age. The conscious and reflective part of the human mind may be convinced that law and arbitration and compromise, and reasonable behaviour in general, form the only road to social salvation and are worth pursuing whenever practicable. The religious mood, under proper stimulation, may fall in love with self-sacrifice and meekness and the effort to love as oneself all one's most irritating enemies. But the profound unconscious springs of emotion in the average man are not much stirred by either of these appeals; what they respond to at once is the cry of heroism, of the passions that count no costs on earth and look for no rewards in heaven.

Let us take one of the most savage incidents in the Sigurd legend. The Niblung brothers, Gunnar and Hogni, were captured by Attila, who wanted the treasure which they had hidden. Attila tried by threats of torture to make Gunnar reveal it. Gunnar said he would speak when they showed him his brother Hogni's heart. They cut out the heart of a churl and brought it to Gunnar; but Gunnar said, "That thing trembles. It is not Hogni's heart." Then they brought Hogni's own heart, and Gunnar knew it and said: "Now that Hogni is dead, none but I knows where the treasure is, and from me you shall never hear it." So they threw him into a pit full of serpents; and he there played his harp to the serpents, and sang aloud, till one old and deaf serpent bit him and he died.

I have known ardent Christians and pacifists and vegetarians moved to the very extreme of admiration by that story. It responds to none of their conscious ideals, only to the ideal of the Heroic Age, pre-Christian, pre-civilized, yet with the makings in it of all greatness, in which the spirit of man rises up invincible against fate or against odds: "Thought shall be the harder, heart the keener, mood shall be the fiercer, as our might lessens." [3] It is not mere fighting-power, for it often goes with that proud generosity which throws away the advantages that mean success. It goes well with sacrifice, as it goes with great love and great hatred. All these things it rates high, despising for their sake safety and comfort and long life and all the common values of the world.

It is a stale sarcasm to point out how extremely small, according to obvious standards, has been the effect of

[3] *The Battle of Maldon.*

Christianity on the ordinary conduct of states and peoples. They have gone crusading against infidels, they have fought interminable and cruel wars against heretics, they have tormented and exterminated Jews readily enough, just as they have eagerly defended the slave-trade as a method of propagating the Gospel; but they will not practise or come near to practising the difficult precepts of the Gospel as if they really believed them. So much we all know, and the fact is matter for serious sociological study as well as for idealist perorations. But it is equally curious that, in the sphere of pure imagination, where an enthusiasm for Christian principles involves no disagreeable practical results whatever, Christianity has had on the whole so little effect. Our popular literature, our songs and our stories, tell of love and of fighting, because it is to the lover and the fighting man that our sympathy and admiration go out. We enjoy *Paradise Lost,* but the part we all like best is the part about Satan. We enjoy the *Pilgrim's Progress,* but we enjoy it most when Apollyon straddles across the path and says, "Here will I spill thy soul!" However much we prize the meek and godly Christian in real life, he has certainly not yet taken possession of the kingdom of poetry.

Of the four great tragedies of Shakespeare none is specifically Christian in theme or spirit. *Hamlet* is based on a pre-Christian story of the duty of revenge clashing with the filial duty. *Lear* is definitely pagan in setting, and based equally on a pre-Christian folk-tale. *Othello* is a story of love and jealousy and murder. *Macbeth,* though tinged throughout with the supernatural, is no more Christian than an average Greek tragedy. Apart from hymns and devotional poems, almost the only great contribution which Christianity has made to imaginative literature is the concept of the Martyr. The Martyr played a very prominent part in the early struggling days of the Christian church. We may remember that martyrdom was held to obliterate all the errors, or even crimes, of a man's previous life. And of course martyrdom appeals at

172

once to the normal human imagination, that is, to the imagination of the Heroic Age. The hero's last fight against overwhelming odds is the most typical motive of the Northern stories, and to a somewhat less degree of the Greek also. It has to be a fight in which honour is saved, and death in some sense accepted and overcome. And that, exactly and word for word, is the last hour of the Martyr. So that here, in its greatest contribution to poetry, it seems that Christianity really took over and made its own one of the oldest and best beloved of the heroic motives. That is all.

No doubt there is a great deal of fine religious poetry written by Christians, though probably, on the whole, not quite so much in proportion to other subjects as has been produced by the Moslems or the Hindus. Yet for the most part it would seem that this poetry in its inspired moments speaks the common language of mystical emotion or communion with God, rather than anything specifically Christian. Such emotion is of course as old as the hills, and was very early in finding expression.

If we consider another point which seems at first sight almost inconsistent with this, we shall perhaps find that the one explains the other. If Christianity has not affected the poetical imagination, it has profoundly affected what we may call the practical imagination. The life of St. Francis might be described as a practical poem; or, one might say, his preaching to the birds is a poem, his kissing of the leper at least a piece of impassioned rhetoric. Similarly, one might think of the fine story of the First Crusade: how Godfrey de Bouillon, after the capture of the Holy City, was elected King of Jerusalem and taken to be crowned in the Church of the Holy Sepulchre; and how, when the time came, he refused the circlet of gold and jewels which was brought to him. Sitting in that place, the only crown he could wear was a crown of thorns. That is imaginative living; it is magnificent and moving rhetoric. It remains, I would suggest, a little too conscious and deliberate to be exactly poetry.

173

It would be rash to lay down an exact boundary line but in general it would seem that every new idea, and certainly every moral or religious reform, must at first be both conscious and self-critical; and that attitude, though precious beyond description for practical life, is almost fatal to poetry. It is like an antiseptic, admirable for cleansing purposes, but poisonous to growing plants. It is easy to feel intense enthusiasm for such subjects as Prison Reform, Universal Insurance, Aseptic Surgery, or the League of Nations. It is possible to make moving speeches about them all, with passages of imaginative rhetoric. But they all imply the use of those parts of the mind, analytic, critical, deliberative, which are both alien and dangerous to poetical inspiration. What we call inspiration seems to depend on elements that are exceedingly old in the history of human development, instincts that lie at the very depths of human nature, before conscious criticism came to prune and train it. This does not mean that poetry is always on the side of conservatism and against reform. The aspiration after a better life, the indignation against injustice, the longing for purity and brotherhood, all these things are *gemeinmenschlich* and as old as the human record. And when we remember this, we can be less astonished at the fact, at first sight so paradoxical, that almost the only great English poet who was really inspired by the ideals commonly called Christian, and built his poetry largely out of them, was Shelley. He cared little for the heroic virtues, and thrilled mainly to the thought of love, meekness, and sacrifice— sacrifice for some cause which is also love. His poetry may indeed be said to have

> speeded hither on the sigh
> Of one who gave an enemy
> His plank, then plunged aside to die;

and he does genuinely prefer to all warrior heroes his "headless patriots and pale youths who perish unupbraiding." But, after all, he does like them to die, and to die game. Such ideals do not come to him directly from Christian doctrine; they come from an element in human nature which is thoroughly ancient and normal. One can find it in ancient Babylon; it is almost the foundation of Buddhism; though among the conquering and successful races of men it is usually present in small and carefully supervised quantities. In Shelley's peculiar temperament it was abundant, some would consider dangerously abundant; and one may perhaps say the same of Blake and of Tolstoy. But fascinating as this attitude is, it has not conquered much territory in the world's imaginative literature.

It seems then that the roots of poetry lie in the deeps of human nature, in time far beyond our earliest record, in psychology deep below our ordinary consciousness. We can trace them back beyond any heroic age known to history, to that primeval Molpê described in the second chapter, in which the scarcely articulate human soul tried to express itself toward the great mysteries of the Tragic Pattern—Love, Strife, Death, and that which is beyond Death. But we can see how the form and content of poetry were affected differently by the diverse experience of different races, and in particular how, in the tradition of poetry in Europe, the influence which seems most profound is that of the Heroic Age. It is not barbarism in itself that has so specially affected poetry; it is not civilization. It is the clash of the two. And further, it is not the orderly rule—a normal process, however unsympathetic—of the barbarian by the civilized. It is the overthrow of order by disorder, of culture by ignorance, of amassed riches by audacious poverty. We cannot expect to analyze the secret of a time about which our knowledge is so scanty, but we can see that it must have forced sensitive and civilized human beings to face unexpected extremes of peril and suffering, while it stimulated the daring of barbaric adventurers with glories and luxuries beyond their comprehension. It provided a combination of rare dangers and rich chances, of indescribable terrors and bewildering hopes, in which, amid the crumbling of external protections, a man had to stand or fall by what he was really worth, by his fighting power, his courage, his strength of will, and the degree to which he could either make his men follow him and his friends love him and die for him, or, if need were, himself follow and love and die.

There would be nothing to surprise us in the case of an individual man who had passed through some intense and soul-stirring experience for a few months in his youth, and found the whole of his later life coloured thereby. And though the parallel is far from perfect, it may serve. We should also find, no doubt, that if the same strain fell on several individuals, some would be crushed by it, some would gain nothing from it, and some few would be strong enough to "learn by suffering." Many nations have passed through times of violent dissolution and passionate hope like the Heroic Age; but very few have turned the experience to spiritual profit, as the Greeks and the Northmen did. It needs toughness and strength to be a poet, as well as exceptional sensibility.

Moreover, there are some important differences between the heroic ages that produced Hector and Gunnar, and ordinary periods of violence and dissolution. In the first place, a heroic age is a time of birth-pangs as well as death-pangs, of hope as well as fear. That would differentiate it from periods like the Thirty Years' War, or the Wars of the Roses, but not from a period like the French Revolution, which was singularly barren in art and poetry. We are credibly informed that

> Bliss was it in that dawn to be alive,
> But to be young was very heaven.

It would seem, however, that the dawn did not last, and the afternoon was sultry and depressing. The next age looked back to the Revolution as a time of crime and courage on the grand scale, but not as a time of beauty and poetry. It is here that the difference lies. The generations that immediately followed the Heroic Age, both in Greece and in Northern Europe, certainly did think of it and sing of it, as a time of splendour. And it looks—though the evidence is conjectural—as if the men of the Heroic Age had themselves felt the world about them to be inspiring and glorious. The singing seems to have begun in the actual lifetime of the Northern heroes, and it may well have been the same with the Greek. One hesitates to use our Iliad and Odyssey in their present shape as evidence; but certainly the feeling in them that the day of the heroes was a great and wonderful day seems to lie deep in the structure of both poems. It is not merely that the heroes wield weapons or throw rocks which "men as they now are" could not even lift; that may mean little. But there is a sense of exhilaration in the narrative, as if in the presence of a beautiful and inspiring world. Things are all good of their kind. The ships are swift and well balanced, the doors and houses well fixed, the armour strong and gleaming, the men, almost without exception, brave and generous, and the women gracious and white-armed and lovely; the sun and the moon shine in beauty, and the West Wind runs shouting over the wine-faced sea. There is a sense of joy in the world, except when definite disasters come from the gods or your enemies, or, of course, from your own Ate.

We cannot, I repeat, be sure that this idealization of the Heroic Age amid all its horrors belongs only to the generations, perhaps still more miserable, that followed it, or whether, as most authorities seem to think, it was actually the spirit of the "heroes" themselves. The Byzantine historian, Priscus, on his famous visit to Attila, passed first through territories which had been depopulated, partly by the massacring Huns themselves, partly by the suicide of whole communities through fear of the Huns, and then, with the horror of this experience still upon him, arrived at headquarters to find the Huns full of joyous enthusiasm and singing songs about their own virtues. A visitor to the camp of the Myrmidons would very likely have had a similar experience. It is curious, in the first book of the Iliad, to look beneath the veil of poetry to the brute facts which it describes: the plague-stricken army pinned to the sea-shore and dependent for its food on precarious raiding, the narrow space choked with dead dogs and mules, the piles of burning corpses, the bitter personal quarrel between the leaders. And the poet makes of it a tale of chivalry and splendour! If such enthusiasm was really characteristic of the contemporaries of Achilles and of Attila, and if the bards' songs were indeed poetry and not a mere journalistic record of passing events, the contrast provided by the Heroic Ages with their miseries and their exhilaration as against our own times, with their comparative comfort and depression of spirits, becomes almost startling.

Perhaps I am pressing this point too hard. No doubt societies, like individuals, are subject to waves of elation and depression, self-confidence and self-abasement; and such feelings, we may remark in passing, have probably as little to do with real merit in the one case as in the other. But through practically all ages the rule seems to hold that, so far as imaginative fiction is concerned, the present is the subject for prose, for realism and for satire; Poetry dwells beyond some dividing veil, among the things which still live after Time has done his worst upon them. Of course a lyric, like *Maud*, or a philosophical poem, like *The Prelude*, may use contemporary events as its material, but their main burden is not narrative at all, but an inner life which is timeless. The thing that cannot live is historical contemporary narrative, like Dryden's *Annus Mirabilis* or Voltaire's *Henriade*.

One can see why the abrupt ups and downs of a man's present material life, however vehement in emotion, are not fit themes for poetry. They are only the rawest of raw material, which needs long treatment before it can be used. But to many imaginative minds it does remain a puzzling doctrine that the things about which they care most, and care, as it seems to them, with the noblest part of their being, are not suitable material for poetry. Many of us have at some time longed to use, or to see others use, the radiance of poetry to illuminate the real lives of men and women and help the causes that now inspire us, instead—one might almost say—of wasting it all on things that might just as well be forgotten or outgrown, however much they were esteemed by our barbaric ancestors.

Yet apparently it cannot be done. Men may well and wisely devote their lives to the emancipation of slaves, or the education of peoples, to the abolition of war or the development of medical or electrical science: excellent objects of devotion, all of them, but somehow too near the surface of experience, too much concerned with criticism and intellect, and the shallow grit of daily vicissitudes, for their roots to work down to the deep places from which poetry springs. Much more sound and beneficent, no doubt, much more calculated to stir the imagination of practical men, than the griefs of Hecuba, or the death of Odysseus' old dog on the dung-heap, or the blast of Roland's horn, or that song that was indeed the lark and not the nightingale. But the kingdom of poetry is not for them. They are new and they argue. They explain and insist and are superseded. Poetry listens to no argument and opens her heart to no strangers. A thousand years in her sight are but as yesterday, and her home is among things that are very old, old as the battle of man against fate, old as love and death and honour, and the kiss of Helen and the dancing of the daffodils.

VIII

HAMLET AND ORESTES [1]

I

IN THE FIRST OF THESE STUDIES WE CONSIDERED THE CON-
scious study and imitation of classical literature revealed
in Milton's poetry. In the second we considered the origin
of that classical literature itself—not indeed the models
which it consciously imitated, but the quarry out of
which its marbles were hewn, or the spring whose waters
ran in its great rivers. In the last chapter we saw how
this original raw material of poetry, the primitive religious
Molpê, for the most part was not wrought to its highest
forms except by passing through fire and torment, and
that for this reason poetry still, in a sense, finds its models
in the Heroic Age. But the unconscious tradition in
poetry is not only greater in extent, it also reaches much
further back into the past, than any deliberate human
imitation.

I propose now to consider the influence of this unconscious tradition in a region where its presence has not
been suspected.

My subject is the study of two great tragic characters,
Hamlet and Orestes, regarded as traditional types. I do
not compare play with play, but simply character with
character, though in the course of the comparison I shall

[1] This study is a reprint, with few changes, of the Annual Shakespeare Lecture for 1914, by kind permission of the British Academy.

naturally consider the situations in which my heroes are placed and the other persons with whom they are associated.

Orestes in Greek is very clearly a traditional character. He occurs in poem after poem, in tragedy after tragedy, varying slightly in each one but always true to type. He is, I think, the most central and typical tragic hero on the Greek stage; and he occurs in no less than seven of our extant tragedies—eight if we count the *Iphigenia in Aulis*, where he is an infant—whereas Oedipus, for instance, only comes in three and Agamemnon in four. I shall use all these seven plays as material: namely, Aeschylus, *Choephoroe* and *Eumenides*; Sophocles, *Electra*; and Euripides, *Electra*, *Orestes*, *Iphigenia in Tauris* and *Andromache*. And we must realize that before any of these plays was written Orestes was a well-established character both in religious worship and in epic and lyric tradition.

As for *Hamlet*, I note, in passing, the well-known fragments of evidence which indicate the existence of a Hamlet tragedy before the publication of Shakespeare's Second Quarto in 1604. These are:

1602. A phrase in Dekker's *Satiromastix*, "My name's Hamlet: Revenge!"

1598. Gabriel Harvey's remarks about Shakespeare's *Hamlet*. The true date of this entry is disputed.

1596. Lodge, *Wit's Miserie and the World's Madness*: "He looks as pale as the ghost which cried so miserally at the theater like an oysterwife, Hamlet, revenge."

1594. Henslowe's Diary records a play called *Hamlet* as acted at Newington Butts Theatre on June 9.

The earliest reference seems to be in Nash's *Epistle* prefixed to Greene's *Menaphon*: it is dated 1589, but was perhaps printed in 1587. "Yet English Seneca read by candle light yeeldes many good sentences, as Bloud is a beggar, and so foorth: and if you intreate him faire in a frosty morning, he will affoord you whole Hamlets, I should say handfuls of tragicall speeches."

The play of *Hamlet* is extant in three main forms:

The First Quarto, dated 1603, but perhaps printed in 1602. It is entitled *"The Tragicall Historie of Hamlet Prince of Denmark* by William Shake-speare, As it hath been at divers times acted by his Highnesse servants in the Cittie of London: as also in the two Vniversities of Cambridge and Oxford and else-where."* It is much shorter than the *Hamlet* which we commonly read, having only 2,143 lines, many of them incomplete, as against the 3,891 of the Globe edition. It differs from our version also in the order of the scenes and to some extent in plot. For instance, the Queen's innocence of her husband's murder is made quite explicit: when she hears how it was wrought she exclaims:

> But, as I have a soule, I sweare by Heaven
> I never knew of this most horride murder;

and thereafter she acts confidentially with Hamlet and Horatio. Also some of the names are different: for Polonius we have Corambis, and for Reynaldo, Montano.

The Second Quarto, dated 1604, describes itself as "enlarged to almoste as much againe as it was, according to the true and perfecte coppie."

Thirdly, there is the Folio of 1623. This omits a good deal that was in the Second Quarto, and contains some passages which are not in that edition but have their parallels in the First Quarto.

Thus *Hamlet*, like most of the great Elizabethan plays, presents itself to us as a whole that has been gradually built up, not as a single definitive creation made by one man in one effort. There was an old play called *Hamlet* extant about 1587, perhaps written by Kyd. It was worked over and improved by Shakespeare; improved doubtless again and again in the course of its different productions. We can trace additions; we can even trace changes of mind or repentances, as when the Folio of 1623 goes back to a discarded passage in the First Quarto. It is a live and growing play, apt no doubt to be slightly different at each performance, and growing steadily more profound, more rich, and more varied in its appeal.

And before it was an English play, it was a Scandinavian story: a very ancient Northern tale, not invented by any person, but just living, and doubtless from time to time growing and decaying, in oral tradition. It is recorded at length, of course with some remodelling, both conscious and unconscious, by Saxo Grammaticus in his great *History of the Danes (Gesta Danorum)*, Books III and IV. Saxo wrote about the year 1185; he calls his hero Amlethus, or Amloði, Prince of Jutland, and has worked in material that seems to come from the classical story of Brutus—Brutus the Fool, who cast out the Tarquins—and the deeds of Anlaf Curan, King of Ireland. But the story of Hamlet existed long before Saxo; for the prose *Edda* happens to quote a song by the poet Snaebjørn, composed about 980, with a passing reference to "Amloði." And it must mean our Amloði; for our Amloði in his pretended madness was a great riddle-maker, and the song refers to one of his best riddles. He speaks in Saxo of the sand as meal ground by the sea; and Snaebjørn's song calls the sea "Amloði's mealbin."

Besides Saxo we have a later form of the same legend in the Icelandic *Ambales Saga*. The earliest extant manuscripts of this belong to the seventeenth century.

Thus our sources for *Hamlet* will be (1) the various versions of the play known to us, (2) the story in Saxo Grammaticus and the *Ambales Saga*, and (3) some occasional variants of these sagas.[2]

II

Now to our comparison.

1. The general situation. In all the versions, both Northern and Greek, the hero is the son of a king who

[2] There are, of course, numerous variants and offshoots of the Hamlet story. See *Corpus Hamleticum* by Professor Josef Schick of Munich.

has been murdered and succeeded on the throne by a younger kinsman—a cousin, Aegisthus, in the Greek; a younger brother, Feng or Claudius, in the Northern. The dead king's wife has married his murderer. The hero, driven by supernatural commands, undertakes and carries through the duty of vengeance.

In Shakespeare the hero dies as his vengeance is accomplished; but this seems to be an innovation. In Saxo, *Ambales*, and the Greek he duly succeeds to the kingdom. In Saxo there is no mention of a ghost; the duty of vengeance is perhaps accepted as natural. In *Ambales*, however, there are angels; in the English, a ghost; in the Greek, dreams and visions of the dead father, and an oracle.

2. In all versions of the story there is some shyness about the mother-murder. In Saxo the mother is not slain; in Shakespeare she is slain by accident, not deliberately murdered; in *Ambales* she is warned and leaves the burning hall just in time. In one of the variants the mother refuses to leave the hall and is burnt with her husband.[3] In the Greek versions she is deliberately slain, but the horror of the deed unseats the hero's reason. We shall consider this mother more at length later on.

3. In all the versions the hero is in some way under the shadow of madness. This is immensely important, indeed essential, in his whole dramatic character. It is present in all the versions, but is somewhat different in each.

In *Hamlet* the madness is assumed, but I trust I am safe in saying that there is something in the hero's character which at least makes one wonder if it is entirely assumed. I think the same may be said of Amloði and Ambales.

---

[3] Halfdan is killed by his brother Frodi, who also takes his wife. Halfdan's sons, Helgi and Hroar, eventually burn Frodi at a feast. See Professor Elton's appendix to his translation of Saxo, edited by York Powell.

In the Greek the complete madness comes only as a result of the mother-murder; yet here too there is that in the hero's character which makes it easy for him to go mad. In the *Choephoroe*, where we see him before the deed, he is not normal. His language is strange and broken amid its amazing eloquence; he is a haunted man. In other plays, after the deed, he is seldom actually raving. But, like Hamlet in his mother's chamber, he sees visions which others cannot:

> You cannot see them: only I can see.[4]

He indulges freely in soliloquies;[5] especially, like Hamlet, he is subject to paralyzing doubts and hesitations, alternating with hot fits. For instance, once in the *Iphigenia* he suddenly wishes to fly and give up his whole enterprise, and has to be checked by Pylades:

> O God, where hast thou brought me? what new snare
> Is this?—I slew my mother, I avenged
> My father at thy bidding. I have ranged
> A homeless world, hunted by shapes of pain. . . .
> . . . We still have time to fly for home,
> Back to the galley quick, ere worse things come.

> #### PYLADES

> To fly we dare not, brother: 't is a thing
> Not of our custom.[6]

Again, in the *Electra* he suspects that the god who commands him to take vengeance may be an evil spirit in disguise:

> How if some fiend of Hell
> Hid in God's likeness spake that oracle?

[4] *Choephoroe*, 1061; cf. *Orestes*, 255–279.
[5] *Iphigenia in Tauris*, 77–94, *Electra*, 367–390; cf. *Iphigenia in Tauris*, 940–978; *Choephoroe*, 268–305, and last scene.
[6] *Iphigenia in Tauris*, 93–103.

One is reminded of Hamlet's words:

> The spirit that I have seen
> May be the devil.[7]

At the moment before the actual crisis he is seized with horror and tries to hold back. In the *Choephoroe* this is given in a line or two:

> Pylades,
> What can I? Dare I let my mother live?[8]

or with a different punctuation: "Let me spare my mother!" In the *Electra* it is a whole scene, where he actually for the moment forgets what it is that he has to do; he only remembers that it has something to do with his mother. Again he vows, too late, after the mother-murder, that, if his dead father had known all, he would never have urged him to such a deed; he would rather

> have knelt down
> And hung his wreath of prayers about my beard,
> To leave him unavenged.[9]

In Shakespeare this belief is made a fact: the Ghost specially charges Hamlet not to kill Gertrude:

> Taint not thy mind, nor let thy soul contrive
> Against thy Mother aught.[1]

Is it too much to say that, in all these strangely characteristic speeches of Orestes, every line might have been spoken by Hamlet, and hardly a line by any other tragic character except those directly influenced by Orestes or Hamlet?

Now what do we find in the sagas? Both in Saxo and in *Ambales* the madness is assumed, entirely or mainly, but in its quality also it is utterly different from that of

---

[7] *Electra*, 979; *Hamlet*, II, 2.
[8] *Choephoroe*, 899.
[9] *Orestes*, 288–293.   [1] *Hamlet*, I, 5; cf. also the tone in III, 4.

Shakespeare's hero. The saga Hamlet is not a highly wrought and sensitive man with his mind shaken by a terrible experience, he is a Fool, a gross Jester, covered with dirt and ashes, grinning and mowing and eating like a hog, spared by the murderer simply because he is considered too witless to be dangerous. The name "Amloði" itself means a fool. This side is emphasised most in *Ambales*, but it is clear enough in Saxo also and explains why he has combined his hero with the Fool, Brutus. Hamlet is a Fool, though his folly is partly assumed and hides unsuspected cunning.

4. The Fool.—It is very remarkable that Shakespeare, who did such wonders in his idealized and half-mystic treatment of the real Fool, should also have made his greatest tragic hero out of a Fool transfigured. Let us spend a few moments on noticing the remnants of the old Fool that subsist in the transfigured hero of the tragedies. For one thing, as has often been remarked, Hamlet's actual language is at times exactly that of the regular Shakespearean Fool: for example, with Polonius in Act II, scene 2; just before the play in Act III, scene 2, and after. But apart from that, there are other significant elements.

(*a*) The Fool's disguise.—Amloði and Brutus and Shakespeare's Hamlet feign madness; Orestes does not. Yet the element of disguise is very strong in Orestes. He is always disguising his feelings: he does so in the *Choephoroe*, Sophocles' *Electra*, Euripides' *Electra* and *Iphigenia in Tauris*. In two passages further, he narrates how, in other circumstances, he had to disguise them:

I suffered in silence and made pretence not to see.[2]

I suffered, Oh, I suffered; but as things drove me I endured.[3]

This is like Shakespeare's Hamlet. It is also very like the

[2] *Iphigenia in Tauris*, 956.
[3] *Andromache*, 980.

saga Hamlet, who deliberately laughs in pretended idiocy to see his brother hanged.

Again, it is a marked feature of Orestes to be present in disguise, especially when he is supposed to be dead, and then at some crisis to reveal himself with startling effect. He is apt to be greeted by such words as "Undreamed-of phantom!" or "Who is this risen from the dead?" [4] He is present disguised and unknown in the *Choephoroe*, Sophocles' *Electra*, Euripides' *Electra* and *Iphigenia in Tauris*; he is in nearly every case supposed to be dead. In the *Choephoroe* and Sophocles' *Electra* he brings the funeral urn that is supposed to contain his own ashes; in the *Iphigenia* he interrupts his own funeral rites.

No other character in Greek tragedy behaves in this extraordinary way. But Saxo's Amloði does. When Amloði goes to England, he is supposed to be dead, and his funeral feast is in progress, when he walks in, "striking all men utterly aghast." [5]

In *Hamlet* there is surely a remnant of this motive, considerably softened. In Act V, 2, the Gravedigger scene, Hamlet has been present in disguise while the Gravedigger and the public thought he was in England, and the King and his confidants must have believed him dead, as they do in Saxo. Then comes the funeral—not his own, but Ophelia's; he stays hidden for a time, and then springs out, revealing himself: "This is I, Hamlet the Dane!" The words seem like an echo of that cry that is so typical in the Greek tragedies: " 'Tis I, Orestes, Agamemnon's son!" [6] One is reminded, too, of the quotation from the pre-Shakespearean *Hamlet* in Dekker's *Satiromastix* of 1602: "My name's Hamlet! Revenge!" It may well be that these melodramatic appearances were more prominent in the tradition before Shakespeare.

[4] *Orestes*, 385, 879, 478 f.; *Iphigenia*, 1361 (cf. 1321).
[5] *Gesta Danorum*, IV, 95.
[6] *Andromache*, 884; *Iphigenia*, 1361; cf. his sudden apparitions in *Choephoroe*, 212 ff., *Electra*, 220, also the recognition scenes.

(b) The disorder of the Fool.—This disguise motive has led us away from the Fool, though it is closely connected with him. Another curious element of the Fool that lingers on is his dirtiness and disorder in dress. Saxo says that Amloði "remained always in his mother's house, utterly listless and unclean, flinging himself on the ground and bespattering his person with foul dirt." [7] Ambales was worse; enough to say that he slept in his mother's room and "ashes and filth reeked off him." [8] We remember Ophelia's description of Hamlet's coming to her chamber:

> his doublet all unbraced;
> No hat upon his head; his stockings fouled,
> Ungartered and down-gyvèd to the ankle,
> Pale as his shirt . . . [9]

Similarly, Orestes, at the beginning of the play that bears his name, is found with his sister, ghastly pale, with foam on his mouth, gouts of rheum in his eyes, his long hair matted with dirt and "made wild with long unwashenness." "Poor curls, poor filthy face," his sister says to him.[1] In the *Electra*, too, he is taken for a brigand,[2] which suggests some lack of neatness in dress; in the *Iphigenia* we hear of his foaming at the mouth and rolling on the ground.[3] In both plays, it is true, Orestes carries with him an air of princely birth, but so, no doubt, did Hamlet, whatever state his stockings were in.

(c) The Fool's rudeness of speech.—Besides being dirty and talking in riddles, the Fool was abusive and gross in his language. This is the case to some degree in Saxo, though no doubt the monk has softened Amloði's words. It is much emphasized in Ambales. That hero's language is habitually outrageous, especially to women.

[7] Saxo, 88.
[8] Hamlet, II, i.
[9] Electra, 219.
[1] Ambales, pp. 73–75, 77.
[2] Orestes, 219–226; cf. 880 ff.
[3] Iphigenia in Tauris, 307 f.

This outrageousness of speech has clearly descended to
Hamlet, in whom it seems to be definitely intended as a
morbid trait. He is obsessed by revolting images. He
does

> like a whore unpack his heart in words
> And fall a-cursing like a very drab,

and he rages at himself because of it.

(*d*) The Fool on women.—Now the general style of
Greek tragedy will not admit any gross language. So
Orestes has lost this trait. But a trace of it perhaps remains. Both Orestes and Hamlet are given to expressing
violently cynical opinions about women.[4] The *Orestes*
bristles with parallels to the ravings of Hamlet's "Get-
thee-to-a-nunnery" scene.[5] The hero is haunted by his
"most pernicious woman." All women want to murder
their husbands; it is only a question of time. Then they
will fly in tears to their children, show their breasts, and
cry for sympathy. We may, perhaps, couple with these
passages the famous speech where he denies any blood
relationship with his mother,[6] and the horrible mad line
where he says he could never weary of killing evil women.[7]

Both heroes also tend—if I may use such an expression—to bully any woman they are left alone with. Amloði in Saxo mishandles his foster-sister—though the
passage is obscure—and utters violent reproaches to the
Queen. (The scene is taken over by Shakespeare.) Ambales is habitually misbehaving in this way. Hamlet bullies
Ophelia cruelly and "speaks daggers" to the Queen. He
never meets any other woman. Orestes is very surly to
Iphigenia;[8] draws his sword on Electra in one play, and
takes her for a devil in another;[9] holds his dagger at the

---

[4] *Orestes*, 246–251, 566–572, 935–942.
[5] *Hamlet*, III, 1.
[6] *Orestes*, 552 ff., based on the quibble in Aeschylus' *Eumenides*,
657–661.
[7] *Orestes*, 1590.
[8] *Iphigenia*, 482 ff.
[9] *Electra*, 220 ff.; *Orestes*, 264.

throat of Hermione till she faints;[1] denounces, threatens, and kills Clytemnestra, and tries to kill Helen. There are not many tragic heroes with such an extreme anti-feminist record.

The above, I think, are, all of them, elements that go deep into the character of the hero as a stage figure. I will now add some slighter and more external points of resemblance.

1. In both traditions the hero has been away from home when the main drama begins, Orestes in Phocis, Hamlet in Wittenberg. This point, as we shall see later, has some significance.

2. The hero in both traditions—and in both rather strangely—goes on a ship, is captured by enemies who want to kill him, but escapes. And as Hamlet has a sort of double escape, first from the King's treacherous letter, and next from the pirates, so Orestes, in the *Iphigenia*, escapes once from the Taurians who catch him on the shore, and again from the pursuers in the ship. Ambales has similar adventures at sea; and the original Amloði seems to have had nautical connexions, since the sea was his meal-bin, and the ship's rudder his knife.[2]

3. Much more curious, and indeed extraordinary, is the following point, which occurs in Saxo, *Ambales*, and the Greek, but not in Shakespeare. We have seen that the hero is always a good deal connected with the dead, with graves and ghosts and funerals. In the sagas on one occasion he wins a great battle after a preliminary defeat, by a somewhat ghastly stratagem. He picks up his dead —or his dead and wounded—and ties them upright to stakes and rocks, so that, when his pursuers renew their attack, they find themselves affronted by an army of dead men standing upright, and fly in dismay. Now in the *Electra*, Orestes prays to his father:

Girt with thine own dead armies wake, Oh wake,[3]

---

[1] *Orestes*, 1575 ff.
[2] See also a pamphlet, *Grotta Söngr and the Orkney and Shetland Quern*, by A. W. Johnston, 1912.   [3] *Electra*, 680.

or, quite literally, "Come bringing every dead man as a
fellow-fighter." One would almost think here that there
was some direct influence—of course with a misunderstanding. But the parallel may be a mere chance.

4. I would not lay much stress on the coincidence
about the serpent. Clytemnestra dreams that she gives
birth to a serpent, which bites her breast. Orestes, hearing of it, accepts the omen: he will be the serpent. And
at the last moment. Clytemnestra so recognizes him:

> Oh, God;
> This is the serpent that I bore and suckled.

We are reminded of the Ghost's words:

> The serpent that did sting thy father's life
> Now wears his crown.[4]

However, Shakespeare abounds in serpents, and I have
found no trace of this serpent motive in the sagas.

5. Nor yet would I make anything of the point that
both Hamlet and Orestes on one occasion have the
enemy in their power and put off killing him in order to
provide a worse death afterwards. This is important in
Hamlet—

> Now might I do it pat, now he is praying;[5]

but only occurs as a slight incident in Sophocles' *Electra*,[6] and may be due merely to the Greek rule of having
no violent deaths on the stage. Nor is there much significance in the fact that in both traditions the hero has
a scene in which he hears the details of his father's death
and bursts into uncontrollable grief.[7] Such a scene is in
both cases almost unavoidable.

Let us now follow this father for a little while. He was,
perhaps naturally, a great warrior. He "slew Troy's thou-

---

[4] *Choephoroe*, 527–550, 928; *Orestes*, 479; *Hamlet*, I, 5.
[5] *Hamlet*, III, 3.
[6] Sophocles, *Electra*, 1491 ff.
[7] *Choephoroe*, 430 ff.; Euripides, *Electra*, 290; *Hamlet*, I, 5, "Oh,
all you host of heaven," etc.

sands"; he "smote the sledded Polacks on the ice." It is
a particular reproach that the son of such a man should
be so slow-tempered, "peaking like John-a-dreams," and
so chary of shedding blood.[8] The father was also generally idealized and made magnificent. He had some manly
faults, yet "He was a man, taking him all in all." He was
"a king of kings."[9] A special contrast is drawn between
him and his successor:

> It was so easy to be true. A King
> Was thine, not feebler, not in any thing
> Below Aegisthus; one whom Hellas chose
> Above all kings.[1]

One might continue: "Look on this picture and on
this."

We may also notice that the successor, besides the
vices which are necessary, or at least desirable, in his
position, is in both cases accused of drunkenness,[2] which
seems irrelevant and unusual.

Lastly, and more important, one of the greatest horrors about the father's death in both traditions is that he
died without the due religious observances. In the Greek
tragedies, this lack of religious burial is almost the central
horror of the whole story. Wherever it is mentioned it
comes as something intolerable, maddening; it breaks
Orestes down. A good instance is the scene in the *Choephoroe*, where Orestes and Electra are kneeling at their
father's grave, awakening the dead and working their
own passion to the murder-point.

ELECTRA

Ah, pitiless one, my mother, mine enemy! With
an enemy's burial didst thou bury him: thy King
without his people, without dying rites; thine husband without a tear!

[8] *Electra*, 275 ff, 336 ff.; cf. 130, 245.
[9] *Ibid.*, 1066 ff.
[1] *Ibid.*, 320 ff., 917, 1080.
[2] *Hamlet*, I, 4; *Electra*, 326.

ORESTES

All, all, in dishonour thou tellest it, woe is me!
And for that dishonouring she shall pay her punishment: by the will of the Gods, by the will of my
hands: Oh, let me but slay, and then perish!

He is now ripe for the hearing of the last horror:

LEADER OF THE CHORUS

His body was mangled to lay his ghost! There,
learn it all . . .

and the scene becomes hysterical.[3]

The atmosphere is quite different in the English. But
the lack of dying rites remains, and retains a strange
dreadfulness:

> Cut off even in the blossom of my sin,
> Unhousel'd, disappointed, unanel'd.

To turn to the other characters: in both the dramatic
traditions the hero has a faithful friend and confidant,
who also arrives from Phocis—Wittenberg, and advises him
about his revenge. This friend, when the hero is threat-
ened with death, wishes to die too, but is prevented by
the hero and told to "absent him from felicity awhile." [4]
This motive is worked out more at length in the Greek
than in the English.

Also the friendship between Orestes and Pylades is
more intense than—between Hamlet and Horatio; naturally, since devoted friendship always plays a greater
part in antiquity. But Hamlet's words are strong:

> Give me that man
> That is not passion's slave, and I will wear him
> In my heart's core, ay, in my heart of heart,
> As I do thee.[5]

[3] *Choephoroe*, 435 ff.; cf. Sophocles, *Electra*, 443 ff.; Euripides, *Electra*, 289, 323 ff.
[4] *Orestes*, 1069 ff.; *Iphigenia*, 675 ff.; *Hamlet*, V, 2.
[5] *Hamlet*, III, 2.

I find no Pylades–Horatio in the sagas; though there is a brother to Hamlet, sometimes older and sometimes a twin. In some of the variants also, such as the stories of Helgi and Hroar, there are pairs of avengers, one of whom is mad, or behaves like a madman.

Next comes a curious point. At first sight it seems as if all the Electra motive were lacking in the modern play, all the Ophelia–Polonius motive in the ancient. Yet I am not sure.

In all the ancient plays Orestes is closely connected with a strange couple—a young woman and a very old man. They are his sister Electra and her only true friend, an old and trusted servant of the dead King, who saved Orestes' life in childhood. In Euripides this old man habitually addresses Electra as "my daughter"—not merely as "child" (παῖς), but really "daughter" (θυγάτηρ),[6] while she in return carefully avoids calling him "Father," because that is to her a sacred name and she will never use it lightly. But in Sophocles she says emphatically:

> "Hail, Father. For it is as if in thee
> I saw my father!" [7]

In the Elizabethan play this couple—if we may so beg the question—has been transformed. The sister is now the mistress, Ophelia; the old servant of the King—for so we must surely describe Polonius or Corambis—remains, but has become Ophelia's real father. And the relations of both to the hero are quite different.

The change is made more intelligible when we look at the sagas. There the young woman is not a sister but a foster-sister; like Electra she helps Amloði, like Ophelia she is his beloved. The old servant of the King is not her father—so far like the Greek; but there the likeness stops. He spies on Amloði in his mother's chamber and is killed for his pains, as in the English.

---

[6] Euripides, *Electra*, 493, 563.
[7] Sophocles, *Electra*, 1361.

We may notice, further, that in all the Electra plays alike a peculiar effect is got from Orestes' first sight of his sister, either walking in a funeral procession or alone in mourning garb.[8] He takes her for a slave, and cries, "Can that be the unhappy Electra?" A similar but stronger effect is reached in *Hamlet*,[9] when Hamlet, seeing an unknown funeral procession approach, gradually discovers whose it is and cries in horror: "What, the fair Ophelia?"

Lastly, there is something peculiar, at any rate in the Northern tradition,—I will take the Greek later,—about the hero's mother. Essentially it is this: she has married the murderer of her first husband and is in part implicated in the murder, and yet the tradition instinctively keeps her sympathetic. In our *Hamlet* she is startled to hear that her first husband was murdered, yet one does not feel clear that she is perfectly honest with herself. She did not know Claudius had poisoned him, but probably that was because she obstinately refused to put together things which she did know and which pointed towards that conclusion. At any rate, though she does not betray Hamlet, she sticks to Claudius and shares his doom. In the First Quarto she is more definitely innocent of the murder; when she learns of it she changes sides, protects Hamlet, and acts in confidence with Horatio. In Saxo her attitude is as ambiguous as in the later *Hamlet*; she is friendly to Amloði and does not betray him, yet does not turn against Feng either.

A wife who loves her husband and bears him children, and then is wedded to his slayer and equally loves him, and does it all in a natural and unemotional manner: it seems somewhat unusual.

And one's surprise is a little increased to find that in Saxo Amloði's wife, Hermutrude, behaves in the same way as his mother has done. On Amloði's death she marries his slayer, Wiglek. Again, there is an Irish king, historical

---

[8] *Choephoroe*, 16; Sophocles, *Electra*, 80; Euripides, *Electra*, 107 ff.
[9] Act V, scene 1.

to a great degree, who has got deeply entangled with the Hamlet story. His name is Anlaf Curan. Now his wife, Gormflaith, carried this practice so far that the chronicler comments on it. After Anlaf's defeat at Tara she married his conqueror Malachy, and on Malachy's defeat she married Malachy's conqueror Brian. We will consider later the Greek parallels to this enigmatic lady. For the present we must admit that she is very unlike the Clytemnestra of Greek tragedy, whose motives are studied in every detail, who boldly hates her husband and murders him. But there are traces in Homer of a far less passionate Clytemnestra.

III

Now I hope I have not tried artificially to make a case or to press my facts too hard. I think it will be conceded that the points of similarity, some fundamental and some perhaps superficial, between these two tragic heroes are rather extraordinary, and are made the more striking by the fact that Hamlet and Orestes are respectively the very greatest or most famous heroes of the world's two great ages of tragedy.

The points of similarity, we must notice, fall into two parts. There are, first, the broad similarities of situation between what we may call the original sagas on both sides; that is, the general story of Orestes and of Hamlet respectively. But, secondly, there is something much more remarkable: when these sagas were worked up into tragedies, quite independently and on very different lines, by the great dramatists of Greece and England, not only do most of the old similarities remain, but a number of new similarities are developed. That is, Aeschylus, Euripides, and Shakespeare are strikingly similar in certain points which do not occur at all in Saxo or *Ambales* or the Greek epic. For instance, the hero's madness is the same in Shakespeare and Euripides, but is totally different from the madness in Saxo or *Ambales*.

What is the connexion? All critics seem to be agreed

that Shakespeare did not study these Greek tragedians directly. And, if anyone should suggest that he did, there are many considerations which would, I think, make that hypothesis unserviceable. Of course, it is likely enough that some of Shakespeare's university friends, who knew Greek, may have told him in conversation of various stories or scenes or effects in Greek plays. Miss Spens suggests the name of Marston. She shows that he consciously imitated the Greek—for instance, in getting a special effect out of the absence of funeral rites—and probably had considerable influence on Shakespeare. This is a highly important line of inquiry, but such an explanation would not carry us very far with Shakespeare, and would be no help with Saxo.

Neither can it be indirect imitation through Seneca. Orestes only appears once in the whole of Seneca, and then he is a baby unable to speak.[1] And in any case Saxo does not seem to have studied Seneca.

Will Scandinavian mercenaries at the Court of Byzantium help us? Or, simpler perhaps, will the Roman conquest of Britain? Both these channels were doubtless important in opening up a connexion between the North and the Mediterranean, and revealing to the Northmen the rich world of classical story. But neither explanation is at all adequate. It might possibly provide a bridge between the traditional Orestes and Saxo's Amloði; but they are not in any pressing need of a bridge. It does not provide any bridge where it is chiefly wanted, between the Orestes of tragedy and Shakespeare's Hamlet.

There seems to have been, so far as our recorded history goes, no chance of imitation, either direct or indirect. Are we thrown back, then, on a much broader and simpler though rather terrifying hypothesis, that the field of tragedy is by nature so limited that these similarities are inevitable? Certain situations and stories and characters —certain subjects, we may say, for shortness—are naturally tragic; these subjects are quite few in number, and,

[1] Seneca, *Agamemnon*, 910–943.

consequently, two poets or sets of poets trying to find or invent tragic subjects are pretty sure to fall into the same paths. I think there is some truth in this suggestion; and I shall make use of something like it later. But I do not think that in itself it is enough, or nearly enough, to explain such close similarities, both detailed and fundamental, as those we are considering. I feel as I look at these two traditions that there must be a connexion somewhere.

There is none within the limits of our historical record; but can there be any outside? There is none between the dramas, nor even directly between the sagas; but can there be some original connexion between the myths, or the primitive religious rituals, on which the dramas are ultimately based? And can it be that in the last analysis the similarities between Euripides and Shakespeare are simply due to the natural working out, by playwrights of special genius, of the dramatic possibilities latent in that original seed? If this is so, it will lead us to some interesting conclusions.

To begin with, then, can we discover the original myth out of which the Greek Orestes-saga has grown? (I do not deny the possible presence of a historical element also; but if history is there, there is certainly myth mixed up with it.) The saga contains two parts:

(1) Agamemnon, "king of men," is dethroned and slain by a younger kinsman, the banished Aegisthus, who is helped by the Queen. (2) His successor, in turn, dreads and tries to destroy the next heir to the throne, Orestes, who, however, comes home secretly and, helped by a Young Queen, Electra, slays him and the Queen with him.

The story falls into its place in a clearly marked group of Greek or pre-Greek legends. Let us recall the primeval kings of the world in Hesiod.

First there was Ouranos and his wife Gaia. Ouranos lived in dread of his children, and "hid them away" till his son Kronos rose and cast him out, helped by the Queen-Mother Gaia.

Then came King Kronos with his wife Rhea. He, too, feared his children and "swallowed them," till his son Zeus rose and cast him out, helped by the Queen-Mother Rhea.

Then, thirdly—but the story cannot continue. For Zeus is still ruling and cannot have been cast out. But he was saved by a narrow margin. He was about to marry the sea-maiden Thetis, when Prometheus warned him that, if he did so, the son of Thetis would be greater than he and cast him out from heaven. And, great as is my love for Thetis, I have little doubt that she would have been found helping her son in his criminal behaviour.

In the above cases the new usurper is represented as the son of the old King and Queen. Consequently the Queen-Mother, though she helps him, does not marry him, as she does when he is merely a younger kinsman. But there is one great saga in which the marriage of mother and son has remained, quite unsoftened and unexpurgated. In Thebes King Laïus and his wife Jocasta knew that their son would slay and dethrone his father. Laïus orders the son's death, but he is saved by the Queen-Mother, and, after slaying and dethroning his father, marries her. She is afterwards slain or dethroned with him, as Clytemnestra is with Aegisthus, and Gertrude with Claudius.

There is clearly a common element in all these stories, and the reader will doubtless have recognized it. It is the world-wide ritual story of what we may call the Golden-Bough Kings. That ritual story is, as I have tried to show elsewhere, the fundamental conception that forms the basis of Greek tragedy, and not Greek tragedy only. It forms the basis of the traditional Mummers' Play, which, though deeply degraded and vulgarized, is not quite dead yet in the countries of Northern Europe and lies at the root of so large a part of all the religions of mankind.

It is unnecessary, I hope, to make any long explanation

of the Vegetation-kings or Year-daemons. But there are perhaps two points that we should remember, to save us from confusion later on. First, there are two early modes of reckoning: you can reckon by seasons or half-years, by summers and winters; or you can reckon with the whole year as your unit. On the first system a Summer-king or Vegetation-spirit is slain by Winter and rises from the dead in the spring. On the second each Year-king comes first as a wintry slayer, weds the queen, grows proud and royal, and then is slain by the Avenger of his predecessor. These two conceptions cause some confusion in the myths, as they do in most forms of the Mummers' Play.

The second point to remember is that this death and vengeance was really enacted among our remote ancestors in terms of human bloodshed. The sacred king really had "slain the slayer" and was doomed himself to be slain. The queen might either be taken on by her husband's slayer, or else slain with her husband. It is no pale myth or allegory that has so deeply dyed the first pages of human history. It is man's passionate desire for the food that will save him from starvation, his passionate memory of the streams of blood, willing and unwilling, that have been shed to keep him alive. But for all this subject 1 must refer the reader to the classic expositions of the *Golden Bough*, and their brilliant development in Dr. Jane Harrison's *Themis*.

Thus Orestes, the madman and king-slayer, takes his place beside Brutus the Fool, who expelled the Tarquins, and Amloði the Fool, who burnt King Fong at his winter feast. The great Greek scholar, Hermann Usener, some years since, on quite other grounds, identified Orestes as a Winter-god, a slayer of the Summer.[2] He is the man of the cold mountains who slays annually the Red Neoptolemus at Delphi; he is the ally of death and the dead; he comes suddenly in the dark; he is mad and raging, like the Winter-god Maimaktes and the November storms. In Athenian ritual, it seems, a cloak was actually woven

[2] *Heilige Handlung*, in the *Archiv für Religionswissenschaft*, 1904.

for him in late autumn, lest he should be too cold.[3] Thus he is quite unlike the various bright heroes who slay dragons of darkness; he finds his comrade in the Bitter Fool—may we say the bitter Amloði?—of many Mummers' Plays, who is the Slayer of the Joyous King.

This is all very well for Orestes; but can we talk thus of Hamlet-Amloði? Is it possible to bring him into the region of myth, and myth of the same kind that we find in Greece? Here I am quite off my accustomed beat, and must speak with diffidence and under correction from my betters. But it seems beyond doubt, even to my most imperfect scrutiny of the material, that the same forms of myth and the same range of primitive religious conceptions are to be found in Scandinavia as in other Arian countries.

There are several wives in the Ynglinga saga who seem to belong to the Gaia–Rhea–Clytemnestra–Jocasta type. For instance, King Vanlandi was married to Drifa of Finland, and was killed by her in conjunction with their son Visburr, who succeeded to the kingdom. (The slaying was done by witchcraft; but no jury could, I think, exculpate Visburr.)

Visburr in turn married the daughter of Aude the Wealthy. Like Agamemnon, he was unfaithful to his wife, so she left him and sent her two sons to talk to him, and duly, in the proper ritual manner, to burn him in his house—just as the Hamlet of saga burned King Feng, just as the actual Northern villagers at their festival burned the Old Year.

Again, there are clear traces of kings who are sacrificed and are succeeded by their slayers. Most of the Yngling kings die in sacrificial ways. One is confessedly sacrificed to avert famine, one killed by a sacrificial bull, one falls off his horse in a temple and dies, one burns himself on a pyre at a festival. Another—like Ouranos and Kronos and the other child-swallowers—sacrifices one of his sons periodically in order to prolong his own life. I cite these

[3] Aristophanes, *Birds,* 712.

cases merely to show that such ideas were apparently current in primitive Norse society as well as elsewhere. But the matter is really clinched by Saxo himself. He not only gives us the tale of Ole, King of the Beggars, who came in disguise, with one servant dressed as a woman, to King Thore's house, got himself hailed as king in mockery, and then slew Thore and took the crown. He definitely tells us, in a story about the Sclavs, that "by public law of the ancients the succession to the throne belonged to him who should slay the king." [4]

So that when we find that the Hamlet of saga resembles Orestes so closely; when we find that he is the Bitter Fool and king-slayer; when especially we find that this strange part of wedding—if not helping—their husband's slayer and successor is played alike by Hamlet's mother, whatever her name, Gerutha, Gertrude, or Amba; and by Amloði's mother and by Ambales' mother, and by the mother of divers variants of Hamlet, like Helgi and Hroar; and by Hamlet's wife, and by the wife of Anlaf Curan, who is partly identified with Hamlet, we can hardly hesitate to draw the same sort of conclusion as would naturally follow in a Greek story. Hamlet is more deeply involved in this Clytemnestra-like atmosphere than any person I know of outside Hesiod. And one cannot fail to be reminded of Oedipus and Jocasta by the fact, which is itself of no value in the story but is preserved both in Saxo and the *Ambales Saga*, that Amloði slept in his mother's chamber.[5]

There is something strangely characteristic in the saga treatment of this ancient Queen-Mother, a woman under the shadow of adultery, the shadow of incest, the shadow of murder, who is yet left in most of the stories a motherly and sympathetic character. Clytemnestra is an exception, and perhaps Gormflaith. But Gaia, Rhea, and even Jocasta, are all motherly and sympathetic. So is Gerutha, the wife of Ørvandil and the mother of

---

[4] *Gesta Danorum*, 254, 277.
[5] Saxo, 88; *Ambales*, p. 119, *et ante*, ed. Gollancz.

Amleth, and Amba the mother of Ambales.[6] So is Groa, the usual wife of Ørvandil, who is probably the same person as Gerutha. "Groa," says Professor Rydberg, "was a tender person devoted to the members of her family." The trait remains even in Shakespeare. "Gertrude," says Professor Bradley, "had a soft animal nature. . . . She loved to be happy like a sheep in the sun, and to do her justice she loved to see others happy, like more sheep in the sun." Just the right character for our Mother Earth! For, of course, that is who she is. The Greek stories speak her name openly: Gaia and Rhea are confessed Earth-Mothers, Jocasta only a few stages less so. One cannot apply moral disapproval to the annual remarriages of Mother Earth with the new Spring-god; nor yet possibly to the impersonal and compulsory marriages of the human queen in certain very primitive stages of society. But later on, when life has become more self-conscious and sensitive, if once a poet or dramatist gets to thinking of the story, and tries to realise the position and feelings of this eternally traitorous wife, this eternally fostering and protecting mother, he cannot but feel in her that element of inward conflict which is the seed of great drama. She is torn between husband, lover, and son; and the avenging son, the mother-murderer, how is he torn?

English tragedy has followed the son. Yet Gerutha, Amba, Gertrude, Hermutrude, Gormflaith, Gaia, Rhea, Jocasta—there is tragedy in all of them, and it is in the main the same tragedy. Why does the most tragic of all of them, Clytemnestra, stand out of the picture?

We can only surmise. For one thing, Clytemnestra, like Gertrude in some stories, has both the normal experiences of the primitive king's wife. She both marries her husband's slayer and is slain by his avenger; and both parts of her story are equally emphasised, which is not the case with the other heroines. Their deaths are generally softened or ignored. But, apart from this, I am

---

[6] In the extant form of the *Ambales Saga* Amba's personal chastity is preserved by a miracle; such an exception approves the rule.

inclined to lay most stress on the deliberate tragic art of Aeschylus. He received perhaps from the tradition a Clytemnestra not much more articulate than Gerutha; but it needed only a turn of the wrist to change her from a silent and passive figure to a woman seething with tragic passions. If Saxo had been a man like Aeschylus, or if Shakespeare had made Gertrude his central figure instead of Hamlet, Clytemnestra would perhaps not have stood so much alone.

And what of Hamlet himself as a mythical character? I find, almost to my surprise, exactly the evidence I should have liked to find. Hamlet in Saxo is the son of Horvendillus or Ørvandil, an ancient Teutonic god connected with dawn and the spring. His great toe, for instance, is now the morning star. (It was frozen off; that is why it shines like ice.) His wife was Groa, who is said to be the Green Earth; he slew his enemy Collerus— Kollr the Hooded, or perhaps the Cold—in what Saxo calls "a sweet and spring-green spot" in a budding wood. He was slain by his brother and avenged by his son. The sort of conclusion towards which I, on my different lines, was groping had already been drawn by several of the recognized Scandinavian authorities: notably by Professor Gollancz (who especially calls attention to the part played by the hero's mother), by Adolf Zinzow, and by Victor Rydberg. Professor Elton is more guarded, but his conclusions point, on the whole, in the same direction. And the whole of the evidence has been greatly strengthened since these words were first published, by the appearance of Miss Phillpotts's remarkable book, *The Elder Edda*.[7]

[7] Gollancz, *Hamlet in Iceland*, Introduction; Zinzow, *Die Hamlet saga an und mit verwandten Sagen erläutert*, 1877; Rydberg, *Teutonic Mythology*, English tr. by Anderson, 1889; Elton, Appendix II to his translation of Saxo, edited by York Powell; Bertha S. Phillpotts, *The Elder Edda* (Cambridge, 1920). Rydberg goes so far as to identify Hamlet with Ørvandil's famous son Swipdag. "Two Dissertations on the Hamlet of Saxo and of Shakespeare" by R. G. Latham contain linguistic and mythological suggestions. I have not come across the works of Gubernatis mentioned in Ward, *English Dramatic Literature*, ii, 165.

Thus, if these arguments are trustworthy, we finally run the Hamlet-saga to earth in the same ground as the Orestes-saga: in that prehistoric and world-wide ritual battle of Summer and Winter, of Life and Death, which has played so vast a part in the mental development of the human race and especially, as Mr. E. K. Chambers has shown us, in the history of mediaeval drama. Both heroes have the notes of the winter about them rather than summer, though both are on the side of right against wrong. Hamlet is no joyous and triumphant slayer. He is clad in black, he rages alone, he is the Bitter Fool who must slay the King.[8]

IV

It seems a strange thing, this gradual shaping and re-shaping of a primitive folk-tale, in itself rather empty and devoid of character, until it issues in a great tragedy which shakes the world. Yet in Greek literature, I am sure, the process is a common, almost a normal, one. Myth is defined by a Greek writer as τὰ λεγόμενα ἐπὶ τοῖς δρωμένοις, "the things said over a ritual act." For a certain agricultural rite, let us suppose, you tore a cornsheaf in pieces and scattered the grain; and to explain why you did so, you told a myth. "There was once a young and beautiful prince who was torn in pieces. . . ." Was he torn by hounds or wild beasts in requital for some strange sin? Or was he utterly innocent, torn by mad Thracian women or devilish Titans, or the working of an unjust curse? As the group in the village talks together, and begins to muse and wonder and make unconscious poetry, the story gets better and stronger and ends by being the tragedy of Pentheus or Hippolytus or Actaeon or Dionysus himself. Of course, an element of history must be present also. Life was not eventless in primitive times any more than it is now. Things happened, and people were moved by them at the time and talked about them afterwards.

[8] I believe this figure of the Fool to be capable of further analysis, but will not pursue the question here.

But to observe exactly, and to remember and report exactly, is one of the very latest and rarest of human accomplishments. By the help of much written record and much mental training we can now manage it pretty well. But early man was at the time too excited to observe, and afterwards too indifferent to record, and always too much beset by fixed forms of thought ever to take in concrete facts exactly. (As a matter of fact, he did not even wish to do so; he was aiming at something quite different.) In any case, the facts, as they happened, were thrown swiftly into the same crucible as the myths. Men did not research. They did not keep names and dates distinct. They talked together and wondered and followed their musings, till an historical king of Ireland grew very like the old mythical Amloði, an historical king of Mycenae took on part of the story of a primitive Ouranos or Sky-King wedded to an Earth-Mother. And in later times it was the myth that lived and grew great rather than the history. The things that thrill and amaze us in *Hamlet* or the *Agamemnon* are not any historical particulars about mediaeval Elsinore or prehistoric Mycenae, but things belonging to the old stories and the old magic rites, which stirred and thrilled our forefathers five and six thousand years ago; set them dancing all night on the hills, tearing beasts and men in pieces, and giving up their own bodies to a ghastly death, in hope thereby to keep the green world from dying and to be the saviours of their own people.

I am not trying to utter a paradox, or even to formulate a theory. I am not for a moment questioning or belittling the existence, or the overwhelming artistic value, of individual genius. I trust no one will suspect me of so doing. I am simply trying to understand a phenomenon which seems, before the days of the printed book and the widespread reading public, to have occurred quite normally and constantly in works of imaginative literature, and doubtless in some degree is occurring still.

What does our hypothesis imply? It seems to imply,

first, a great unconscious solidarity and continuity, lasting from age to age, among all the children of the poets, both the makers and the callers-forth, both the artists and the audiences. In artistic creation, as in all the rest of life, the traditional element is far larger, the purely inventive element far smaller, than the unsophisticated man supposes.

Further, it implies that in the process of *traditio*— that is, of being handed on from generation to generation, constantly modified and expurgated, re-felt and re-thought—a subject sometimes shows a curious power of almost eternal durability. It can be vastly altered; it may seem utterly transformed. Yet some inherent quality still remains, and significant details are repeated quite unconsciously by generation after generation of poets. Nay, more. It seems to show that often there is latent in some primitive myth a wealth of detailed drama, waiting only for the dramatist of genius to discover it and draw it forth. Of course, we must not exaggerate this point. We must not say that *Hamlet* or the *Electra* is latent in the original ritual as a flower is latent in the seed. The seed, if it just gets its food, is bound to develop along a certain fixed line; the myth or ritual is not. It depends for its development on too many live people and too many changing and complex conditions. We can only say that some natural line of growth is there, and in the case before us it seems to have asserted itself both in large features and in fine details, in a rather extraordinary way. The two societies in which the Hamlet and Orestes tragedies arose were very dissimilar; the poets were quite different in character, and quite independent; even the particular plays themselves differed greatly in plot and setting and technique and most other qualities; the only point of contact lies at their common origin many thousand years ago, and yet the fundamental identity still shows itself, almost unmistakeable.

This conception may seem strange; but after all, in the history of religion it is already a proved and accepted fact, this "almost eternal durability" of primitive conceptions and even primitive rites. Our hypothesis will imply that what is already known to happen in religion may also occur in imaginative drama.

If this is so, it seems only natural that those subjects, or some of those subjects, which particularly stirred the interest of primitive men, should still have an appeal to certain very deep-rooted human instincts. I do not say that they will always move us now; but, when they do, they will tend to do so in ways which we recognize as particularly profound and poetical. This comes in part from their original quality; in part, I suspect, it depends on mere repetition. We all know the emotional charm possessed by famous and familiar words and names, even to hearers who do not understand the words and know little of the bearers of the names. I suspect that a charm of that sort lies in these stories and situations, which are—I cannot quite keep clear of metaphor—deeply implanted in the memory of the race, stamped, as it were, upon our physical organism. We have forgotten their faces and their voices; we say that they are strange to us. Yet there is that within us which leaps at the sight of them, a cry of blood which tells us we have known them always.

Of course, it is an essential part of the whole process of Tradition that the mythical material is constantly castigated and rekindled by comparison with real life. That is where realism comes in, and literary skill and imagination. An element drawn from real life was there, no doubt, even at the beginning. The earliest myth-maker never invented in a vacuum. He really tried—in Aristotle's famous phrase—to tell "the sort of thing that would happen"; only his conception of "what would happen" was, by our standards, a little wild. Then, as man's experience of life grew larger and calmer and more objective, his conception of "the sort of thing that would happen" grew more competent. It grew ever nearer to the truth of Nature, to its variety, to its reasonableness, to its infinite subtlety. And in the greatest ages of literature there seems to be, among other things, a power of preserving due proportion between these opposite elements—the expression of boundless primitive emotion and the subtle and delicate representation of life. In plays like *Hamlet* or the *Agamemnon* or the *Electra* we have certainly fine and flexible character-study, a varied and well-wrought story, a full command of the technical instruments of the poet and the dramatist; but we have also, I suspect, a strange, unanalyzed vibration below the surface, an undercurrent of desires and fears and passions, long slumbering yet eternally familiar, which have for thousands of years lain near the root of our most intimate emotions and been wrought into the fabric of our most magical dreams. How far into past ages this stream may reach back, I dare not even surmise; but it seems as if the power of stirring it or moving with it were one of the last secrets of genius.

POETRY

AND CAN WE, AFTER ALL THIS, MAKE OUT WITH ANY
clearness what Poetry is? For one thing, I feel sure that,
for the purposes of the poet or artist himself, we must
frankly assume the real existence of the external world
and the real difference between beauty and ugliness. I
fear that the metaphysicians and the writers on abstract
aesthetics will despise us for this. They have all gone wandering after Professor Croce, who explains art on a monistic basis. Croce holds that art is not a representation of
beauty, but is absolutely identical with beauty. It is merely
an experience; but an experience expressing itself. The
rose that I see is my creation, just as Raphael's picture is
his creation. Also there is no difference between Raphael's
conception and his execution: his conception simply is
his execution, just as my rose is simply what I see and
smell. Furthermore, since all art is just this single experience, which is both intuition and expression at the same
time, and since beauty is the same thing as art, the only
characteristic that beauty has is expressiveness. To be
expressive is to be beautiful, to be inexpressive is to lack
beauty.[1] The difference between beauty and ugliness thus
disappears, because obviously you might express very effec-

---

[1] Croce would not speak of "expressing" an object: a picture of
an ugly object, with him, only expresses the author's "intuition" of
that object. This does not appear to be much more than a verbal distinction.

tively an ugly object. The only opposite to beauty is in-expressiveness.

I mention this theory because it is so widely current that it cannot be ignored. It is accepted, for instance, by my friend Mr. Carritt, in his admirable book on the Theory of Beauty. It seems to me—as so much philosophy seems to a mere grammarian—to be based on a system-atic misuse of ordinary language, though I am quite glad to admit that it is an interesting and instructive, and even an intellectually stimulating, misuse. I will go further and say that it is a misuse of language which can be kept up with almost perfect consistency through several volumes of philosophical writing. Yet it does seem to me to involve inconsistencies. For example, when a poet or artist is work-ing over his poem or picture, what is he doing? He would probably say, and I should say, that he was trying to make it express his conception more adequately; but, on Croce's theory, I do not see what the man is doing. His work already expresses perfectly his conception, since his intui-tion and execution are always absolutely the same thing. There is no conception still unexpressed to lead him on. And of course the theory is exposed to the other usual criticisms which apply to any monistic philosophy.

There are philosophic answers, of course, to all these difficulties; still they trouble me, and consequently I fall back into the fatherly arms of Aristotle. I think a picture is a picture of something. A picture has a subject and is not absolutely identical with its subject, though of course the subject may be treated with any amount of selection and imagination; I think that a poet may have, and al-most always has, prior to his execution, some conception which he tries his best to execute or express; that it changes and grows while he expresses it; and that he never fully succeeds in his task. And as for the theory, now almost overwhelmingly accepted, that art is self-expression, I venture to think that it is a truism and a dangerously misleading one. Everything that a man does is self-expression. The way a man laces his boots, the way he writes, the way he says, "Good-morning," is probably different from the way followed by any other man, and is thus expressive of his personality. But it need not be good art, for that reason. Imagine a pompous and egotistic man in a state of personal irritation, having to make an after-dinner speech. It would probably express him only too well, but it might not be a good speech. At the same time, I think that there is almost no more dangerous doctrine to be preached to young poets and artists than this doctrine that art is self-expression. It makes them think of the one thing of all others which they ought to forget. The artist ought to be thinking of his subject and his work, and not of himself at all.[2]

Poetry, in the old, commonplace Aristotelian view, is an "artifact"—I mean, it is a thing made. The poem consists in the written or spoken words, and the chief art of the poet consists in choosing and arranging these words. When we say that the *Ode to the Nightingale* is a beautiful poem, I think it is most convenient to agree that we mean the words, either as they run in our heads or as they stand on the printed page. Of course, there are all sorts of puzzles that can be put to the supporter of this view. Suppose the words were written accidentally, by some one who did not know their meaning, or, say, by a typewriting machine being jolted in a train. Suppose (what is too often the case) some old poet wrote them, and now no one understands them. Are they still beautiful? Suppose, like certain phrases in the Old Testament, they are mistranslations. If "The iron entered into my soul" is a mere mistake for "I was put into the stocks alive," is the phrase still beautiful? These dialectical problems can be raised against any theory which accepts the reality of the external world. They are not essentially different from the question whether a rose is beautiful when no one sees it, nor that again

---

[2] Croce, I imagine, would say that the boot-lacing and the speech only "express" the man if they are put into a work of art with the intention of "expressing" him. But at any rate they reveal him, which to most people seems much the same thing.

from the question whether it exists at all when no one is aware of it. Aristotle—to whom I dutifully return—gets out of the difficulty by saying that he calls a rose beautiful whether it is seen or not, because it is at any rate "potentially" so. So I would regard the words as being the poem, because they have power, if read, to produce a certain effect.

Of course, we all recognize that poetry itself is an activity of the mind and not a printed page. But the inconvenience of talking always in terms of the mental activity is so enormous that I wish instead to speak in terms of the "artifact," the external result. If, when we speak of the *Ode to the Nightingale*, we agree to mean the printed poem, we shall understand one another. At worst there may be some questions of misprints, or different editions or versions. But if we mean Keats's own mental activity, or his "intuition," the air grows thick with misunderstandings and ambiguities. Do we mean his first conception of the ode, or the very long series of mental efforts by which he composed each stanza and each line and rewrote those that he did not like, or his "intuition" of the poem as a whole when he first read it through, or one of the innumerable occasions when he remembered it afterwards, and if so, which? Or what do we mean?

And, further, is it really Keats's intuition that we wish to mean? Is it not mine or yours? Surely I mean my series of intuitions of the ode, and you mean yours; and each of those series again is infinite. The finished material work of art, the written or printed page, does provide us with one fixed solid amid this infinite flow of "intuitions" or mental experiences; therefore we choose it as the point to talk about.

This point provisionally settled, let us go back to a question raised in an earlier chapter: is the world of poetry a revelation or an illusion? Is poetry a pretence, or a creation, or a discovery?

Is it all a pretence? Well, pretence has at least two

meanings. R. L. Stevenson once paid a visit to a South Sea Island chieftain who was also a poet, and asked him in the course of conversation what his poetry was about. "Sweethearts and the sea," said the old chief; "sweethearts and the sea. Not all same true, you know; all same lie." And Stevenson remarks that that is a very fair description of all poetry.

Still the royal poet's command of English, at least of philosophical English, was not quite perfect. The statements that he made in the poems were not really lies; they were pretence. And they were not pretence in the sense that they were intended to deceive other people and make them believe that the author was feeling something which he did not feel. When we call them pretence, we mean that the poet was pretending as children in their games pretend; he was moving in an imaginary world and playing there as children play. In this sense of the word, poetry is pretence, and need not be ashamed of being so. Play is the most important, or at least the most absorbing, part of life to young children, and poetry and art constitute the play of the grown-ups. Of course, it is a grown-up sort of play, more difficult and serious and deep-reaching, but just as vitally important and just as mysterious in its relation to the rest of life as play is among the young. If it is true that they whom the gods love die young, it must be that they preserve their power to play. Dante, when he pretended to go to the Inferno and Purgatorio and Paradiso, and to see all that there befell his friends and enemies and others in whom he was interested, was playing a game, a very magnificent game, and one which we are still able to play with him. And Homer and Vergil and Milton are all there for us to play with, if we have the good will and the intelligence, in different parts of the same splendid playing-ground.

Poetry then is a pretence. But is that all? Is it not also a creation? The word has a touch of bombast about it; it was made to suit modern tastes. But still I think we must admit that it is true. When Shakespeare wrote *Hamlet,* he made something, something which had not existed before and which has proved to be very important. But what was it exactly that he created? Did he create people? I think not. Did he create real murders and agonies and suicides? I think not. I do not see how to improve on the perfectly simple way in which the matter is put in Aristotle and Plato. He made a real poem, he made real verses; but he did not make, he only "imitated" or "represented," kings of Denmark and ghosts and murders. The murder that he made was not a real murder of a real king, but an imitation murder of an imitation king; and it is a misleading modern exaggeration when we say that he created real persons.

Modern critics seem to hate the thought of "imitation" or "representation." They are in love with the idea of "self-expression," self-assertion, the revelation of personality, and the like. I might content myself by quoting the answer of an eminent French artist who was head of the Slade School, to a student who defended careless drawing on the ground that she wanted to express her personality: "*La personnalité de mademoiselle n'intéresse qu'à maman.*" The truth seems to be, that whatever you do, you will inevitably reveal your personality, but that if your work is good, it will be an interesting personality, and if not, not. Therefore you can safely concentrate on doing the work as well as possible, and let your personality look after itself.

But I should like to go rather deeper into the matter. I am delighted to find that Shelley, who came as near as any one to knowing what poetry really is, actually says that the opposite of poetry is egotism.[3] I had never ventured actually in so many words to say that, but I had long held that the great obstacle to writing good poetry was egotism. You cannot enter into the kingdom of poetry

[3] "Poetry and the principle of self are the God and Mammon of the world."—*Defence of Poetry.*

except by losing yourself. And you lose yourself in something which you contemplate, which you admire and love, which, as the Greeks put it, you "imitate" and seek to become one with. For Μίμησις, "Imitation," we must remember, is the same thing as Μέθεξις, "Communion." Shelley is following exactly the same line of thought when he derives all poetry, and indeed all creation, from Love, for he defines Love as "a going out of our own nature (ἔκστασις) and an identification of ourselves with the beautiful which exists in thought action or person, not our own."

To me personally this group of conceptions is completely satisfying. If I may speak of myself as a poet, even of a humble order, I should say that my experience is somewhat as follows. I will take the case of a translation, because I can make that clearer. I begin to see differently some poem which I already, in the ordinary sense, know pretty well. I see it differently, more charged with meaning and beauty. It occupies my whole mind and I feel a sort of μέθεξις or union with it. If any one told me I had not myself written it, I think I should for the moment feel hurt and surprised. It seems like a very important truth which I have seen and possess, and wish to express. Then bits of it, turns of phrases, fragments of rhythm, begin to sing themselves in my mind in English. And so the poem gets started. I do not think that this experience would be essentially different if I were contemplating something quite unliterary, such as my mistress's eyebrow or the Retreat through Serbia, as the raw material of my poem. I seem to see the inspiration toward poetic creation as caused by something which I contemplate, love, and strive somehow to be at one with. Of course I may be misled by the somewhat peculiar limitations of my experience.

And, lastly, is Poetry, as Shelley and the Romantic school of poets mostly thought, a revelation of truth, a Discovery? The poet, says Shelley, "strips the veil of familiarity from the world and lays bare the naked and sleeping beauty which is the spirit of its forms." It strips off a veil, and shows what is really beneath. "What the imagination seizes as beauty," says Keats, "must be truth." "Vision or imagination," wrote Blake, "is a representation of what eternally exists—really and unchangeably." Other passages to the same effect I have already quoted.

Let us try to make out what element of truth there is in this theory. First of all, there can be no pretence of maintaining that the particular statements made in all good poems are true. It is only too patent that they are "not all same true, you know; all same lie." Some critics, however, have argued, especially some of the German idealist philosophers, that poetry utters universal or generic truths, though not particular truths. This is based, I think, on a misunderstanding of Aristotle, who says quite truly that a poet should make his characters act in a probable manner, that is, in the way in which that sort of person would act. He should thus aim at a sort of generic truth, though not, like a historian, at particular facts. That is simple enough. But idealist philosophers have transformed this common-sense statement into a doctrine that poetry in some mysterious way utters universal truths, and that the poet sees and understands the world as a whole.

This seems to me quite untrue. A poet is generally one who sees or feels and even understands certain things intensely, but he is usually very limited in his interests and his knowledge, and a bad hand at adding up results. He sees vividly and deeply, but not widely and judiciously. I would any day sooner take the opinion of a lawyer or historian or economist about the world or human nature as a whole than that of a poet.

Let us take some of the great and celebrated generalizations of poetry:

Ay me, for aught that I could ever read,
Could ever hear by tale or history,
The course of true love never did run smooth.
For either it was different in blood,

Or else misgraffèd in respect of years,
Or else it stood upon the choice of friends;
Or, if there were a sympathy in choice,
War, death, or sickness did lay seige to it,
Making it momentary as a sound,
Swift as a shadow, short as any dream,
Brief as the lightning in the collied night,
That, in a spleen, unfolds both heaven and earth,
And, ere a man hath time to say, "Behold!"
The jaws of darkness do devour it up.
So quick bright things come to confusion!

Is that true? The answer is, Who cares? It is not
meant to be a "true" statement; it is meant to express
a state of mind or feeling with which the reader will imaginatively sympathize; and it does. It is also, no doubt,
meant to be beautiful, and it most certainly is. But as for
truth, the same poet who here says that love passes swift
as a shadow, short as any dream, makes elsewhere a statement which is practically just the opposite.

Love's not Time's fool, though rosy lips and cheeks
    Within his bending sickle's compass come;
Love alters not with his brief hours and weeks,
    But bears it out, even to the edge of doom.

Is that true? Who cares? It is certainly beautiful, and
it is the kind of sentiment that suits the place. But if
you want information on the probable duration of human love under various conditions, go to a sociologist or
a statistician, not to a poet.

This criticism may seem obvious, but it takes us an
important step forward. It is not through the statements
which it makes that poetry reaches any degree of truth.
If truth or falsehood is to be understood simply as an
attribute of propositions or statements, then the preten-
sions of poetry become extremely small. "Twice two are
four" is true. "It is warmer here than out of doors" may
be true; but a sonata is not true or false, nor an imagina-

219

tive painting, nor a poem. A photograph can be "true," in the sense that it might be used as evidence in court and certain true propositions deduced from it. But in this strict sense of the word no art is either true or untrue. To say that Beauty is Truth is like saying that a tune smells or that time is blue, or that the number 4 is angry.

But this strict sense of the word truth is being constantly broken down, not by the mere carelessness of colloquial speech, like other exact uses, but by the pressing need for a word to denote something slightly different. When you really know something, when you know a person, or a poem, or even a scientific subject, your knowledge can never be comprised in a definite number of true statements: it is something almost different in kind from that. Your knowledge is not a series of propositions about the subject; it is a conception of the subject. And your conception is never completely true, like the statement $2 + 2 = 4$. It may be comparatively true, or "truer" than some one else's, in the sense that it is more generally adequate or more really like the subject in question. Suppose you say: "I know John Tomkins better than his own mother does"—that means, I think, that your general conception of Tomkins's character is more "true," or adequate, than his mother's, and probably also that there are depths in Tomkins which you have sounded and his mother has not. You have, as it were, come intimately into contact with Tomkins—though you might find it difficult to put your knowledge into the form of definite statements.

Now it seems to me clear that Poetry—or any other form of Art or appreciation of Beauty—does bring you into contact with reality. To say over to yourself a snatch of very beautiful poetry gives you an intense experience; and it is, it must be, experience of something. After it there is something that you have discovered or gained; something which you now possess, which you can go back to and find waiting for you, and can use as it should be used.

This contact with reality which comes through art is not so very different from ordinary scientific knowledge. If you know the multiplication table, you can understand certain calculations and deal in a perfectly successful manner with certain problems that arise in ordinary life. You can also explain your knowledge to a third person. If you know, or are fond of, a certain poem, you can understand certain feelings, and meet more successfully than before certain problems of human experience; but you cannot explain your knowledge to other people except imperfectly and inarticulately. You communicate it, perhaps, much as a dog communicates to another dog the suggestion that it would be well to go off hunting. But, in sum, you have got into touch with something real; you have gained an experience of something unrevealed before.

Now when this happens with an art like music, which has no words attached to it and tells no story, people are not deceived. But in judging of poetry they go wrong because poetry is made up of words, and the words form statements, and people imagine that it is those statements which are true or false. That, I suggest, is a complete mistake. The "truth," or contact with reality, which you reach through Keats's *Nightingale* is entirely different from the information conveyed by any of the statements in it. Even where the poem professes to consist of definite philosophic statements about life, like FitzGerald's *Omar Kháyyám*, their objective truth or falseness does not vitally matter. What does matter is that they should express well a feeling which we want to have expressed. For example, *Omar Kháyyám* consists mostly of dogmatic statements about life which seem to me to be probably untrue and certainly most depressing; but I love the poem and am exhilarated by reading it.

> Come, fill the Cup and in the fire of Spring
> Your Winter Garment of Repentance fling.
>   The Bird of Time has but a little way
> To flutter—and the Bird is on the wing.

This does not make me wish to violate the Eighteenth Amendment, or throw my clothes into the fire: it makes me just thrill with delight, and perhaps like life a little better. The words and statements are only the stuff of which the poem is made.

Does this mean that the words are only sounds and the poem a collection of sounds? That is clearly nonsense —a form of nonsense that is admired in certain French coteries, and is called "dadaism." It only means that, in poetry, every word is full of associations, memories, overtones, and the same is true of every statement. In good poetry no single statement bears its face value. It means indefinitely more. Imagine some exile or prisoner of war in Siberia, picking up a torn fragment of an old railway timetable giving the times of trains to and from various places where he had lived and played as a boy. Each name in the list would have a kind of magic; each statement, that you changed here or could have refreshments there, would be of value, not for what it said, but for what it recalled or suggested. The language of poetry has much of that quality; and the more so, the more deeply it is steeped in the tradition. Then, one must always remember that the words are not alone: there is also the regular rhythm of the verse, corresponding, as we are now told, to the various physiological rhythms of the living body and deriving therefrom a mysterious power over the emotions. There is also, as I have tried to explain above, a quality of rhythm or architecture in the composition itself, which is quite different from mere plot-interest and corresponds, I think, to the real rhythms of life, as revealed in one part or another of the Tragic Pattern. All these elements, and doubtless others also, combine to make the felt but indefinable contact with reality or truth conveyed by the poem.

The mistake which poets of the Romantic school, like Coleridge and Shelley, sometimes make is not to distinguish this contact with reality from the definite statements contained in the poem. It cannot be translated into words any more than, say, the feeling of a dive into deep water on a hot day. It is just an experience, and an experience of something real. And the mistake I speak of is like one which is often made in connexion with experiences of religious emotion. Many people, belonging to totally different religions, have had the experience of religious ecstasy; and most of them have always translated it into a dogmatic message, given in person by one of their own saints, and confirming the beliefs of their own sect.

But, if it cannot be translated into words, does this contact with reality really explain or teach anything? I think it does. In the first place you will have noticed that the ancient Molpê, from which our poetry seems to be descended, was concerned especially with those subjects about which we care most and know least, or at any rate are least able to make explicit statements. Love, Strife, Death, and that which is beyond Death: these are the great mysteries of the world.

It seems to me a reasonable belief that, as Bergson and others have argued, there are whole ranges of existence which human language cannot express. Our language is a biological product for certain practical ends; it is a collection of tools for enabling man to communicate with man. This is not to deny for a moment that in its primary and obvious use, as in prose, language is the greatest of all human inventions, a thing of enormous range and subtlety. But it is capable of a further range of expression, indefinitely wider, subtler, and higher, when used with all its associations and half-meanings and overtones and its accompaniments of rhythm and "music," as in poetry. I would say, then, that any good poem is, first, a set of definite propositions given by the words in their first meaning; and secondly, beyond that, a revelation of beauty. The beauty of the poem is a part of the beauty of the universe. To use the word beauty in both cases is perhaps unsatisfactory, because, of course, every poem expresses something different from every other. Every work of art is

223

entirely individual and what it expresses is a beauty of
its own. It follows that, wherever poetry is created,—
and here we may use poetry to cover all forms of art,—
wherever poetry is created, it reveals beauty and in every
place a special and different detail of beauty. It reveals,
as Shelley said, the hidden beauty that is at the heart of
existence.

Would you say that it does not reveal; it only invents?
In thinking long over this point, I cannot in the end see
that there is really any difference. If a blind man suddenly received his sight and saw for the first time that a
rose was red, you could argue for ever whether the rose
had really been red all the time though he did not see it,
or whether the redness did not exist until there was both
a subject which saw and an object seen. It is simpler at
any rate to speak in terms of external things, as the ancients would, and to say that poetry reveals the beauty of
the world.[4]

I have not a specially high opinion of professional poets.
I think the claims sometimes put forward on their behalf
are quite insufferable, as, for instance, that they are the
wisest lawgivers and the only true teachers of human duty.
I could never feel much excited over the question in Mr.
Yeats's play, whether Seannachan should go in to dinner
before the bishop and the general, or they before Seannachan. But poetry, in the sense in which we have been
using it, is something that belongs, in varying degrees, not
only to professional poets but to all human beings. And
if it is the quality which reveals the hidden beauty of the
world, it is certainly a thing of very great importance.

Beauty is a thing, or an element in things, that cannot be defined but only experienced. The Muses, when
they attended the wedding feast of Pleus and Thetis,
made a remark about it which seems to me not common-

---

[4] If good poetry reveals the beauty, does bad poetry reveal the
ugliness of the world? I should say bad poetry failed to reveal much
of anything, but that a really ugly poem (e.g., one that was mean,
spiteful, or obscene) might well reveal some ugliness. The painting
of a really ugly picture doubtless makes the world uglier.

place, but profound: Ὅτι καλὸν φίλον ἀεί·: Beauty is that which when seen is loved. As an element in experience, it makes the whole experience precious.

One characteristic it seems to have in common with other of the best things: it cannot be directly pursued. It comes only when certain other things go right. We all know that if you directly pursue happiness—happiness by itself, in a vacuum—you will not be happy. It is equally true that if you similarly pursue virtue, you become tiresome rather than virtuous. I think it is no less dangerous for a poet or artist to pursue beauty *per se*; if you express what you have got to express, if you tell your story or paint your picture, and do it well in the spirit of love or worship, then beauty will result. We are thrown back again to Aristotle: it is an ἐπιγιγνόμενον τέλος, a completion or fulfilment that comes on things when they are done right. But when it is there, it has perhaps above all other earthly things a power of reconciliation, as a great tragedy reconciles man to his own death and the frustration of what seemed to be his best hopes. If death can be beautiful, so that, when seen, it is loved, one does not mind dying.

I will not deal with the argument that beauty is merely what happens to please the eye, as, for instance, a particular brand of tobacco or chocolate may please the palate. I have indicated already the line I should be disposed to take about it. The alternative view is that beauty is a reality which we experience first and most obviously with the eye, but which we can also divine in other ways and particularly through the use of the imagination. If so, if the beauty of things is a reality which we gradually learn to see and to create, and can see and create more and more as we learn, the result is surely momentous for our practical philosophy of life. The Greek philosophers of the fourth century were constantly discussing the nature of τὸ ἀγαθόν, the "Good," the element in things which makes them valuable and which ultimately gives meaning to the long process of nature. Some of them found it in happiness, or well-being, some in virtue, or well-doing, and later philosophers have never got much further into the subject; everyone is at heart either a Stoic or an Epicurean, or a mixture of the two. But on the hypothesis we have taken, it looks as if beauty might have a greater claim than either happiness or virtue to be in itself the solution, or the nearest approach man can comprehend to a solution, of the ultimate secret of the world. Happiness is a terribly frail foundation on which to build any theory of life; and it seems to the plain man that happiness cannot be the ultimate goal because it has so often to be sacrificed for something better than itself. Virtue, or moral goodness, is too purely human a thing; and has too much the air of a means to an end beyond itself. Beauty is in things human and non-human, and seems almost omnipresent in the natural world. Now, if we ask Aristotle or Plato why a man should act righteously, or why he ought sometimes to sacrifice his happiness or to welcome martyrdom, they will answer, in language which to a Greek is perfectly simple though possibly strange to us, that he should do so ἕνεκα τοῦ καλοῦ, "for the sake of the beautiful." You have to choose, let us say, between betraying a friend and facing pain or danger. To do one thing will be αἰσχρόν, ugly; to do the other will be καλόν. We have no exact word for καλόν. "Beautiful" sounds a little priggish; "pretty" is too small in meaning. In French one could say, quite simply, of one action "c'est beau," and of another "c'est laid." We can say that one is ugly, but we have no good word for the opposite.

It is always a comfort to me that Shelley in his writings about poetry assumes as a matter of course that there is beauty in human action and thought just as much as in a picture or a landscape. He does not see, as I confess I have never been able to see, though people have tried to point it out to me for forty years, any real difference between the moral and the aesthetic.[5] And if we

---

[5] The difference is said to lie in the sense of responsibility which always attaches to the moral act. Suppose I refuse a bribe, or jump

take the best-developed and most genuinely popular art of the present day, the novel, I think we shall find that it is predominantly interested and occupied in representing beauty and ugliness in the sphere of human character. There is no subject about which most of us have such keen perception and such strong feelings. I believe as a matter of fact, amid the immense variety of religious, moral, and social beliefs in which we live, and the marked weakening of many of them, that the actual motive that works most genuinely among good men and women is this avoidance of the conduct which they feel to be ugly and this love of that which they feel to be "fair" or "decent" or "straight," or some other of those modest synonyms which in our shyness we use instead of the word "beautiful." No doubt in practice they are more concerned to avoid the ugly than to choose the beautiful; nevertheless, τὸ καλόν is to such people the guide of life.

The discussion has brought us to that wider conception of poetry from which in the first of these studies I shrank back, as a presence in all life, practically equivalent to beauty. There is something in the world which, as it is seen, is loved; something which, as Pindar says, is better than riches; as Plato says, better than happiness or life itself. Shelley has described it, imperfectly, in the *Hymn to Intellectual Beauty*, and Wordsworth in the *Intimations of Immortality*. Most people, I think, put it to themselves in terms of religion, or of some social faith that inspires them. Plato was content to call it τὸ καλόν.

But the special subject of these studies has been the Classical Tradition in Poetry. By emphasising the word tradition I mean to regard Poetry as a thing that unites

---

into the sea to save a dog: if I refuse the bribe because it would be "dirty" to accept it or because I wish to serve my country honestly, if I save the dog because I like the dog or because it would be a mean thing to let the dog drown, such behaviour, they say, is merely aesthetic; it only becomes moral if I have the feeling of some judge who sees or some law which must be obeyed. In reality, I should have thought, this sense of an over-watching judge or law is merely a refined and disguised form of the fear of punishment, and as such rather an impurity in the moral motive than a characteristic of it.

and not separates. It is not a competition in which each individual writer is expected to produce something new, to assert his personal claims, to outstrip his neighbour, and to put the old poets into the shade. It is a common worship wherein all servants of the Muses labour, a common service wherein each can help another, and wherein "a thing of beauty" lives on and is "a joy for ever," on one condition only, that it is still studied and loved and understood. By tradition the old beauty is kept alive and used for the discovery of new beauty.

The Tradition also makes us realize that Poetry is not a new thing, not an accomplishment or refinement of civilization. It is a need of the human soul, and apparently about as old as that soul itself. And the greatest poetry seems to be that which has its roots deepest in human nature, deepest in passion, deepest in wonder and in worship, deepest among the infinite reverberations of the past.

But the Classical Tradition implies something more. It implies that in this long service, this "Song in which all men join," both the poets and the listeners, there have been ages and individuals with greater powers than others. There are works of beauty that stand out above the ordinary changes of taste and fashion and have approved themselves to be of permanent value. For us the Tradition has flowed through a fairly clear channel: from Greece through Rome, with a confluent stream from Israel, through Christianity, with some bright torrents from the pagan North, and then, broken into many languages and local variants, down to modern Europe and America. And on the whole, in the long history certain achievements stand out as greatest, and certain characteristics mark the central stream.

I can hardly believe, in spite of temporary appearances, that civilization will ever permanently and of set purpose throw aside the great remote things of beauty just because it needs some time and effort to read and understand them; that the whole world will ever deliberately

turn away from the best because it is difficult, and feed
contentedly on second- and third- and twelfth-rate substitutes. It would surely be too dire an apostasy.

We must keep and love, in all art and thought, not
only in that of Greece and Rome, the great things that
have become classic. But I would not for a moment urge
either of two claims that are sometimes made by devoted
classicists. I do not recommend the conscious imitation
of classical authors: such imitation may be good or bad
—good in Vergil or Milton or Keats or Tennyson, bad
in Wilkes's *Epigoniad* and most of the poems of the
Renaissance. Neither do I profess that by studying classical models a man can form a standard of unerring taste,
which will guide him straight in the quest of that light
that never was on sea or land. Any gleam you follow may
be a false gleam; any path you select for finding it may
be a misleading path; though, of course, the more you
have studied, the more intimately you have conversed
with those who have seen and made some true beauty,
the more likely you will be to know true beauty when you
see it. But, when all precautions are taken, *humanum
est errare*; to make mistakes is a natural attribute of man,
and it is vain for a fallible and erring creature to expect
to devise or find any rules which will save him from his
own fallibility. He must go in love, he must go in rever-
ence, he must work and give ungrudgingly; but even then
there is no certainty of arriving. He who seeks the spiritual
kingdom must take his life in his hands.

INDEX

Index

Bible, absence of explanatory comment on early books of, 169

Blake, William, 63, 127, 175, 217

Blank verse, in English, metre of, 72, 86

Boccaccio, Giovanni, *Decameron*, 16

Bouillon, Godfrey de, 173

Bradley, Professor, 204

Bridges, Robert, 104, 106

Browning, Robert, 6

Buddhism, 175

Bunyan, John, *Pilgrim's Progress*, 172

Butler, Samuel, a rebel against the tradition, 127

Byron, George Gordon, Lord: mentioned, 157; *Don Juan*, 91, 134

C

Carritt, Mr., 212

Catharsis, see Katharsis

Catullus, 153

Chadwick, Professor, 162

Chambers, E. K., 206

Chanson de Roland, 134, 160, 179

Character, and story, relative importance of, 131–3

Chariton, 134

Chaucer, Geoffrey, 63, 83, 111, 134

Chinese poetry: metre in, 77–8; rhyme in, 78, 84

Choral dances, 28–9, 30

Choral songs, 28, 32

Choruses, 32, 130

Christianity, effect of, considered in divers aspects, 171–4

Clemens, S. L. (Mark Twain), *A Connecticut Yankee in King Arthur's Court*, 159

Cleophon, 109

Clough, Arthur Hugh: *Amours de Voyage*, 92; *The Bothie of Tuober na Vuolich*, 92

Coleridge, S. T., 222

Colloquial language and slang, 113

Comedy: nature of, 33–4, 47, 50–2; form in, 59–60; *see also* Tragedy, Comedy

Comment and explanation, absence of, in early literatures, 168–70

Communion, 40, 217

Comos, 33, 34, 46, 47, 48

Competition in art, 124

Confusion, as opposed to unity, 137–40

Congreve, William, 50, 63

Conrad, Joseph, 161

Consciousness, double, 43

Cornford, F. M., *Origin of Attic Comedy*, 33, 49–50; *From Religion to Philosophy*, 40

Crabbe, George, 109

Croce, Benedetto, 211 and n., 212, 213 n.

Cruelty, man takes pleasure in, 54

D

Dactylic hexameters, 84, 93

"Dadaism," 222

Dance: importance of, 27–32, 120–1; and ancient metres, 70–1, 120; *see also* Chapter II

Dante Alighieri: mentioned, 95, 107, 108, 127; *Divina Commedia*, 134, 157, 215; *Vita Nuova*, 19

Darius, King, 159

Daudet, Alphonse, the Tartarin series, 132

"Dead wood," in classical literature, 136–7

Death, in tragedy, 33–6

Dekker, Thomas, *Satiromastix*, 181, 188

Delian Maidens, 28, 29, 31

Detective stories, 155

Dickens, Charles: mentioned, 63; "blank-verse" prose in *Bleak House*, 89

Diction, poetic, 17, 108–29

Diderot, Denis, 63, 68

Digressions and retardations as defects in unity, 135

Dionysius of Halicarnassus, 75 n., 79

Dionysus: mentioned, 33, 35, 36, 47, 120, 206; and Pentheus, 56

Dochmiac metre, 81

Index

Index

Index

THE TEXT of this book was set in Electra, a Linotype face designed by W. A. Dwiggins. This face cannot be classified as modern or old-style. It is not based on any historical model, nor does it echo any particular period or style. It avoids the extreme contrast between thick and thin elements that marks most modern faces, and attempts to give a feeling of fluidity, power, and speed. Composed, printed, and bound by THE COLONIAL PRESS INC., *Clinton, Massachusetts.* Paper manufactured by S. D. WARREN COMPANY, *Boston, Massachusetts.* Cover design by ALFRED ZALON.

Vintage Books